Praise f

IF YOUR ENEMY HUNGERS, FEED HIM

"*If Your Enemy Hungers, Feed Him* is being published at a time when reaching across borders and cultural boundaries is increasingly difficult. In chronicling an episode from history when mission-minded Americans succeeded in crossing barriers of bias and distrust, Robert E. Hooper has written a particularly timely book that will inform and surprise. I highly recommend it to scholars as well as the general public."

    —**Timothy D. Johnson,** University Research Professor, Lipscomb University

"Robert E. Hooper has accomplished a monumental task in gathering the history of the Churches of Christ in the Far East. Carefully researched and filled with first-person accounts, this book should inspire future efforts to continue the Lord's work around the world. That is why this book is so important. The sacrifices made by these heroes of the faith leave the reader desiring to have the courage to do likewise."

    —**Bonnie Miller,** author of *Messengers of the Risen Son in the Land of the Rising Sun*

"This work of serious scholarship fills a much-needed gap in our understanding of Church of Christ missionary activity in Japan. Professor Hooper's meticulous documentary research and personal interviews with the handful of surviving missionaries give us a nearly complete picture of this important chapter in church history."

    —**Howard Miller,** Assistant Professor and Academic Chair of the Department of History Politics and Philosophy at Lipscomb University

"Robert E. Hooper, considered by many to be the dean of church historians in Churches of Christ, has immortalized a small band of male and female missionaries who took the message of Jesus to Japan during one of the most difficult periods in the history of the world. Their example inspires us to live our lives for the sake of the gospel."

    —**Howard W. Norton,** retired Professor of Bible and Missions at Harding University

"From J. M. McCaleb to Sarah Andrews to Ibaraki College, Robert Hooper tells the fascinating narrative of Japanese Christians and their missionaries from Churches of Christ from their pre-WWII origins to the 1970s. Each story is filled with faith and conviction, and each one forms our own faith. Particularly captivating are the stories of immigration, war, and internment. The plot, though about previous generations, rings true today and, through history, sounds a warning for how we exclude or welcome people in the present."

    —**John Mark Hicks,** Professor of Theology at Lipscomb University

"Robert E. Hooper has written an invaluable account of the work of Churches of Christ in Japan and among Japanese Americans. As a consummate historian, he sets the story squarely into its global context, demonstrating how we inevitably reflect larger social, cultural, political and economic events. But beyond facts, *If Your Enemy Hungers, Feed Him* provides readers with a moving spiritual experience, one that will prove both inspiring and transformative as Christians today discern how to take Christ courageously into our own world."

—**Douglas A. Foster,** Professor of Church History, Director of the Center for Restoration Studies at Abilene Christian University

"Many of the stories in *If Your Enemy Hungers, Feed Him* would have been forgotten if Robert E. Hooper had not tracked them down and rescued them from oblivion. Thank you for reminding us of the power of stories and for bearing witness to God's present and coming kingdom."

—**Jerry Rushford,** Director of the Jerry Rushford Center for Research on Churches of Christ and the Stone-Campbell Restoration Movement at Pepperdine University

IF YOUR ENEMY HUNGERS
FEED HIM

CHURCH OF CHRIST MISSIONARIES *in* JAPAN, 1892–1970
IF YOUR ENEMY HUNGERS
FEED HIM

R O B E R T   E .   H O O P E R

Abilene Christian University Press

In memory of the
young men and women
who knew,
with the help of God,
Ibaraki Christian College would become a reality.

Harry Robert, Jr., and Gerri Fox
Logan and Madeline Fox
Virgil and Lou Lawyer
Charles and Norma Doyle
Joe and Rosa Belle Cannon
Carroll and Pauline Cannon

IF YOUR ENEMY HUNGERS, FEED HIM

Church of Christ Missionaries in Japan, 1892–1970

ACU PRESS

Copyright © 2017 by Robert E. Hooper

ISBN 978-0-89112-495-5

Printed in the United States of America

LIBRARY OF CONGRESS CATALOGING-IN-PUBLICATION DATA
Names: Hooper, Robert E., 1932- author.
Title: If your enemy hungers, feed him : Church of Christ missionaries in
  Japan, 1892-1970 / Robert E. Hooper.
Description: Abilene : Abilene Christian University Press, 2017.
Identifiers: LCCN 2017004219 | ISBN 9780891124955 (pbk.)
Subjects: LCSH: Churches of Christ—Missions—Japan—History—20th century. |
  Missions—Japan.
Classification: LCC BV3445.3 .H66 2017 | DDC 266/.6652—dc23
LC record available at https://lccn.loc.gov/ 2017004219

Cover images from the Bob Hunter Collection, Center for Restoration Studies, Abilene Christian University.

Maps of Japan and Japanese Administrative Divisions provided by United States, Central Intelligence Agency, 1996.

Cover design by ThinkPen Design, LLC
Interior text design by Sandy Armstrong, Strong Design

For information contact:
Abilene Christian University Press
ACU Box 29138
Abilene, Texas 79699

1-877-816-4455
www.acupressbooks.com

17 18 19 20 21 22 / 7 6 5 4 3 2 1

CONTENTS

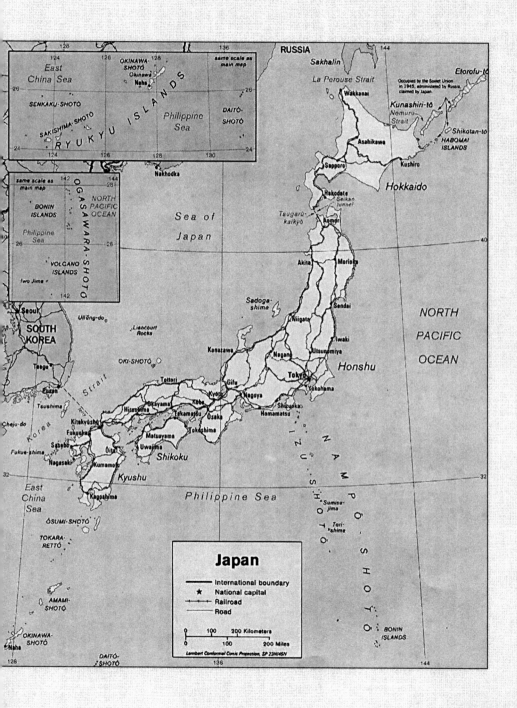

East China Sea

OKINAWA-SHOTŌ
Okinawa
Naha

same scale as main map

SENKAKU-SHOTŌ

RYUKYU ISLANDS

SAKISHIMA-SHOTŌ

Philippine Sea

DAITŌ-SHOTŌ

same scale as main map

OGASAWARA-SHOTŌ

NORTH PACIFIC OCEAN

BONIN ISLANDS

Philippine Sea

VOLCANO ISLANDS

Iwo Jima

RUSSIA

Sakhalin

La Perouse Strait

Occupied by the Soviet Union in 1945, administered by Russia, claimed by Japan.

Etorofu-tō

Wakkanai

Kunashiri-tō

Nemuro Strait

Shikotan-tō

HABOMAI ISLANDS

Asahikawa

Sapporo

Kushiro

Hokkaido

Hakodate

Seikan Tunnel

Tsugaru-kaikyō

Aomori

Nakhodka

Seoul

Ullŭng-do

SOUTH KOREA

Taegu

Pusan

Tsushima

Cheju-do

Fukue-shima

Nagasaki

Sasebo

Kumamoto

Kagoshima

ÓSUMI-SHOTŌ

TOKARA-RETTŌ

AMAMI-SHOTŌ

OKINAWA-SHOTŌ

Naha

DAITŌ-SHOTŌ

Liancourt Rocks

OKI-SHOTŌ

Strait

Korea

Tottori

Hiroshima

Okayama

Takamatsu

Kitakyūshū

Fukuoka

Ōita

Uwajima

Matsuyama

Shikoku

Kyushu

Sea of Japan

Sadoga-shima

Akita

Morioka

Niigata

Sendai

Iwaki

Kanazawa

Nagano

Utsunomiya

Honshu

Gifu

Kyoto

Kobe

Ōsaka

Nagoya

Tokushima

Shizuoka

Hamamatsu

Tokyo

Yokohama

IZU-SHOTŌ

NAMPO-SHOTŌ

Philippine Sea

Sumisu-jima

Tori-shima

BONIN ISLANDS

NORTH PACIFIC OCEAN

East China Sea

Japan

— International boundary
★ National capital
╬ Railroad
— Road

0   100   200 Kilometers
0   100   200 Miles

Lambert Conformal Conic Projection, SP 23N/45N

11

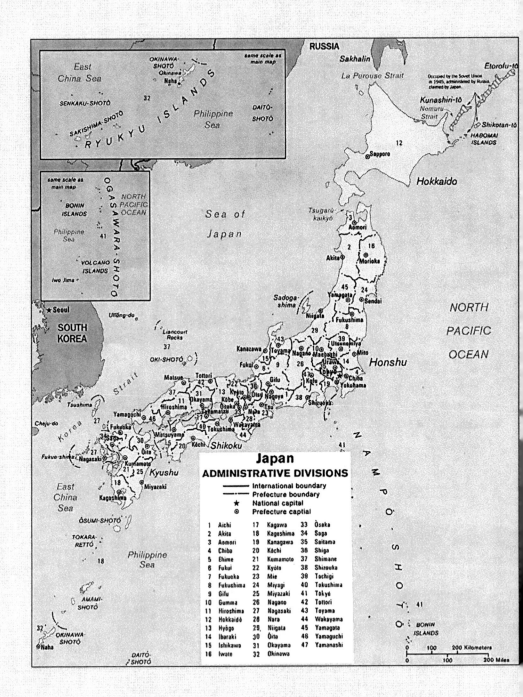

Japan
ADMINISTRATIVE DIVISIONS

—————— International boundary
—·—·— Prefecture boundary
★ National capital
◉ Prefecture captial

1	Aichi	17	Kagawa	33	Ōsaka
2	Akita	18	Kagoshima	34	Saga
3	Aomori	19	Kanagawa	35	Saitama
4	Chiba	20	Kōchi	36	Shiga
5	Ehime	21	Kumamoto	37	Shimane
6	Fukui	22	Kyōto	38	Shizuoka
7	Fukuoka	23	Mie	39	Tochigi
8	Fukushima	24	Miyagi	40	Tokushima
9	Gifu	25	Miyazaki	41	Tokyō
10	Gumma	26	Nagano	42	Tottori
11	Hiroshima	27	Nagasaki	43	Toyama
12	Hokkaidō	28	Nara	44	Wakayama
13	Hyōgo	29	Niigata	45	Yamagata
14	Ibaraki	30	Ōita	46	Yamaguchi
15	Ishikawa	31	Okayama	47	Yamanashi
16	Iwate	32	Okinawa		

PREFACE

I was a young eighteen-year-old freshman at David Lipscomb College during the winter quarter in 1951 when Otis Gatewood, missionary to Germany, spoke at the winter lectures to an overflow crowd. We had come to hear a man who had led a host of men and women to war-torn Europe after World War II. Everyone sat enraptured as Gatewood told of the response of a defeated people to the gospel of Christ. I can't remember if the audience applauded—probably not—when he finished his presentation. We should have. These dedicated missionaries embodied the spirit of "love your enemy" in the name of Christ. The circumstances were brutal under less-than-ideal circumstances. It was clear that everyone in the room was moved deeply by Gatewood's presentation. After the presentation, baskets were passed for a special collection to support mission efforts in Germany. Willard Collins, vice-president of Lipscomb, told me years later that a number of watches had been contributed—evidently those persons did not have ready cash, but they wanted to help.

Had Gatewood asked for a show of hands of those who wished to go to Germany right then, half of the students present that night would have responded. I know I would have. The presentation was just that moving, just that important. Here was a true embodiment of Matthew 5:44 (NIV): "Love your enemies and pray for those who persecute you" amid countless obstacles. These missionaries broke down all boundaries to spread the word of Christ to Germany and around the world, regardless of national boundaries, color of their skin, or languages they spoke. That night was the first time I had really come face to face with foreign missions, particularly missions carried out amid incredible adversity overcome by the power of Christ's gospel. From that time forward in my life, I would pay extra attention to missionaries who had left home to go far away and share the gospel with others under difficult circumstances.

I did not become a missionary myself. But throughout my academic career, I became more and more intrigued by the mission field. Whether it was Germany, Italy, China, Korea, or Japan, the stories of committed men and women who traveled the world sharing Christ caught my attention. In 1960 I returned to Lipscomb as a member of the history faculty. I also entered graduate school in pursuit of my PhD in history. At dissertation time, I chose to research David Lipscomb's political and educational ideas. In reading through religious journals, especially the *Gospel Advocate,* I became interested in the American Christian Missionary Society, organized in 1849. Although David Lipscomb would oppose the Missionary Society, this was the first attempt by anyone in the Stone-Campbell movement to venture into foreign missions.

Following the Civil War, Lipscomb asked churches to help minister to the Cherokees and other tribes in what is now Oklahoma. Later in the 1880s, Lipscomb encouraged three Nashville churches to support a mission to Armenia, with missionary Azariah Paul traveling home to share the gospel with his people.

In the next decade, John M. McCaleb of Hickman County, Tennessee, a graduate of the College of the Bible, approached Lipscomb and Churches of Christ to support him and his wife as voluntary missionaries to Japan.

As opposed to a missionary society, Lipscomb liked the volunteer nature of McCaleb's mission—the real beginning of foreign missions among Churches of Christ. When I first learned of Sarah Andrews, who as a young lady decided to travel halfway around the world to join McCaleb as a missionary to the Japanese people, she became my hero. Not only did Andrews go to Japan at age twenty-one; she lived in very primitive housing for Americans during her early years in Japan. But the most incredible part of her story was her desire to remain in Japan during World War II, undergoing cruel treatment by Japanese authorities. When discovered after the war, she was near death. But she was so incredibly devoted to spreading the gospel and assisting the Japanese people in their time of need that nothing could deter her efforts.

I became "hooked" on the study of foreign missions among Churches of Christ. When I produced the biography of David Lipscomb, published as *Crying in the Wilderness: A Biography of David Lipscomb* in 1979, I began to focus on mission efforts in Churches of Christ—especially in Japan. With my interest in Sarah Andrews, I produced an unpublished paper on women missionaries in Japan—Andrews, Lillie Cypert, and Hettie Lee Ewing. I presented this paper on a number of occasions, even in Warsaw, Poland. In 1993, Howard Publishing Company issued my *Distinct People: A History of Churches of Christ in the Twentieth Century.* Although I did not focus on missions, it was a theme in the book, with a section emphasizing the efforts of Sarah Andrews in Japan.

While engaged in research on the larger story of Churches of Christ, I took notes on mission work happening all over the world. I increasingly focused on Japan, the Far East, and Europe in particular because these regions were highly contested in World War II. I was inspired by the missionaries who were carrying out Christ's message in often difficult circumstances. They walked in the steps of Jesus, who sat at dining tables with tax collectors, associated with prostitutes, dared to touch lepers, and reached out to outcasts. When these missionaries stepped over societal boundaries, across "enemy" lines, to embrace brothers and sisters in the name of Christ, they carried on that legacy.

The longer the hours I spent in Beaman Library at Lipscomb, Brackett Library at Harding University, and the Harding School of Theology's Graves Library in Memphis, the narrower my focus became. Because of my early interest in missions to Japan, I began to focus on the Far East. Amazingly, the journals and papers of Churches of Christ covered and supported mission work across the Pacific Ocean, although at times the only news reports were in the back pages of the publications. The more I searched and the more notes I took, the more I realized there was sufficient coverage to tell the engaging stories of missions and missionaries in the Far East and Japan in particular. Add to the focus on Christian missions the political history of the region, the adverse conditions, and often hostility endured by the missionaries during these times, and it became an even more exciting study.

Usually during the process of most undertakings, there is a defining moment. Mine came in the spring of 2013 while standing in the first floor hallway of the Ezell Center at Lipscomb University. I was discussing my research with Dr. Timothy Johnson, professor of history at Lipscomb and a foremost scholar on American involvement in the Mexican War. Excitedly, I told him about the sixteen members of Churches of Christ held in Japanese internment camps during World War II. I shared with him the story of Sarah Andrews remaining in Japan during the conflict between Japan and the United States. I shared with him the experiences of Japanese American Christians who were interned at Camp Amache in Granada, Colorado, during World War II. He said to me, "Dr. Hooper, your stories would make a great movie. Limit your study to mission work among the Japanese, in Japan and America. The stories need to be told in greater detail." I then knew what I would be doing over the next two years—telling the stories of missionaries in Japan and the internment of Japanese Christians in camps across the western United States.

With this in mind, I faced another decision: How would I organize the chapters so as to fit the missionary efforts into the larger context of history—especially given the hostilities during the nineteenth and early twentieth centuries that made these efforts that much more pivotal and important? The more I read the political and social history of the relationship between the United States and Japan, the more I knew that the attack on Pearl Harbor by the Japanese on December 7, 1941, had to mark the beginning of my narrative. For this reason, the Prologue is about political history, the development of Japanese nationalism, and the movement of the United States into the Far East, culminating in the attack on Pearl Harbor.

Following the political prologue, the narrative chapters telling the stories of the missionaries before the advent of World War II look backward to 1892 and the coming of J. M. McCaleb to Japan. Thus five chapters culminate in the coming of World War II and the reaction to the world conflict. These are stories of which heroes are made—heroes on the front line in Japan and the United States. These heroes are both Japanese nationals and American missionaries. And the Japanese Christians interned in American camps must not be overlooked.

The years after the war, 1945 to 1970, provide us with different stories of young men and women, most from Christian colleges within the fellowship of Churches of Christ, going with enthusiasm to Japan amid horrendous conditions to uplift the sick, the oppressed, the hurting and offering them the healing found in Jesus Christ. One powerful story is that of Harry R. Fox, Sr., a missionary to Japan before World War II, who was recruited by the US military as a translator in Nagasaki in late 1945. Fox worked directly with survivors of the nuclear bomb dropped on August 9, 1945, which destroyed the city beyond recognition. Surveying the dead and dying—the helplessness of the survivors—Fox wrote urgently to Christians in America that the only hope for Japan was Jesus Christ. He then challenged Churches of Christ with a verse from Romans 12:20: "If thine [your] enemy hungers, feed him." Hence the title of this volume—timeless wisdom from God's word, exemplified and carried out by those who heeded the call to reach out to a wounded and desolate people in need and suffering beyond measure.

Heeding the call to carry Christ's light in a dark world, some missionaries who formerly served in Japan returned to resume their work, but the majority was made up of fresh young volunteers from US Christian colleges where they heard about the spiritual and physical needs of the people of Japan. They responded with compassion. Several volunteers had served in various branches of the military in the Far East—they knew firsthand the needs of the people there. Defying nationalistic ties and notions of "the enemy," these brave servants of Christ chose instead to pursue compassion and love for their fellow man against all odds. For the most part, the missionaries were welcomed with open arms. The Japanese people's once unwavering trust in the divinity of their emperor waned in the face of defeat and destruction, and they were left searching for answers. Who was this Christian God that espoused love and compassion? Missionaries who went to Ibaraki Prefecture had a decided advantage. There were a number of Japanese nationals who kept churches alive during the war. To know the stories of six young couples who, without backgrounds in education, began, operated, and built a high school and college from nothing that became Ibaraki Christian College in Omika, Japan, is thrilling. All the while these brave people of faith were preaching to and baptizing hundreds of people up and down the Kuji River Valley. These are gripping stories of faith and endurance against overwhelming odds.

ACKNOWLEDGMENTS

The stories I tell in the following chapters could not have been told had they depended totally on my research of books, journals, and newspapers. For my understanding of Japan before and after World War II, I am ever grateful to Harry Robert Fox, Jr. Through our conversations and the many printed resources he shared with me, I have been better able to tell the stories of Ibaraki, Japan. Also important to my understanding have been my conversations with Lou Lawyer, the wife of Virgil Lawyer; she and her husband were among the pioneering couples who as young college graduates accepted the challenge of mission work in Ibaraki.

I first met Harry Robert Fox, Jr., in the spring of 2010 at the Pepperdine University Bible Lectures. He was ninety years of age. Born in Japan, he was just the person I needed to give me a personal insight into mission work in Japan before and after World War II. But more than information he shared with me, we became very good friends. I am so thankful that Jerry Rushford, director of the Pepperdine Bible Lectures, encouraged me to travel to Malibu in 2010.

Coming into contact with the Los Angeles Japanese Church of Christ through columns in the *Gospel Advocate* by S. H. Hall (the minister of the Russell Street Church of Christ in Nashville) added another dimension to the story of missions among Japanese people. Hall was responsible for encouraging the formation of a church among the Japanese in Los Angeles. Through these articles and a lengthy story in the *Christian Chronicle*, I encountered the Shigekuni family, pillars of the Japanese church in Los Angeles and, through a nephew, mission work among their own people in Japan. Through correspondence with Thomas Shigekuni in recent years, the stories of the Japanese internment in the Amache Detention Camp in Granada, Colorado, are able to be told through the personal experiences of a young teenager.

Libraries are essential to historians—they are our laboratories. Without the support of the entire staff of Beaman Library, Lipscomb University, under the direction of my good friend Carolyn Wilson, I could not have finished this book. I have spent days, weeks, months, and years in the depths of Beaman and before that, Crisman Library. In recent years, while my wife and I lived half of the year in Little Rock, Arkansas, I've had the privilege of working in the Brackett Library of Harding University. Members of the library staff, led by Jean Waldrop, have been very helpful in finding items I could not locate on my own—especially some rather rare volumes not available elsewhere. The consummate librarian is Don Meredith of the Harding School of Theology. He knows the history of Churches of Christ as well as anyone within the fellowship and where research materials can be found, whether in his library or elsewhere. I could never have accomplished my research without these libraries and their more-than-helpful personnel.

An author cannot perform the final read-through of a manuscript—he would leave too many mistakes. There must be friends and critics who are willing to read, comment on, and criticize the makeup and content of the chapters in the manuscript. I am grateful to Dr. Douglas Davis, now deceased; Tom Hook, longtime missionary in Chile; and Elbert Grimes, a friend in Little Rock, for volunteering their time to read my writings. Harry

Robert Fox, Jr., has read selected chapters on Japan. I also must add a special comment for Bonnie Miller, a published author. She is the proofreader and editor every writer dreams about. Her reading of the manuscript made a tremendous difference in the finished product. Jim Turner, a longtime newspaper editor, author, and my son-in-law, read the manuscript on two occasions. Their comments, criticisms, and corrections have made this a better contribution to the history of Churches of Christ and, on a larger scale, an amazing collection of stories that document the power of the gospel to triumph and break down barriers in trying circumstances.

In years past my children have listened to me tell about my research and have even endured listening to me read from rough drafts. While researching and writing the following chapters of church history, only one person has had to endure a constant "Listen to what I've found," or "Listen to what I've written." And she has been an attentive listener and encourager throughout the months—even years—of the birth of this book. She read and commented on each chapter. I will ever be grateful to you, Bonnie Cone Hooper, for what you mean to me and for your contributions to the completion of this study of mission efforts among Churches of Christ in Japan.

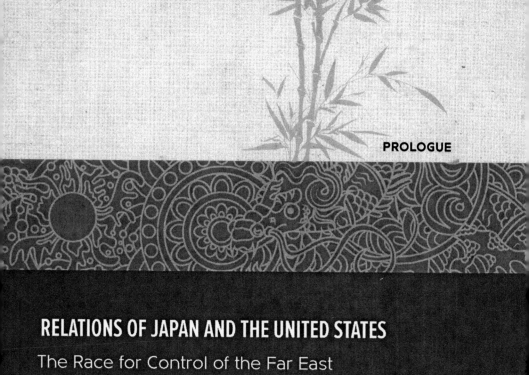

RELATIONS OF JAPAN AND THE UNITED STATES

The Race for Control of the Far East

Most Americans think of Pearl Harbor as a surprise attack, but it was long in the making. President Franklin D. Roosevelt knew conflict with Japan was a distinct possibility, considering the events of the 1930s. Equally, Japan believed the actions of the United States from 1937 to 1941 made World War II inevitable. Both were right.

How did the United States get involved in the Far East? The natural development of the United States was westward. Thomas Jefferson believed this to be true when he made the Louisiana Purchase a first concern, sending Meriwether Lewis and William Clark in 1804 to explore the great land purchase of 1803. As Stephen Ambrose states in *Undaunted Courage*, "What was at stake here was the whole of the Louisiana Purchase, the great western empire of the United States."[1]

Jefferson's desire for Louisiana caused Americans to envision a great nation stretching from the Atlantic to the Pacific. By the 1840s this idea became commonly known as Manifest Destiny: the belief that God willed that the United States should control the entire region from Canada to Mexico. Secretary of State Daniel Webster likely voiced the feelings of all knowing Americans when he suggested that the United States should "command the oceans, both oceans, all the oceans."[2] However, one nation stood in the way of American movements into the Far East in its quest for trade with China.

For 250 years, Japan had been closed to all but an occasional Dutch trading ship. The United States not only advocated open trade with the island nation; Japan was also needed as a fueling station for US steamships on the way to China. Secretary of State Webster advocated the opening of Japan, believing that God had placed coal "in the depths of the Japanese islands for the benefit of the human family."[3]

In 1853, Commodore Matthew Perry and four steamships, belching great clouds of black smoke, sailed into Edo Bay—present-day Tokyo Bay. Rebuffed, Perry returned in 1854 to continue his quest, even if he needed to use force, to open Japan for trade. This time he came with seven ships. And Japan, against her desire, opened her ports, although only slightly, for trade. On February 13, 1860, a seventy-seven-person delegation boarded an American ship on their way to Washington, DC, to formally ratify a treaty between Japan and the United States. This was the first time in 250 years that Japan had exited seclusion. Japan now entered the race for power among the nations of the world.[4]

Soon after the Civil War, at the insistence of Secretary of State William Henry Seward, the United States purchased Alaska from Russia for $7.2 million. With the United States controlling Alaska, Japan was much nearer to the United States than it had been prior to the Civil War[5]—a fact not unnoticed by Japan.

Missionaries followed the opening of China and Japan in increasing numbers, likely spurred on by Manifest Destiny. From 1858, when only eighty-one missionaries were in China, the number grew to 1,296 in 1889. Although Catholic missionaries had come to Japan many years before,

Protestant missionaries crossed the Pacific in the nineteenth century, including missionaries from Churches of Christ.

Manifest Destiny took on new meaning with the coming of the Spanish-American War of 1898. The sinking of the USS *Maine* in Havana Harbor in February 1898 fueled American fervor for war. Assistant Secretary of the Navy Theodore Roosevelt resigned his office to lead the "Rough Riders" in storming San Juan Hill. In the same move, the United States gained control of Puerto Rico.[6]

Prior to resigning his naval office, Theodore Roosevelt, with McKinley's approval, ordered Admiral George Dewey to sail his fleet, made up of six new ships, into Manila harbor in the Philippines. The Spanish offered light resistance. America's Manifest Destiny had gained its most significant holding in the Far East. This extended America's line of advantage from Alaska to the Philippines. This move certainly gave Japan concern.

For Japan, the year 1868 changed the direction of their nation. With the overthrow of the Shogun government, a fifteen-year-old emperor began his rule by proclamation on October 23. Thus began the Meiji Restoration, converting Japan from a feudal society into a modern nation-state.[7]

With the Meiji Restoration, the Japanese began to modernize, industrialize, and build a modern military, fashioned on Western models. In 1894–1895, Japan defeated China and initiated their rise to power. Southward, Formosa became Japan's first imperialistic trophy.[8]

Focus on China

European nations had moved into China before the United States showed interest. In fact, Great Britain used the Opium War in the 1840s to gain a strong foothold in China. Soon other European countries, Japan, and the United States discovered opportunities for profit in China. Japan saw China, specifically Manchuria, as a prospective major sphere of influence. At the same time, American trade followed Christian missionaries to China, and the Far East country became a good market for the abundance of cotton grown in the American South.

Into the breach opened by Japan, Russia and western European countries joined the United States in entering China in the 1890s. Instead of agreeing to carve up China among various nations, Secretary of State John Hay issued his Open Door Notes in 1899, calling for an open China for all nations.[9]

Although the Open Door Policy seemed to favor China in the battle among nations wishing to gain physical space in that country, it was the United States' means of protecting her interests in the most populous country of the world. The Chinese, however, were not impressed. In 1899, the Boxer Rebellion was an attempt to drive foreign nations out of China.

To counter the rebellion, the nations, including Japan and the United States, joined forces to put an end to the uprising. Into this fray President McKinley, without congressional approval, sent a large contingent of troops from the Philippines to aid in the put-down of the Boxers. The Japanese sent the largest military force, 22,000 men, to show its strength in the Far East. The allied nations, now including Russia, defeated the rebellion in Peking. Secretary Hay issued another Open Door Note. Everyone agreed to the open door—even Russia, although in fact she did not abide by the spirit of the agreement.[10]

With Japan becoming a major player in the world, the Far East in the early twentieth century had three nations vying for superiority in the region: China, Japan, and Russia. Japan wanted an empire. Thus Japan moved to control Manchuria, as did Russia. European nations, especially England, viewed Russian expansion into Manchuria with concern. They were building the Trans-Siberian Railroad, looking for entry into the Far East and a port on the Pacific Ocean. Great Britain signed a mutual defense treaty with Japan in 1902 to strengthen Japan's ability to thwart Russia's desire to control Manchuria.

Control of Manchuria led to conflict between Russia and Japan. Japan economically controlled south Manchuria; Russia sought a free hand in Manchuria. To gain her goals, Russia proposed giving Japan a free hand in Korea. Not satisfied with this arrangement, the Japanese government worked its people into a war frenzy. The Japanese chanted, with Britain in mind: "Lion, Lion, the King of the Beasts [now] approves of us, and America sympathizes with us in the war for civilization."[11] The Japanese leadership knew the United States favored them.

In a clash known as the Russo-Japanese War, Japan won numerous important battles. But these costly conflicts left Japan economically strapped. Had it not been for the monetary help of American bankers, Japan could not have continued the war. To win the conflict for dominance in Manchuria, the Slavic nation felt it necessary to transfer its Baltic Sea fleet some 18,000 miles to the Sea of Japan, anticipating easily defeating Japan. Far from home, the Russian fleet was defeated.

A Growing Power in the East

Although Japan did not achieve all its goals, the nation was now a power.[12] As a warning for the future, an Asiatic nation had, for the first time, defeated a European nation.

Desiring to expand, Japan had her eye on Korea. After promising to help Korea gain independence from China, the United States, in the 1910 Root-Takahira Treaty, joined England and France in giving control of Korea to Japan. With southern Manchuria, Formosa, and now Korea, Japan was becoming an even stronger player in the Far East.[13]

As long as the people of Japan remained in their home nation and focused on the Far East, the United States was not overly concerned with small conflicts across the Pacific. But the Japanese did not remain in Japan. The Japanese people began venturing to Hawaii, where they were needed for growing commercial crops in the islands. The first Japanese workers arrived in Hawaii in 1868, when 148 men, women, and children came to the island country. The population increased to 60,000 in 1900.[14] After annexation of Hawaii by the United States in 1898, it became easier for the Japanese to cross the Pacific Ocean to the West Coast of the United States. One estimate placed the number of Japanese who emigrated to the mainland at 40,000.[15]

A Preview of Things to Come

Even though the total number of Japanese immigrants was not overwhelming in the early years of the twentieth century, opposition to all Asians in San Francisco became volatile in 1906. In the fall of that year, Chinese, Japanese, and Korean students were segregated into so-called Oriental public schools. This was not a good move considering that the Japanese

Red Cross had just sent $250,000 to aid victims of the 1906 San Francisco earthquake. In response, a Tokyo newspaper spoke strongly: "Stand up, Japanese nation! Our countrymen have been HUMILIATED. . . . Why do not we assist [with] sending [war] ships." Theodore Roosevelt, although not personally favorable toward Asians, was angry at the San Francisco School Board, calling the board "idiots."[16]

President Roosevelt attempted to mollify the tensions of California and Japan over the racial issue prevalent on the West Coast. He was able to get Japan to accept a "Gentleman's Agreement" to restrict Japanese immigration to the United States. Fortunately for both nations, in the early twentieth century, the Japanese government cut the flow of laborers to the United States.[17]

In the same year as the San Francisco earthquake, Roosevelt and his advisors began planning sessions for a possible war with Japan. As a two-ocean nation, the United States constructed the Panama Canal. To impress the world with the naval prowess of the United States, in 1907 Roosevelt sent the Great White Fleet around the world, with an important stop in Japan. Pronouncing the voyage a success, Teddy Roosevelt was impressed with the new navy.[18]

Even though the United States became involved late in World War I, she emerged as the leading nation of the world, with the largest navy and greatest economic power. Japan, however, desired to join the "greatest nation league." This desire had implications for the 1920s and afterward.[19]

The 1920s: Increased Negative Feelings between the United States and Japan

Preparing for natural disasters is often left for the future, including ever-concerned Japan, located on one of the largest geological faults in the world. No one expected what happened on September 1, 1923, when the cities of Tokyo and Yokohama were devastated by an earthquake and a tidal wave, followed by widespread fire. Some 200,000 Japanese lost their lives, and two million were left homeless. Starvation and disease killed thousands. The US government and its people quickly sent $11.6 million in relief. It was hoped that such a response would help the relationship between the two nations. One Tokyo newspaper's response to the American aid was optimistic: "[They have behaved] like the Americans of old. They have been efficient, sentimental and generous in giving and forgetful of everything else in their zeal to help helpless sufferers."[20]

Japan spent much of the 1920s recovering from this devastating earthquake. During the 1920s, Japan's economy had become more and more closely tied to Wall Street. When Wall Street took its tumble in October 1929, the reverberations were felt around the world, especially in Japan. As Walter LaFever states, "Japan's economy now found itself tied to sinking stones." Some Japanese families faced starvation. Unemployment escalated to 47.5 percent in 1925. On average, five hundred persons committed suicide each month in 1930. Japan was in an economic bind.[21]

Japan, even more, began looking toward Manchuria for economic survival. The history of the Far East might have been different had Japan taken a different direction in her relationship with China. Japanese historian Saburō Ienaga, in his *The Pacific War: 1931–1945*, condemns Japan's desire to control the whole of Manchuria, not unlike Western imperialist nations. Japan already had an army, the Kwantung, in Manchuria to protect its interests, especially the South Manchurian Railway. In the spring of 1931, the army called for a covert operation in Mukden. On September 18, 1931, a train was derailed by an explosion on the South Manchurian Railway. The preplanned blast was blamed on the Chinese. The government in Tokyo did nothing to stop the advance of the Kwantung Army throughout Manchuria. World War II in the Far East had begun,[22] and the military was well on its way to having complete control of Japan.

The Japanese Military Gains Control of Japan

How did the Japanese Army and Navy gain control of Japan? The World War I era and the 1920s were more open in Japan, but education came under the strict control of the national government, and the emperor became a monarch with sacred authority. Rituals, written by the government, were used to instill a reverence among the people for the emperor and the state.[23]

In 1917, the nation's leadership introduced military training into the schools. Japanese wars were emphasized in the classroom to instill nationalism. In 1925, military officers were assigned for all schools, from middle through high school. Military training became an integral part of the curriculum. All youngsters, from the poorest to the upper classes, were included in the program. Saburō states, "These laws and public education, used as instruments of coercion and manipulation, were the decisive factors that made it impossible for the Japanese people to stop their country from launching the Pacific War."[24]

The United States, paralyzed by events in Manchuria, understood the importance of China to the economies of both Japan and Russia. Japan continued driving deeper into Manchuria, even beyond the Great Wall, whetting their appetite for more territory—even all of Manchuria. When the League of Nations voted overwhelmingly for Japan to withdraw from Manchuria, Japan walked out of the assembly. In March 1933, Japan withdrew from the League.[25]

During the 1930s, Japan moved deeper into China, shelling and bombing Shanghai. Supporting the Open Door Policy toward China, the United States sent reinforcements to support American interests. Did anyone think this a prelude to 1941? In Tokyo, the civilian government breathed its last. Using the assassination of Prime Minister Inukai, the military gained total control of Japan. They would be in charge of Japan until 1945, the conclusion of World War II.[26]

On the mainland, China was in the midst of its own civil war. In the late 1920s, the communism of Mao Zu Dung and the nationalism of Chiang Kai-shek vied for the upper hand. By the end of the 1920s, Chiang moved to consolidate his power throughout China. Although Japan was an enemy, Japan was also strongly opposed to the communism of the Soviet Union, which was China's enemy in Manchuria.[27] In reality, Chiang viewed as his foremost enemy Mao and communism. Thus Chiang welcomed Japan's control of Manchuria, forming a wall against the Soviet Union.

Ever the imperialist, Japan believed China could be easily defeated. For the most part, the Japanese had contempt for the Chinese and believed that sending a few divisions against the Chinese would cause them to quit. However, the Chinese developed a strong nationalistic consciousness in the 1930s. Even more disconcerting, however, was the strength of the Communist Eighth Route Army, made up of Chinese men who were experiencing freedom for the first time. In the midst of a civil war between the communists and the nationalists, the Japanese found themselves in conflict with both Chinese armies.[28]

Japan Becomes Deeply Involved in China:
The United States Responds

The year 1937 was a telling time for Japan. On July 7, Japanese and Chinese forces clashed at Marco Polo Bridge near Peking. Instead of this being an isolated event, it escalated into a wider war—the Second Sino-Japanese War. In the meantime, Roosevelt continued to provide arms for China and oil and raw materials for Japan.[29]

The Japanese government likely had no idea that the Marco Polo Bridge incident near Peking would escalate into a broader war. The Japanese attacked Chiang Kai-shek's capital city of Nanking. On December 12, Japanese airplanes sank an American gunboat, the *Panay*, on the Yangtze River. The ship was responding to a call from foreigners to aid them in escaping Nanking. In the melee, three Americans were killed. While Congress debated the US response to the sinking of the *Panay*, the Japanese massacred 150,000 Chinese, often referred to as the "Rape of Nanking."

President Roosevelt reacted quickly to the attack. He outlined for his cabinet three motives Japan had for the attack. According to historian Ted Morgan, "in the first place, an arrogant and unrebuked assault on the United States would impress the Chinese with the power and strength of Japan. In the second place, Japan wanted to make it uncomfortable for any Western power to stay in the Yangtze or in any other part of China. In the third place, Japan wanted to force all Westerners out of China." Secretary of Navy Claude Swanson wanted war with Japan immediately.[30]

Japan apologized profusely for killing Americans, paying the United States $1.1 million in reparations. The war continued southwest to Canton, where on May 28 and June 4, 1938, Japanese planes bombed the city, killing at least 1,500 people.

The United States responded by increasing financial aid to China and placing an embargo on selling airplane parts to Japan. American trade with Japan peaked in 1937. Japan was growing more dependent on the United States for oil and scrap metal in pursuit of her goals.[31]

In July 1940, President Roosevelt asked Congress for a $4 billion increase for the military. In the same month, the president signed the National Defense Action Act, giving him the power to deny the export of goods he deemed necessary to support the US defense goals. By the passage of the act, Roosevelt stopped the sale of necessary items Japan needed to pursue its goals. In response, Japan joined the European Axis powers, Germany and Italy. Signing a treaty with the Nazi puppet Vichy France, Japan moved troops into northern Indochina, a move to solidify its hold on that nation and also surrounding China. As LeFever states, "[t]he Japanese were. . . to be the final arbiter of what the 'open door' in China meant."[32]

The year 1941 would be the year of no return. The United States had broken Japanese secret codes; the American government knew Japan's dilemma. Without American trade, Japan would lose the economic and military race for the Far East. The only answer was the invasion of the British, Dutch, and French territories of Southeast Asia. There they could have the raw materials, especially oil, to pursue a war with the United States. With Japan locating troops in Indochina, the "hawks" in Washington chose to force the Japanese to acquiesce or face war. This left Japan in a difficult situation—concession or war.[33]

Japan would not agree to leave China, as they had spent ten years gaining a foothold. Needing a decisive prowar leader, the government chose the war minister Tojo Hideki to become prime minister late in October 1941. He had spoken with emotion against concessions in China in order to keep the peace: "He warned that any withdraw of troops would be a condemnation of all Japan's efforts in China, and would also threaten Manchukuo, perhaps even Korea."[34]

Throughout 1941, Secretary of State Cordell Hull and Kichisaburo Nomura were engaged in talks designed to forestall conflict between the two nations. The Japanese Imperial Conference on November 5 agreed to go to war early in December if diplomacy failed. On November 26, Hull handed Nomura a memorandum calling for Japan to withdraw from China and Indochina. The Japanese leadership now accepted the fact that war was inevitable.

Missionary families affiliated with Churches of Christ had called Japan home since the early 1890s. But after the bombing at Pearl Harbor, only two women remained behind: Sarah Andrews and Lillie Cypert. It is to Sarah Andrews's remarkable story, along with those of the earliest US missionaries to Japan, that we turn next.

Endnotes

[1]Stephen Ambrose, *Undaunted Courage: Meriwether Lewis, Thomas Jefferson, and the Opening of the American West* (New York: Touchstone, 1996), 442.

[2]George C. Herring, *From Colony to Superpower: U.S. Foreign Relations since 1776* (New York: Oxford University Press, 2008), 205–7.

[3]Walter LaFever, *Clash: U.S.–Japanese Relations through History* (New York: W. W. Norton & Company, 1997), 12.

[4]Ibid., 23.

[5]George C. Herring, *From Colony to Superpower*, 257, 258.

[6]Ibid., 312, 313.

[7]Walter LaFever, *Clash*, 29, 30; George C. Herring, *From Colony to Superpower*, 224.

[8]George C. Herring, *From Colony to Superpower*, 268.

[9]Ibid., 69.

[10]Ibid., 332, 333; Walter LaFever, *Clash*, 68, 69.

[11]Walter LaFever, *Clash*, 77.

[12]Ibid., 78–84.

[13]Walter LaFever, *Clash*, 51, 91, 92.

[14]US Office of the Historian, "Japanese-American Relations at the Turn of the Century, 1900–1922," accessed December 22, 2016, https://history.state.gov/milestones/1899-1913/japanese-relations.

[15]Ibid., 164.

[16]Ibid. *Clash*, 88, 89.

[17]George C. Herring, *From Colony to Superpower*, 356.

[18]Ibid., 349.

[19]Ibid., 99.

[20]Ibid., 467.

[21]Ibid., 155, 156.

[22]Saburō Ienaga, *The Pacific War: 1931–1945* (New York: Pantheon Books, 1978), 58–65.

[23]Ibid., 19–22.

[24]Ibid., 22–32.

[25]Ibid., 66.

[26]Walter LaFever, *Clash*, 161–73.

[27]Ibid., 150.

[28]Saburō Ienaga, *The Pacific War*, 88–96.

[29]Walter LaFever, *Clash*, 184.

[30]Ted Morgan, *FDR: A Biography* (New York: Simon and Schuster, 1985), 488.

[31]Ibid., 186–88.

[32]Ibid.

[33]George C. Herring, *From Colony to Superpower*, 534, 535.

[34]Walter LaFever, *Clash*, 205; Saburō Ienaga, *The Pacific War*, 134.

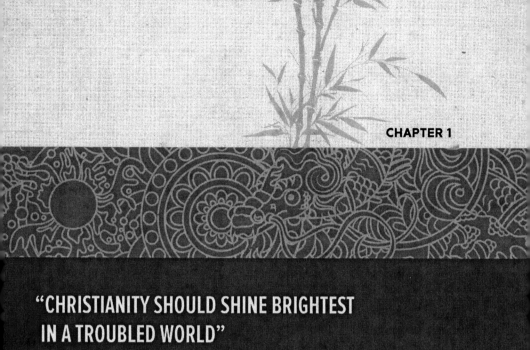

CHAPTER 1

"CHRISTIANITY SHOULD SHINE BRIGHTEST IN A TROUBLED WORLD"

Sarah Andrews and Early Missionaries to Japan

On October 28, 1945, William Billingsley, an American GI, along with a fellow soldier crossed the mountains from Yokohama to Shizuoka. Billingsley was looking for Sarah Andrews, who had been missing since the outbreak of the war. Knowing her physical weakness, her family had feared she was dead.

A 1944 edition of Nashville, Tennessee's *World Vision*, a Christian magazine published by former missionary to Japan Barney Morehead, commemorated Andrews's brave efforts, fearing the worst: "[N]o word has come directly from [Sarah Andrews] since the war began. . . . Through what trials she passed we may not know, but her faith was strong and her courage undaunted. . . . And wherever she lies there rests a faithful soldier of the Cross. She went to a foreign shore, not with missiles of hate and destruction, but with a message of hope."[1]

Andrews, a missionary for Churches of Christ in Japan since 1916, wrote about the severe conditions endured by the Japanese people in 1939: "The pall of war hung over the land, with its black-outs, strict police force, scarcity of commodities, soldiers everywhere, the odor of sulphur from ammunition factories filling the air." Japan had been at war since 1931, and Andrews carried out her work spreading the love of Christ amid the harsh realities of a war-torn nation greatly in need of Christ's love: "Indeed, evidences of the burden and sorrows of war were everywhere depressing."[2]

As she struggled to carry out her work in the face of such great obstacles, Sarah Andrews and those who worked alongside her composed the beginning of a second wave of missionaries arriving in Japan representing Churches of Christ. To fully appreciate her long tenure as a missionary in Japan from 1916 onward, it is important to first trace the beginnings of missionary work of the Churches of Christ in Japan, dating back to 1892—a legacy that Andrews dared to continue and carry on amid the horrors of World War II.

The First Church of Christ Volunteer Missionaries Arrive in Japan (1892)

Japan was the first major destination for foreign missions among Churches of Christ. From the time of the Civil War, the conservative Disciples of Christ, especially in the southern states, opposed mission work done through missionary societies. These churches would later be designated Churches of Christ and were often chided for not doing mission work, which became a cause for concern. The *Gospel Advocate* of Nashville, Tennessee, began supporting independent mission work, first among the Cherokee Indians, as early as the 1850s when James J. Trott moved westward to the Oklahoma Territory. After the Civil War, the paper encouraged churches to support the work of Robert W. Officer, also in the Oklahoma Territory. Influenced by John W. McGarvey, David Lipscomb, editor of the *Gospel Advocate*, urged Nashville churches to supply funds for an Armenian, Azariah Paul, a former student at the College of the Bible in Lexington, Kentucky, in his desire to return to his home country to preach the gospel to his people. The Nashville churches agreed to support the mission.

In the early 1890s, Wilson K. Azbill, a Kentuckian and a graduate of the College of the Bible, initiated the concept of the Volunteer Band for foreign missions to spread the gospel of Christ worldwide. Azbill traveled widely across mid-America, visiting churches and soliciting support, particularly for Japanese missions. Of the total $3,300 raised, the promise of $1,475 came from Tennessee. In the meantime, John M. McCaleb, also a recent graduate of the College of the Bible, and a native Tennessean, listened to his former classmate Eugene Snodgrass, a Kentuckian, announce to his fellow students at the College of the Bible his intention to go to Japan as a missionary. For the first time, McCaleb thought about foreign missions. McCaleb strongly considered joining Azbill's newly organized Volunteer Band to go as an unattached missionary to Japan. Before he made his decision, McCaleb felt it important that editor David Lipscomb favored the Volunteer Band approach advocated by Azbill. Lipscomb believed the Azbill plan to be scriptural.[3] As a result, McCaleb and his wife Della sailed to Japan on March 26, 1892, along with Azbill, Lucia Scott, and Carme Hostetter, the last two graduates of Hiram College in Ohio.[4]

Arriving in Japan, McCaleb soon learned that Snodgrass had separated from the missionary society. He refused to accept the use of instrumental music in worship. As a result, McCaleb had an unexpected associate with experience who understood something of missionary needs in Japan. Snodgrass, arriving in Japan in 1888, had already established the Kamitomizaka church in Tokyo. In 1893, soon after the McCalebs' arrival, Snodgrass and his wife returned to the States on furlough. Even though the Broadway church in Lexington, Kentucky, did not support him as a volunteer missionary, he used the church as his base while away from Japan. Traveling to Nashville, David Lipscomb and Snodgrass met for the first time. Growing from the visit, Snodgrass began writing a weekly foreign missionary column for the *Advocate*.[5] In 1895, he and his wife returned to Japan.

The Kanda Ward of Tokyo became the center of McCaleb's work. Here he would establish schools for the education of the poor and teach the children who would, hopefully, reach their parents.[6] These schools were especially important because the Japanese government, at the time, did not provide education for the poorer classes.

With the absence of the Snodgrass family for two years, the burden of the work fell on the shoulders of McCaleb, Carme Hostetter, and Lucia Scott. Both young ladies quickly became involved in educating the Japanese poor. Lucia opened a school in Yotsuya Ward. In 1893, McCaleb raised $600 from churches in America to construct a building for worship and a school. In its second year, fifty students enrolled. However, McCaleb, lacking funds to support his family, found it necessary to travel 400 miles to Kanazawa, on the west coast of Japan, to teach English. Thus the Kanda Ward work and the operation of the school while McCaleb was away from Tokyo became Carme Hostetter's responsibility.[7]

Answering the call, on October 14, 1899, William Bishop, a graduate of the Nashville Bible School, sailed with his wife, Alice, for Japan. He would add tremendously to the Japanese mission endeavor. While a student in the Nashville school, he had worked in a print shop, a talent especially needed in Japan. The young missionary received the blessings of David Lipscomb, as his former student.[8] As the Bishops arrived, the McCalebs returned to the United States on furlough. They had been in Japan seven years. Leaving Japan on August 4, 1899, the McCalebs would remain in the States until July 1901.

Working in the Kanda Mission, Bishop, purchasing a small printing press from Eugene Snodgrass, began providing printed materials for the Japanese. As expected, Bishop proved to be a valuable addition to the efforts of the Volunteer Band. But soon grief engulfed William's life. Alice, not well when she left the States, died on March 9, 1900, tuberculosis claiming her life. William buried her in foreign soil in Tokyo's Aoyama Cemetery.[9]

Bishop grieved the loss of Alice, finding some consolation in his work and printing Christian materials for the Japanese, including John W. McGarvey's *Commentary on Acts*. His grief, however, could not be contained.

Within a year, Bishop began corresponding with Clara Mae Elliott of Paris, Texas, the daughter of J. D. Elliott, an elder of the Paris church. Bishop had preached for the church prior to going to Japan. By November 1901, the possibility of marriage was in the air. In the spring of 1902, Bishop left for America to claim his new bride. Married on April 1, 1902, they sailed for Japan in October, arriving in Yokohama on November 24, 1902.[10]

These three men—McCaleb, Snodgrass, and Bishop—and their families formed the backbone of the mission efforts of Churches of Christ in Japan for the first 15 to 20 years. However, because of his wife's illness, it was necessary for Eugene Snodgrass to return to the United States in 1903. Without warning, in 1905 Eugene suffered a major brain hemorrhage, dying on March 25, 1906.[11] Ten years after the Snodgrasses left Japan, William Bishop quickly left Japan on January 2, 1913, on his way to a sanatorium in Monrovia, California. The medical professionals were unable to save his life. He died on April 4, 1913, a victim of tuberculosis, a common illness in Japan, especially for those who lived and worked in the poorer sections of the cities.[12] Other missionaries came to Japan during the early years, but McCaleb, Snodgrass, and Bishop were the most influential in ensuring the success of the Church of Christ Japanese missions.

J. M. McCaleb, remaining in Japan even when his family returned to America, was the person who served as the cohesive factor for the mission efforts in Japan from 1892 until World War II.[13] His tenure spanned fifty years. During that era, the call of Japan made that country the most prominent destination of missionaries from Churches of Christ. From 1892 to 1916, twenty-two individuals from Churches of Christ went from the United States to Japan as missionaries. Besides the original members of the Volunteer Band, plus Mr. and Mrs. Eugene Snodgrass and William Bishop and his two wives, the missionaries included the following:

Alice Miller (1895), serving thirty-three years
F. A. Wagner (1897), serving four years (died in Japan)
Mr. and Mrs. R. L. Pruett (1896), serving one year (joined
    missionary society)
Nettie Craynon (1896), serving one year
Dr. Gertrude Remington (1904), serving three years
Mr. and Mrs. C. C. Klingman (1908), serving four years
Mr. and Mrs. B. W. Hon (1910), serving one year
Mr. and Mrs. C. G. Vincent (1911), serving four years

The twenty-two missionaries who served from 1892 to 1915 had a total of 153 years on the mission field. There were 720 baptisms during those years. They established eight churches.[14]

And when Sarah Andrews arrived in Japan in January 1916, her work built off the legacy of those brave souls who had served before her, in increasing politically tense times. Upon her arrival, only J. M. McCaleb remained of the original twenty-two missionaries who earlier had come to Japan.

Sarah Andrews Answers the Call of Japan

Sarah Andrews, twenty-three years of age and knowing only J. M. McCaleb, made her way to Japan in January 1916, determined to fulfill her long-held desire to be a missionary. She had no training for mission work beyond high school, except a short time at the State Normal School in Memphis and her personal reading on Japan and its people. Leaving Dickson, Tennessee, alone on December 25, 1915, she boarded a ship in Vancouver, British Columbia, on January 1, 1916, arriving in Japan on January 15.[15]

From childhood, Sarah's mother had talked excitedly about McCaleb, the missionary. Then in 1909, McCaleb made a visit to Dickson. The young Andrews, born in 1892 (the exact year McCaleb first went to Japan) excitedly told him of her plans to be a missionary. And, of course, she dreamed of going to Japan. When I. B. Bradley, the preacher at Dickson, baptized her at age fourteen, he recalled Sarah saying to him, "I hope someday to go to Japan as a missionary to help teach them about the true God and the Savior; and I am going to work for that and try to prepare myself for the work." She never wavered from her dream.

Many friends and family, naturally, questioned why a young woman who had never been out of the United States would choose to go so far away to do Christian work. Her response was always, "There is certainly a vast amount of work to be done at home; but please compare the number of workers in the United States with the number of workers among forty million idolaters in Japan. . . ." She added, "If the Lord permits and my health continues, I hope to have a long life to give to the work in Japan, since I am twenty-two years of age at this time." Even though she would have major health problems in Japan, she realized her dream of service among the Japanese people.

True of most missionaries who went to Japan, Sarah Andrews settled in Tokyo, where McCaleb had established a mission post and a church called Zoshigaya. For the next two years, she studied the Japanese language. Andrews, writing to America, revealed some of the conditions a young American faced in Japan: "I love Japan and love the work but find the language quite difficult although it is easier now than at first." Two weeks later, she described her living conditions: "We are conforming to Japanese habits to some extent, but not entirely. We prefer beds and chairs to sitting and sleeping on the floor, and a stove during cold weather rather than a wee firebox."[16]

But she was never satisfied to remain in Tokyo. Like the Apostle Paul, she desired to work in "one of the untouched towns." She did not, however, move blindly. She wrote to a number of chiefs of outlying towns, "praying all the while that the Lord would lead us to the very place where he would have us go." After settling on Okitsu, Andrews stated, "I believe he did lead us."

Okitsu, a town of 8,600 people, was about 100 miles south of Tokyo. Andrews moved to Okitsu on July 10, 1919, with her helper, O'iki San, the affectionate name given by Andrews to her friend. O'iki San's widowed mother also moved with them to their new home. Sarah had taught and converted O'iki San, a.k.a. O'iki Nemura, during her learning time in Tokyo. Their goal was to teach children in a Sunday school and then form a small kindergarten: "We will sow the seed in the homes." Because of her understanding of biblical teachings in Churches of Christ, Andrews always called native preachers to come to Okitsu for extended periods of preaching and then baptizing the converts, many who had been taught by Andrews. She dreamed of the time when she and O'iki San would have fellow Christians with whom they could share the Lord's Supper.[17]

Sarah and O'iki San vigorously entered into their work. But first, they needed to overcome the prejudice of a Buddhist town toward Christianity. However, the people wanted a kindergarten, and it was Sarah and O'iki San's goal to form one. Sarah indicated, "I am glad we accepted the invitation to come, and believe the Lord's hand is in it all." The call for students resulted in eighty-five applicants, even though they could accept only thirty-five youngsters. Then they began a Sunday school and before long had an impressive 150 enrollees. The two women "believed that much depends upon the work among the children in getting into the homes of the people and teaching the grown people."

During the first year, the women held three Bible classes each week in their home. In December 1919, Oto Fujimori, from Takahagi in the Chiba Prefecture, came to baptize two believers. (Fujimori's importance as a native preacher is the subject of Chapter 2.) He came again in February for another baptism—and in the following week, several more.[18] Now there were multiple Christians to share the Lord's Supper.

O'iki San's own mother soon responded to the call for baptism. One account describes the scene beautifully: "It was a beautiful sight to see them buried with Jesus in the waves of the sea, between ten and eleven one evening, by the light of candles, and the dashing waves lending solemnity befitting the occasion."[19]

Noting her success in Okitsu, I. B. Bradley, preacher for the Dickson, Tennessee, Church of Christ, exulted, "Sarah Andrews is one of God's noble women—godly, modest, faithful, and loyal to the truth as it is written." Now, he said, it was time for her to return to the United States on furlough.[20] Andrews left Japan on January 7, 1921, with plans to remain in the United States only one year. Two hundred persons from Okitsu gathered at Sarah's residence to see her off, including McCaleb and Fujimori. Sunday school children lined the railroad tracks to bid her good-bye and to bow as the train left the station. Andrews had made a decided impact since the fall of 1919 when she arrived in Okitsu.[21]

Sarah was not well when she sailed for the United States. After arriving in America, she decided to remain longer than one year. An important part of her stay was a year's study at David Lipscomb College. While in America, she also encouraged support for the construction of a church building in Okitsu. It was needed not only for worship but also for the kindergarten and daily Bible classes. And many of her supporters, including Margaret Lipscomb, the wife of David Lipscomb, called for the construction of a Western-style house for Andrews. By December 15, 1921, she began planning her return to Japan: "The Japanese seem anxious for my return, and I am hungry to go back to work." However, her plan did not prove possible. Not until late 1922 did her health begin to improve. Only then did she schedule December 24, 1922, as a sailing date from Seattle.[22] Andrews's letters were circulated widely in Christian publications. And in March 1922, the editors of the *Gospel Advocate* asked her to write on "Woman's Work as a

Missionary." Her conclusions were, "Though she [a woman] does no public preaching, she has a place to fill especially in the house-to-house work and work among children. Until the citadel—the home, where character is formed and destiny shaped—is approached, heathenism cannot be put down." She stated further, "Of course woman's work is the quiet, unassuming type, done in a private way, and the true Christian woman seeks none other."[23] And yet Andrews and other woman missionaries were involved in church activities in Japan that would not have been possible in America.

Andrews's second leaving from home was much better publicized than her going in 1915. The church in Huntsville, Alabama, where her brother-in-law, T. B. Thompson, was the minister, held a reception for her and made a pledge to provide her with regular support. On the afternoon of December 10, the students and faculty held a rally on the campus of David Lipscomb College, resulting in an additional $500 for her home fund. It was the conclusion of a good visit to America.

Arriving in Japan, the American missionary faced horrible weather. The winter of 1922 and 1923 was extremely cold in Okitsu, in an area of Japan often thought tropical. Andrews had to sit wrapped in blankets with her feet propped on the brazier. These conditions encouraged Margaret Lipscomb to urge the construction of a house for Sarah before next winter. The money began to mount. In early 1924, a house had been ordered from the Aladdin Company of Portland, Oregon, to be shipped on February 24.

In the meantime, Andrews, O'iki San, and O'iki San's mother decided to move to Shizuoka, a much larger city than Okitsu. The prefabricated house, however, did not reach Shizuoka until June, after being delayed in Yokohama for two months. Andrews considered the reasons for this to be political, with her work jeopardized by international political turmoil, perhaps only a mere precursor of the struggles still to come: "Some opposition to Christian work has been excited by the immigration bill recently passed by the United States Congress. Some efforts have been made to break up the Sunday school and all the work at Okitsu." Finally on October 11 and 12, 1924, Sarah and her Christian friends moved into their new home. Remembering the cold winter of last year, Sarah stated: "I had a grate put in and hope to keep warm this winter and get real strong and well."[24]

43

Sarah Andrews was ever a dreamer, even with her physical limitations. She looked forward to the time when she could build a center for a kindergarten, a Sunday school, and a place for worship in her new home city, Shizuoka. She had already constructed a small building in Okitsu. But the winter of 1924–1925 saw Sarah's health deteriorate even more, affecting both of her lungs. Doctors encouraged her to return to the United States, but this was not her desire, and she did not wish to impose on the churches supporting her. She wrote, "I have faith, by God's mercy and grace, I can get well in Japan. . . . All I want to live for is for service, and I believe, God helping me, I will get able to serve. . . . I love the Lord, and I want his will to be done, whatever may be my wish. He knoweth best."[25]

A year later, Andrews continued her torrid schedule, except she gave up her summer classes. Her appetite was better, and she even gained weight. But O'iki San became ill, causing Sarah to say, "I felt my right hand was gone." Both women needed rest. For the past two years, Andrews had been doing her work from her home and often from her bed. After a few months, Sarah, along with O'iki, decided to travel to the United States. They spent time in Nashville, where she and O'iki attended Lipscomb for a semester. Early on, Sarah even went to the Mayo Clinic, but most of her three years in the States were spent in Los Angeles with the relatively new Westside Church of Christ, the first Japanese Church of Christ in the United States. In the summer of 1930, Sarah and O'iki returned to Japan.[26]

The 1930s were difficult years for Sarah Andrews. Churches of Christ were divided over the issue of premillennialism. Thus, I. B. Bradley, who had originally baptized Sarah, found it necessary to affirm her "soundness" in the faith: "She is not, nor has she ever been, guilty of 'being carried away with divers and strange doctrines.' . . . She is not tainted . . . with any of the theories that are now causing trouble in our churches."[27] Nonetheless, support for missionaries became increasingly difficult to find. The use of the term "missionary" came into question by some, including Foy E. Wallace, editor of the *Gospel Advocate*. There was less and less space in the papers for foreign missions.

The economic depression in the United States cut deeply into Andrews's support. In 1934, for instance, the average monthly amount sent to Sarah Andrews and O'iki San was only $46.09. As a result, she had given her house to the native preacher and his family to save money. Sarah and O'iki San lived in two rooms in the meetinghouse.[28]

In 1935, Sarah looked forward to getting some much-needed preaching help in Shizuoka. Tokuo Mazawa had been in Tennessee attending David Lipscomb College. He returned to Japan on August 4 to join his wife, who had already moved to Shizuoka. Mazawa had earlier studied to be a Buddhist priest but then began his career as a teacher and went to the United States to make his fortune. In Los Angeles, he came under the influence of Hirosuke Ishiguro, minister of the Westside Church of Christ. Converted in 1927, he returned to Japan where he established a church, eventually growing it to forty-five members with their own building. However, he believed he needed more education, especially in the Bible.[29] He chose to enroll in Lipscomb during the same time period as Orville D. Bixler, since 1918 a missionary to Japan (discussed in more detail in Chapters 3 and 7).

Mazawa's return to Japan allowed Sarah Andrews to return in 1936 to the United States. She traveled as quickly as she could to be with her mother in Alabama and restore her health. Upon her departure, she told McCaleb that she would return to Japan only on the condition that her health was fully restored. McCaleb lamented her departure, indicating, "I especially regret to see her go, and I shall feel lonely without her."[30]

More than three years after Sarah Andrews left Japan, she felt herself well enough to return to Japan and to her adopted people. In a well-structured and feeling article that appeared in the *Christian Leader*, Andrews began by quoting John Ruskin's first verse of "Called Aside":

Called Aside—
From the glad workings of a busy life,
From the world's ceaseless stir of care and strife
Into the shade and stillness by my Heavenly Guide,
For a brief space I have been called aside.

She announced to Churches of Christ that she would, on November 20, 1939, leave from Los Angeles for Japan. She certainly had no idea what the immediate future held for her. Japan had changed dramatically since she left her adopted country three years prior; the Japanese military was now on an aggressive campaign to control China.

Andrews's visit to America was not confined to rest. As her health improved, she enrolled in classes in practical nursing. Returning to Nashville, she attended Peabody College where she took classes in public health. She explained why these areas of study were important to her work in Japan: "In helping the people physically I hope primarily to help them spiritually."[31]

Returning to her Japanese home in Shizuoka, she was warmly welcomed by the churches. She listened to fellow missionary Hettie Lee Ewing describe the political conditions in Japan. How the attitudes of the people had changed since Sarah left for the United States in 1936! The two missionaries, however, could not dwell on the political issues. A horrible fire consumed much of the area of Shizuoka where Andrews lived. Fortunately, her house survived. The losses experienced by the Japanese people gave an opportunity for Ewing, Andrews, and the churches in the city to reach out to the refugees.[32] Probably sooner than she expected, Sarah used her public health and nursing knowledge to help the people of Shizuoka.

Sarah Andrews's commitment to serve in Japan had a direct impact on at least two other women missionaries: Lillie Cypert and Hettie Lee Ewing. Their stories are faith driven, both detailing a strong desire to serve the Japanese people. Both Cypert and Ewing, like Andrews before them, are a source of inspiration for all Christians, showing how on faith they left America for a life among the people of a different, and at times despised, culture.

Lillie Cypert: A Missionary from Arkansas
Like Sarah Andrews, Lillie Cypert was another dedicated missionary who dared to leave the United States for Japan to follow a lifelong dream. On October 5, 1917, she left the United States for Japan. She arrived in Yokohama on October 25. Commenting on her arrival, McCaleb wrote, "She and Andrews are happily located in the Zoshigaya mission home, and both are busy at the language." The most difficult problem facing Cypert was a lack of funds for her support in Japan. When she left home, on faith, she carried with her only one month's support. Thankfully, in 1919, Nellie Straiton of Fort Worth, Texas, accepted the responsibility for soliciting funds for Cypert and transferring them to her.

Born in Oak Flat, Arkansas, in 1890, Cypert attended Freed and Hardeman's school in Henderson, Tennessee. While teaching school in 1916, she first indicated a desire to do mission work in Japan. Asked when she would like to go, she quickly responded, "As soon as possible." She left her home in Leslie, Arkansas, a year later for Japan.[33]

Cypert served her entire mission experience in Tokyo. She remained for a time with McCaleb's Zoshigaya church, where she focused on the Sunday school and a sewing school operated by McCaleb. From her first outreach on reaching Japan, she cared for orphaned children, supporting them and the Sunday school from her $100 monthly fund from America. Being adventurous, she even purchased a bicycle to assist her in the scattered nature of her work.

After five years, in 1922, Cypert decided to take a furlough to the United States. Arriving in San Francisco on June 11, she quickly made her way to Leslie, Arkansas, where her mother eagerly awaited her arrival. Soon after reaching home, Lillie witnessed with gladness her mother's baptism. In Texas, where she visited with Nellie Straiton, she also attended classes at Abilene Christian College. While in Abilene, she heard of the earthquake destruction of Yokohoma and Tokyo. Even though education was important to her, the destruction of Tokyo by an earthquake in September 1923 called her to return to Japan.

What Cypert saw on arrival in Yokohama overwhelmed her. That city and Tokyo were extensively damaged. Cypert stated, "The great disaster is an awful thing, far beyond our imagination. . . . I cannot think of the whole city of Yokohama being gone, yet it is true. . . . I have heard nothing from my kiddies at all, indirectly or otherwise." With relief, she heard that the Christians within the churches where she worked had all survived, although many had lost their homes. She also learned that all the missionaries were safe. Most were out of the city vacationing in the mountains.[34] Before leaving the ship in Yokohama, the missionary observed, "We have been peering through our field glasses for hours to see the ruined city, and desolation it was–nothing left to make it like the place we sailed from less than a year and a half ago."[35] (The earthquake is discussed in more detail in Chapter 2.)

In Tokyo, Lillie Cypert quickly resumed her work. Not only did she continue with the Zoshigaya Sunday school; she also taught a Sunday school in the barracks where the earthquake sufferers lived. Each time she handed out clothing, she gave a religious tract. However, she believed the goodwill that came from the help given by Americans following the devastation of the earthquake was cancelled by the 1924 Exclusion Act passed by the Congress of the United States. She bemoaned what had happened in America: "The Japanese people 'lost their confidence' and decided that the help they had received was only deceitfulness and that the Christian religion was the 'prompter' of the immigration bill also. As a result, where formerly there was interest manifested in the teaching of our Bible, now there is indifference and prejudice."[36]

By the 1920s, Japan was becoming more nationalistic, a trend that struck fear in the hearts of many Americans. Negative US reactions aimed at the Japanese people, such as the Exclusion Act, aroused strong feelings in Japan toward the United States. This and similar actions would not soon be forgotten by the nation on the rise in the Far East. It is evident that missionaries in Japan felt the rising tide of nationalism from both sides of the growing conflict.

Yet even in the face of growing indifference and prejudice, Cypert's work continued to grow. Roy Lanier, a Church of Christ preacher, reported in 1929 that her ministry had resulted in as many baptisms as any mission point in Japan. She had begun a new work in Tanashi, an area of Tokyo. Within a short while, she had 150 children enrolled in her Sunday school. Following intense urging, she formed a kindergarten in the town—the first school in Tanashi. Because of her efforts and that of native preachers from other areas, the small church added six members in 1929, raising the membership of the church to twenty-three.[37]

Little is known about Lillie Cypert's ministry during the 1930s because she was ill with scarlet fever in 1935 and other illnesses followed. She may have suffered a small stroke. During these difficult times, she continued to be funded quite well by churches in Texas. Unlike Andrews, she rarely reported through the church papers. During the 1930s, Cypert's concern for homeless Japanese children was well known. She continued caring for several orphaned youngsters as her own children until the day she was repatriated to the United States in 1943. It can be concluded that through her tireless efforts as a servant of Jesus Christ amid adversity and opposition, she cared for her brothers and sisters in the faith, surpassing the stigma of nationalism and false notions of separation—as children of God.

Hettie Lee Ewing: "Maybe This Is My Call"

In May 1924, Hettie Lee Ewing heard O. E. Phillips of Abilene, Texas, read a letter from Lillie Cypert about her work in Japan. The letter raised questions and concerns in Ewing's mind: "Maybe, maybe this is my call. Maybe I should go. Maybe I'm the one." Later she talked with Phillips. She asked, "But could I do it? . . . I'm just a grown-up country girl. I don't have a college degree. . . . I don't think I could *begin* to learn the Japanese language." At the conclusion of Phillips's sermon on a Sunday night a few days later, the preacher told the congregation that a young lady would like to be a missionary. He then said: "Sister Hettie Lee, stand up!" Although there would be hurdles and problems, this was the beginning of Hettie Lee Ewing's adventure as a missionary to Japan, before and after World War II.[38]

Unlike Sarah Andrews, Ewing was not a young lady when she answered the call of Japan. She was twenty-eight years of age. Born on October 11, 1896, in Johnson County, Texas, she was fourteen years old when she, along with nine other girls of the same age, responded for baptism under the preaching of Joe Warlick. Reading the religious papers, she discovered foreign missions. She learned with concern that Churches of Christ had only forty missionaries in foreign countries, counting husbands, wives, and single women.[39]

Ewing, however, faced a very high hurdle in her desire to go to Japan. She was the only person to care for her widowed father. But fortunately for Ewing, her father removed the hurdle when he remarried. She was now free to pursue her dream, but she needed funds for transportation and then for monthly support. The church in Cleburne, Texas, responded, although in a small way, to her plea. When she visited the church, they placed a cup on a table before the congregation, allowing the members to contribute to Ewing's dream. The cup contained $11—her first money to support her move to Japan. In faith, she made her way to Los Angeles where she lived and worked with the recently established Japanese church. Here she gained experience among Japanese people.

Funds began to arrive, although not in abundance, from Texas and Tennessee. Finally on August 13, 1926, she had sufficient money to travel to Japan on the *Siberia Maru*. She sailed on the same ship as Ethel Mattley, a missionary to China. Mattley attempted to persuade Hettie Lee to travel on to China with her, but her mind was set. Japan was her destination. On September 2, she arrived in Yokohama, where she was met by McCaleb, Cypert, and Barney and Nellie Morehead, who had arrived in Japan in 1925.[40] (Their story is found in Chapter 3.)

From the first day, Ewing was anxious to reach out to the Japanese people. After only four months, she realized she could learn the language easier by going among the people, even learning while walking the streets of Tokyo. For health reasons, Sarah Andrews needed to return to the United States in 1927, and McCaleb suggested that Ewing go to Shizuoka to occupy Sarah's house until she returned. This was ideal for Ewing. There were two Christians there who would have a deep impact on Ewing: a brother and sister, Kinji and Michiko Tashiro. Kinji, an excellent communicator, taught his people from the Japanese Bible; Ewing, while studying the Japanese language, taught from an English Bible. Hettie Lee, Kinji, and Michiko continued their work together, traveling to Los Angeles for academic endeavors and settling on the north island of Hokkaido. But on October 23, 1931, Kinji died as a result of typhoid fever, an epidemic that ravaged Japan that year.[41]

The loss was devastating, and Ewing went into a deep depression. Finding peace through her faith and with the help of her friends, after her recovery, Ewing found her calling in Shizuoka and established a church in the Nakahara Ward in the southeast section, while Sarah Andrews established a church in the northwest area of the city as well as a church in Shimizu. Together, the two women were responsible for establishing four churches prior to World War II.[42]

Hettie Lee Ewing, at the age of thirty-eight, returned in 1934 to the United States where, as a freshman, she enrolled in Abilene Christian College. She asked President James F. Cox if she might get the same tuition discount as preacher students. Not only did he answer "yes" to her question, but offered even more—free tuition. At graduation in 1937, Charles R. Roberson stated as she received her degree "I would like to say that in all my teaching years, it gives me more pleasure to present this degree than any I have ever presented."[43]

The years between Hettie Lee Ewing's return to Japan in 1937 and her leaving Japan in 1940 were years of great concern for American missionaries. Ewing discovered that she had to be careful what she wrote to friends and family in the United States, lest she be considered an enemy. A war raged with China, and the Japanese army committed horrible atrocities in Nanking. When she left Japan in 1934, there was little hostility toward Americans. However, as the years progressed, leading up to World War II, there was an outpouring of anti-American sentiment, and American citizens could no longer travel without special permission from the government. During 1939 and 1940, the government often interrogated foreigners. For Hettie Lee Ewing, it was time to return to the United States. Japanese nationalism had made it almost impossible to share Christ with a war-crazed nation. On October 4, 1940, she sailed from Yokohama to America.[44]

Sarah Andrews and Lillie Cypert Choose to Remain in Japan

Two of the single missionary women chose to remain in Japan, even when the American government constantly urged women and children to return to the United States. Even as late as February 1941, when the US government knew conflict was imminent, Andrews and Cypert chose not to heed the American Consulate General's warning. I. B. Bradley, Andrews's American contact, urged her in the spring of 1941 to come home. Andrews, with determination, responded to her dear friend: "I don't believe war will come, but granting it does, CHRISTIANITY SHOULD SHINE BRIGHTEST IN A TROUBLED WORLD [emphasis supplied] and not retreat in hiding when clouds are overcast. . . . I believe it was God's will for me to come to Japan and [I] just can't forsake my post of duty as long as needs and opportunities prevail. . . . Has He not already shown me that I should stay?" She added in a note on October 13, "The church work progresses very nicely at the three stations in this section with all church services maintained."[45] Sarah Andrews established churches in Okitsu, Shizuoka, and Shimizu.

Andrews knew her future in Japan would not be easy. Because Japan froze all her bank accounts, support could not reach her. She encouraged those who had fellowship with her to send money to I. B. Bradley to deposit in her account so it would be available when Japan lifted the freeze. She had cut her expenses to the very minimum. Sarah wrote to American Christians: "My personal expenses are amazingly small and therefore by dismissing my helper I can make the Japanese money on hand last for a few months." Knowing their fears, she encouraged her friends not to be concerned about her. "I am getting along fine among many friends, with God over all. His promises are sure and steadfast."[46]

Little was heard from Andrews and Cypert during the first two years of World War II, although Cypert's sister received a letter from her dated January 29, 1942.[47] Somewhat later, Andrews's name appeared on a list for exchange.[48] This never materialized. An anonymous note received by the *Christian Leader* in November 1942 confirmed Andrews's safety. When the person last saw Andrews, she was asked to relay the message, "I'm fine and give them my love."[49] In 1943 it was Cypert, not Andrews, who was exchanged for Japanese nationals.[50] From this point forward until late in 1945, nothing was heard from Andrews.

It was only after World War II that Andrews could tell her harrowing story of her existence in her adopted country. Even before the outbreak of war, Andrews questioned the attitudes of the Japanese government toward religion in the country—especially as it would impact Churches of Christ and more specifically the three churches she had established. The Department of Education, through the Religious Body Law, proceeded to organize all religion in Japan under three headings—Shinto, Buddhist, and Christian. This move would eliminate all divisions and sects within each group. Now all Christian communities would be identified broadly as "The Japanese Christian Church." Andrews attempted to explain to members of the three churches how they would lose their identity if this should happen: "[I]f the churches entered such a federation, they ceased thereupon to be churches of Christ. I encouraged them to stand for the New Testament order and trust God for the consequences, even if they were ordered to disband and must worship God in secret as in days of old Rome."[51]

The churches seemed to be in total agreement with Andrews, until one of the leaders became what she called "a veritable turncoat." Through clandestine ways, he did all he could to take the churches into the national union. "My heart was burdened, and prayers and tears went up to God for Zion's cause."[52] The opposition never ceased. In September 1942, the government sent Andrews, along with three Catholic nuns, to a concentration camp in Yokohama. Transported by train for one hundred miles, four soldiers guarded them, one for each woman. After two weeks in camp, because of her health, the officials returned Andrews to Shizuoka. They did not expect her to live. Interned in her home, she remained there for the duration of the war.

The missionary's sudden return to her home in Shizuoka was, she said, "a sore disappointment to those who were striving to enter the federation and to those who were eager for my property."[53] They did everything imaginable to remove her from her Western-style home. She wrote, "Various schemes, plottings, and trickery were resorted to in an endeavor to get me out again."[54] They tried to prove she was not sick and should be returned to the internment camp. Failing in this ruse, they attempted to send her to a sanitarium. When American planes began to bomb Shizuoka, they wanted her evacuated to the mountains. Next they falsely accused her of plotting against the Japanese government and tried to send her to prison. Finally, they pronounced her insane and tried to send her to an asylum in Manchuria. Yet every effort to gain her property and to undermine her opposition to the religious federation failed. Even though she was forced to live alone for the final two years of the war "and food was scarce," she still prevailed and continued with her mission, unfazed by any obstacle.[55]

The years of war limited her missionary outreach. Beginning early in the morning of December 8, 1941, when a neighbor told her that war had been declared between Japan and the United States, Sarah Andrews's situation until 1945 was poor at best. As she told it, "American assets were frozen, foreign postal service was suspended, American nationals were advised to evacuate." Her commitment was firm. "I was not afraid; besides, the cause was at stake, so I had no thought of leaving."[56] On December 10, 1941, she was called to report to the police station where she was ordered to discontinue all teaching. She was not allowed to gather with Christians in any of the three churches. She had to abandon her Bible class. But with grit, she would never be stopped. She used the time to prepare Bible study guides that could be used at the war's end. Isolated from her Christian friends, she was very lonely. But she recalled that John in his loneliness and in exile penned Revelation. And Paul, as a prisoner of the state in Rome, wrote many of his New Testament letters. Thus her forced seclusion gave her an opportunity to do as Paul and John did in confinement—write Bible lessons for Japanese Christians.

Early on, her greatest concern was the fear the authorities would confiscate her books, including her Bibles. The Finance Department required her to list all her property, "even to the number of handkerchiefs."[57] The policeman, quizzing the prisoner, wanted to know why she had more than one copy of the Bible. Fortunately, he did not take her Bibles, but he did confiscate her manuscripts, "Notes on Galatians and Ephesians." Sarah, however, would not be discouraged. She finished her "Bible-Study Topics" before she was sent to the concentration camp in September 1942.

For the next three years, Sarah Andrews would live a life of solitude, with 1944 and 1945 being the most difficult. There was very little food. "My garden space," she related, "was confiscated."[58] Thus her one means of having a balanced diet was taken from her. During the final two years of the war, with the US Air Force putting pressure on the islands of Japan by bombing her cities, Sarah had to use rather drastic methods to stay alive. She recalled, "I had never experienced hunger until I was caught in the throes of war. My weight reached the low ebb of seventy-five pounds, and my body became very edematous from malnutrition."[59] To supplement the little food she received from the Japanese, she boiled tree leaves for food, processed corn stalks for sugar, boiled sea water for salt, and cooked grasshoppers for meat.[60]

Andrews's finances soon became nonexistent. The weeks, months, and years that American funds did not come caused her to take drastic actions during 1942—and probably into 1943. She sold her furniture, piece by piece, to have meager funds available to purchase necessities, especially scarce food. Even then, she had to have permission from her guards to sell the furniture. In the meantime, funds sent to Bradley to provide for Andrews's needs dried up. Everyone thought she was dead.

The one thing that helped Sarah keep going was the time she spent writing. She left a manuscript, possibly the topical lessons, with a friend for safe keeping. When intense bombing began in the region of Shizuoka, her friend placed the manuscript in a basket of clothing and moved north, attempting to escape the ravages of war. The manuscript was lost. In the meantime, Andrews continued writing, this time a history of the church. But the confinement to her house, the stress and strain associated with her situation, and especially the starvation made work almost impossible.[61]

In the meantime, Lillie Cypert's time in Japan was coming to an end—she would never return. Cypert's experiences were not as difficult as Andrews's. From sometime in 1942 until she was repatriated in the fall of 1943, the Japanese interned her in a small camp. The majority of the internees were missionaries and teachers. For the most part, the prisoners were treated well. Cypert told how each internee received a pound of bread a day. And each day, they had a sufficient supply of tea, and each person had a spoon of sugar and butter. They received, occasionally, a tangerine and a few grapes. At other times they had half an apple or half a pear. She told how they would save rinds from the tangerines and hoard their sugar to make jam for their bread. From time to time, they were provided a few vegetables—the kind the Japanese would not eat, including celery, cauliflower, asparagus, and sometimes spinach.[62]

That isn't to say that everything went well in camp. The Japanese had fifteen soldiers guarding the internees: "A few of these were not always nice to us, but most of them were, as long as we obeyed the rules and restrictions. But we did have to obey or they made it hard for us." Cypert continued by saying, "In that time I had . . . no occasion to be unhappy except on account of privations and lack of conveniences."[63] Lillie stated that the meanest thing anyone said to those in the internment camp was a response by a policeman when the internees were told they would not have sufficient wood to keep warm during the winter: "This is only a bunch of old women; let them die."[64]

Even while imprisoned in the camp, she felt it important to share the message of Jesus, whether with internees or Japanese guards. Often she gave the guards religious tracts. When she did not have an entire Bible to give away, she would give sections of the Bible to encourage reading of the Scriptures.

Lillie Cypert's internment came to an end in 1943. Some Americans were freed from the camps when the United States agreed to repatriate Japanese Americans who chose to return to Japan. Repatriation would be a one-for-one arrangement. Cypert boarded a ship on September 13 or 14 and arrived in New York on December 2, 1943. She traveled most of the journey on the MS *Gripsholm*, a Swedish ship especially servicing repatriated persons from both Japan and the United States. The journey required eighty days on two ships, first on the *Teia Maru* from Tokyo to Goa, India, and then aboard the *Gripsholm* to New York by way of Rio de Janeiro, Brazil.[65]

Arriving in New York, she traveled by bus to Louisville, Kentucky, then on to Dallas where she met with Christians from that city, and then with her sponsoring Central Church of Christ in Fort Worth. As late as December 1943, the church continued to raise $1000 to finance her trip from Tokyo to California, where she would spend the remainder of her life, with the exception of working a short time in a Japanese internment camp in Arkansas.[66]

From the beginning, the majority of Cypert's work in Japan had been among children, especially teaching kindergarten. But she carried her interest in children even farther and cared for three orphaned children as if they were her own. When she left Japan, their ages ranged from sixteen to twenty years of age. As she recalled her time in Japan, she was concerned about the three young people she left behind. She had not heard from them since she left in 1943. In America, she told her audience in Dallas that all the children were Christians.[67] After the war, she located the young men, even arranging for Steve, the youngest brother, to attend George Pepperdine on scholarship.

But even after the joy of reuniting with her adopted children, Lillie Cypert was never in good health following her return to the United States. The Central church in Fort Worth continued her support—$50 a month. After her return, in a letter to the church, although she seemed somewhat bitter, she did say, "It is through [Central church's] good offices that I am able to look forward each month to the assurance that I shall have at least my sustenance."[68] Having suffered a stroke, she lived in a trailer behind the building of the Westside Church of Christ in Los Angeles. She also suffered with high blood pressure. Her Christian friends moved her to a nursing facility in Porterville, California, where on August 13, 1954, she died in her sleep after a long, lingering illness.[69] Her desire to return to Japan would not be realized.

The War Is Over!

Sarah Andrews's situation became even more dangerous as the war came closer to her home. In June 1945, B-29 bombers increased the number of daily flights over Japan. America targeted and destroyed by incendiary and megabombs the largest cities of the enemy. From her home, Sarah Andrews, caught in the midst of war, watched a devastating raid over a neighboring town. Fires were everywhere. The raids were getting nearer to her home.

Then there were two raids on the outskirts of Shizuoka, where she lived. On the night of June 19, bombs fell on Shizuoka, leaving much of the city in flames. Amazingly, Sarah slept through the bombing, although houses burned within sixty feet of her home. She knew her ability to sleep through the raid was due to the providence of God. Had she attempted to escape the devastation that night, likely she would have been mobbed by angry Japanese citizens—and killed.

Many of her fellow residents died that night, and many more were wounded. Naturally, emotions were running high among the people. The Japanese residents of Shizuoka remembered June 19 as "that night of horror."[70] Anger became channeled toward Sarah Andrews, the American in their midst.[71]

The following day, the officials brought seventeen wounded persons to Andrews's house, ordering her to provide care for them. The chapel where the church had met before the war, located on the property with Sarah's home, became a clinic. She said of her efforts: "I did my best, but the food supply was so scarce and I was so weak that after a fortnight I broke down and the city moved these patients out."[72] Her body was swelling—a sign of starvation. She weighed, as mentioned earlier, only seventy-five pounds![73]

After August 6, 1945, Andrews noticed the B-29 bombers no longer filled the skies. The Japanese woman who delivered her small allotment of food also brought good news. The war was over! Interestingly, she gave the emperor credit for calling an end to the conflict. The emperor, she said, "in sympathy for his people had graciously delivered them."[74] Sarah observed that the people of Shizuoka, so weary of war, were now so relaxed that many laid down in the streets, or wherever they happened to be, and went to sleep. By the first of September, the police told Andrews that overtures for peace were underway. No longer was she harassed by anyone. It was a new day for Sarah Andrews.

Japan had undergone major destruction; there were few places to live. Sarah opened her home to a Japanese lady and her daughter—refugees from a decimated Tokyo. Not only could she provide housing; food became available in sufficient supply to feed the displaced family. Sarah was starving a few weeks before, but now the Japanese government delivered food daily to her house. Christians, no longer harassed by the government, came freely to visit her. Worship resumed in all three churches, although the church in Shimizu lost its building by bombing in July 1945. The churches had not met for the duration of the war. Only when she met with the churches did Andrews realize "that a dark curtain of war had lifted and liberation had come."[75]

The young American soldiers who had been sent on a mission to check on Sarah Andrews arrived on October 28, 1945. Not until June 1946 would she be strong enough to make the long trip across the Pacific Ocean to her family. Only after the GI from Tyler, Texas, confirmed Sarah to be alive did she begin to hear from America. In turn, she corresponded with family in Texas, Tennessee, and Florida. She had received during the war only three short twenty-five-word letters through the Red Cross. These were received in early 1942—her only contacts with America and her family during the last three years of confinement. While she regained her health, the US Army supplied Sarah her every need. She gained twenty-five pounds.[76]

The Japanese people of Shizuoka were greatly impressed with the care the American military showered on Andrews. They attributed the blessings to God: "Surely the Supreme Being is with that woman!" This response caused Sarah to rejoice that she was "considered worthy to suffer." But she gave all credit to God. "God showed himself strong. He saved my life. He saved the [church] property. But the victory of God's will as regards his church in Japan is the source of greatest joy and thanksgiving." Religious freedom was again alive in Japan. Her Japanese Christian friends impressed her by their vision for the future and what Christianity could mean for a new Japan.[77]

The day finally arrived when Sarah Andrews, after seven years in Japan, left her home in Shizuoka for America. On that day in June 1946, Christians surrounded her, people she nurtured for more than twenty-five years. She observed that "a group of prominent women in Shizuoka City came to bid me farewell before I left Japan." They encouraged her to return as soon as possible. "God willing," she said, "I hope to return. The call comes ringing."[78]

Endnotes

[1] Charles R. Brewer, "Editorial," *World Vision*, April, May, June 1944, 3.

[2] Ibid., 1076.

[3] W. K. Azbill, "The Voluntary Mission to Japan," *Gospel Advocate*, December 3, 1891, 767; David Lipscomb, "The Japan Mission," *Gospel Advocate*, December 17, 1892, 792. Information on the early years of Japanese missions is found in Robert E. Hooper, "The Land of the Rising Sun: The Volunteer Band Goes to Japan." A copy of the paper is in Beaman Library, Lipscomb University, Nashville, Tennessee.

[4] No editor, "Miscellaneous," *Gospel Advocate*, January 21, 1892, 40; David Lipscomb, "Mission to Japan," *Gospel Advocate*, February 4, 1892, 73; W. K. Azbill, "The Japan Voluntary Band," *Gospel Advocate*, March 24, 1892, 183; W. K. Azbill, "The Departing Mission Band," *Gospel Advocate*, April 21, 1892, 255; Della McCaleb, "Letter from Japan," July 7, 1892, 419.

[5] E. Snodgrass (ed.), "Foreign Mission Column," *Gospel Advocate*, July 25, 1895, 471.

[6] A personal story of McCaleb's work in Japan is found in his *Once Traveled Roads* (Nashville, TN: Gospel Advocate Company, 1934).

[7] Callie Hosteller, "From Japan," *Gospel Advocate*, June 28, 1894, 401.

[8] J. M. McCaleb, "Letter," *Gospel Advocate*, January 26, 1899, 57–59; William J. Bishop, "Letter," *Gospel Advocate*, March 30, 1899, 196.

[9] Editor, "Miscellany," *Gospel Advocate*, March 22, 1900, 181; William J. Bishop, "Letter," *Gospel Advocate*, April 5, 1900; 213; William J. Bishop, "Letter," *Gospel Advocate*, April 22, 1900, 229.

[10] Gary Owen Turner, "Pioneer to Japan: A Biography of John M. McCaleb" (unpublished MA thesis, Abilene Christian College, 1972), 59, 60.

[11] Ibid., 61.

[12] Ibid., 81–83.

[13] Yukikazu Obata has written an excellent study on J. M. McCaleb's views on race and missions. See his "The Gospel Is For All? The Problem of Universality in J. M. McCaleb's Views on Missions and Race," in *Reconciliation Reconsidered: Advancing the National Conversation on Race in Churches of Christ*, edited by Tanya Smith Brice (Abilene TX: Abilene Christiann University Press, 2016), 57–66.

[14] C. G. Vincent and J. M. McCaleb, "Facts and Figures Regarding Missionary Work," *Christian Leader*, February 1, 1916, 11.

[15] The biographical information on Sarah Andrews and Lillie Cypert is from a paper the writer presented at the Pan-European Lectures in Warsaw, Poland, August 2005. Robert E. Hooper, "Single Women in Missions: Japan as a Case Study." A copy of the

paper is located in Beaman Library, Lipscomb University, Nashville, Tennessee. A survey of Sarah Andrews's life is found in Bonnie Miller, *Messengers of the Risen Son in the Land of the Rising Sun* (Abilene TX: Leafwood Press, 2008). A more in-depth study of Sarah Andrews is Fiona Soltes, *Virtuous Servant: Sarah Sheppard Andrews, Christian Missionary to Japan* (Franklin, TN: Providence House Publishers, 2009).

[16] Nellie Stratton, "Peculiar Customs in Japan," *Gospel Advocate*, June 27, 1918, 607; Sarah Shepherd Andrews, "Report for March and April," *Gospel Advocate*, July 18, 1918, 677.

[17] Sarah Shepherd Andrews, "Okitsu," *Christian Leader*, October 28, 1919, 16.

[18] Sarah Andrews, "Financial Report for First Quarter, 1920," and "Report of Work in Okitsu," *Gospel Advocate*, May 20, 1920, 494.

[19] Nellie Stratton, "Japan News Items," *Gospel Advocate*, September 2, 1920, 867.

[20] I. B. Bradley, "The Sarah Andrews Mission," *Gospel Advocate*, August 5, 1920, 757.

[21] J. M. McCaleb, "From Day to Day," *Christian Leader*, February 15, 1921, 8.

[22] I. B. Bradley, "The Japanese Work," *Gospel Advocate*, August 25, 1921, 803, 804; Sarah Andrews, "Okitsu Japan Mission," *Gospel Advocate*, December 15, 1921, 1220; I. B. Bradley, "An Urgent Call for Mission Funds," *Gospel Advocate*, October 19, 1922, 1006; Sarah Andrews, "An Endorsement of Appeal Made," *Gospel Advocate*, November 2, 1922, 1037; I. B. Bradley, "Report of Funds for the Japan Work," *Gospel Advocate*, November 30, 1922, 1133.

[23] Sarah Andrews, "Woman's Work as a Missionary," *Gospel Advocate*, March 9, 1922, 222.

[24] Robert S. King, "No Title," *Gospel Advocate*, February 14, 1924, 156; Margaret Lipscomb, "Sister Andrews Needs Assistance," *Gospel Advocate*, May 29, 1924, 509; August 21, 1924, 795; Sarah Andrews, "Letter from Sister Andrews," *Gospel Advocate*, November 20,1924, 1116.

[25] Robert S. King, "Illness of Sister Andrews," *Gospel Advocate*, May 14, 1925, 462.

[26] I. B. Bradley, "Don't Forget the Old Ones," *Gospel Advocate*, March 7, 1929, 220; S. H. Hall, "The Japanese Church of Christ, Los Angeles, Cal.," *Gospel Advocate*, March 21, 1929, 268; Hettie Lee Ewing, "It Is Good to Be Remembered," *Gospel Advocate*, October 1930, 977; Soltes, *Virtuous Servant*, 25, 26.

[27] I. B. Bradley, "Appeal for Japan Work," *Christian Leader*, September 4, 1934, 10; I. B. Bradley, "Appeal for Japan Work," Gospel Advocate, September 6, 1934, 861.

[28] S. H. Hall, "A Letter from Sister Andrews," *Gospel Advocate*, December 15, 1932, 1332.

[29] Robert S. King, "Tokuo Mazawa," *Gospel Advocate*, October 5, 1935, 949.

[30] J. M. McCaleb, "A Sheet of News," *Christian Leader*, March 31, 1936, 12.

[31] Sarah Andrews, "A Noble Plan," *Christian Leader*, October 15, 1939, 8.

[32] Don Carlos Janes, "Missionary Notes," *Word and Work*, April 1940, 96.

[33] Don Carlos Janes, "Our Newest Missionary," *Christian Leader*, October 30, 1917, 4; Lillie Cypert, "Report for January, February, and March," *Gospel Advocate*, July 10, 1919, 660.

[34] Nellie Straiton, *A Missionary Report, 1923* (Morrilton, AR: Living Message Publishing, 1924).

[35] Lillie Cypert, "From Honolulu to Tokyo," *Gospel Advocate*, February 14, 1924, 161.

[36] Lillie Cypert, "A Mission Statement for 1924," *Gospel Advocate*, April 2, 1925, 330, 331.

[37] Roy H. Lanier, "Sister Cypert in Japan," *Gospel Advocate*, June 13, 1929, 566.

[38] Orlan and Nina Sawey (ed.), *She Hath Done What She Could: The Reminiscences of Hettie Lee Ewing* (Dallas: Gospel Teachers Publications, 1974), 30–32.

[39] Ibid., 5, 19, 29.

[40] Ibid., 35, 39, 40, 44, 45, 49, 50.

[41] Ibid., 55, 58, 61, 62; Carl L. Etter, "Kinji Tashiro's Passing," *Oriental Christian*, December 1931, 7, 8.

[42] Orlan and Nina Sawey, *She Hath Done What She Could*, 57–69.

[43] Ibid., 77–79.

[44] Ibid., 86–94.

[45] I. B. Bradley, "Sarah Andrews Remains in Japan," *The Christian Ledger*, December 23, 1941, 4, 5.

[46] Ibid., 6.

[47] W. E. Brightwell, "Sister Cypert Carries On," *Gospel Advocate*, April 23, 1942, 400.

[48] W. E. Brightwell, "Sister Andrews to Return," *Gospel Advocate*, January 7, 1943, 16.

[49] No author, "Sarah Andrews Is Safe," *Christian Leader*, November 24, 1942, 11.

[50] John Stratton, "Sister Cypert Returns from Japan," *Christian Leader*, December 7, 1943, 9.

[51] Sarah Andrews, "Japanese Experiences," *Gospel Advocate*, November 14, 1946, 1076.

[52] Ibid.

[53] Ibid.

[54] Ibid.

[55] Ibid.

[56] Ibid.

[57] Ibid.

[58] Ibid., 1077.

[59] Sarah Andrews, "My Maintenance during the War," *Gospel Advocate*, November 13, 1947, 919.

[60] Ibid.

[61] Ibid.

[62] No author, "Lillie Cypert Tells Inside Story of Japanese Internee Camp; Japan Running Low on Resources at Home," *Christian Chronicle*, January 5, 1944, 1, 3.

[63] Ibid.

[64] Ibid.

[65] Ibid., 1.

[66] John Stratton, "Cypert," *Christian Leader*, December 7, 1943, 9.

[67] Ibid.

[68] Elders, Central Church, Fort Worth, Texas, "Lillie Cypert Fund," *Gospel Advocate*, July 4, 1946, 638.

[69] Walter Corbin, "Sister Lillie Cypert Passes," *Gospel Advocate*, August 26, 1954, 676.

[70] Sarah Andrews, "Relates Japanese Experiences," *Gospel Advocate*, November 14, 1946, 1076.

[71] Ibid., 1077.

[72] Ibid.

[73] Ibid.

[74] Ibid.

[75] Ibid.

[76] Ibid.

[77] Ibid.

[78] Ibid.

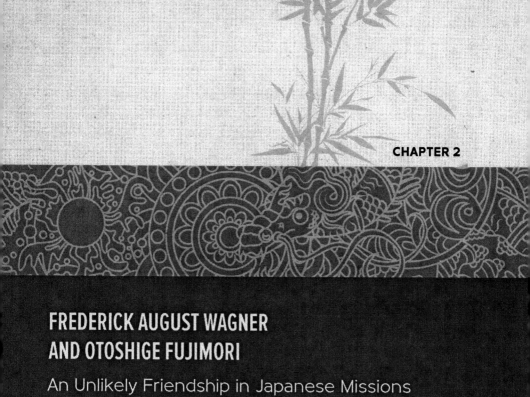

CHAPTER 2

FREDERICK AUGUST WAGNER AND OTOSHIGE FUJIMORI

An Unlikely Friendship in Japanese Missions

t all began as an unlikely story in Detroit, Michigan, at the Plum Street Church of Christ. Two men from opposite sides of the world met and became close friends because of their common commitment to Christianity. Frederick A. Wagner, born in Germany on October 21, 1836, came to the United States at the age of forty. Soon after arriving in America, he read McGarvey's *Commentary on Acts* and, as a result, accepted Christ. He settled in Detroit, Michigan. Even though a bachelor, he became an influential member of the Plum Street church.

In 1889, a young man left Japan for America looking for his fortune and hopefully to support his parents in their old age. Otoshige Fujimori, born on February 18, 1872, had gone to a school in Japan where a female Baptist missionary introduced him to the Bible.[1] In America, he frequented a number of Christian churches but concluded, "Christianity is only a humbug." He did not hear what he had read in his own New Testament. On a Sunday night, he happened to visit Detroit's Plum Street Church of Christ. He became convinced that W. D. Campbell's preaching agreed with his reading of his Japanese Testament. On May 13, 1894, he confessed his faith in Jesus Christ and responded for baptism.[2]

Shortly thereafter, F. A. Wagner and Oto Fujimori became close Christian friends. Recalling the visit three years after their first meeting, Wagner remembered, "In the pleasantly smiling face of the young brother I read the honesty of an uncorrupted mind, and the beauty of purity and chastity, which made him dear to everyone who got intimately acquainted with our Oto."[3] Soon they began discussing the possibility of going to Japan to share the gospel with the Japanese people. In an apostle Paul and Timothy relationship, the two men found a quiet place on a farm near Yale, Michigan, where Wagner instructed his young friend in the Scriptures and in the art of preaching.

Wagner, with confidence in the abilities of his brother Fujimori, exclaimed, "All who know him consider him as a gift of Divine Providence to the Church, being the very material the brotherhood should appreciate by sending and supporting him as a truly *Christian* missionary in the Land of the Rising Sun!"[4] Fujimori continued to grow in his ministry and taught and baptized Naozo Imamura, who would accompany Wagner and Fujimori to Japan. Wagner wrote favorably of the two men: "Both have a sanctified zeal for God according to knowledge, prayerfully desiring to preach the gospel to their own people." He added, "The Lord willing, I shall live and go with them as their gospel servant."[5]

Frederick A. Wagner Joins Oto Fujimori as Missionaries to Japan

In October 1896, of the $400 needed for the trip, the three men had only $40. Wagner had faith in their mission and did not despair. "But we are poor. Have no money to pay our traveling expenses. . . . May the Church in general be blessed with an active enthusiasm and practical zeal for missionary work, is the humble prayer of your brother in Christ, F. A. Wagner."

Soon, a number of churches agreed to support their mission in Japan.[6] By February, with the needed funds in hand, they began making travel plans. The two Detroit churches—Plum Street and Vinewood Mission—gathered to wish the men Godspeed. At the evening meeting, Oto baptized a young lady. Then all three men were asked to stand on the platform. "There we stood," recalled Wagner, "an old, gray haired man in the midst of blooming, hopeful youth, one European with two Asiatics [*sic*], a German with two Japanese, before an assembly of Americans, forcibly illustrating the uniting and amalgamating influence of God's power in the gospel of salvation." Then the congregation sang, "God be with you till we meet again—at Jesus's feet." Tears filled the eyes of all those gathered. Wagner remarked, "We parted! I, for my part, know very well that I never shall see these dear friends again while I am in this body."[7] Frederick A. Wagner was truly a man committed to Christ and the new mission to Japan.

The Japan Mission team sailed from Seattle on February 25, 1897, on the *Wakanonra Maru*, "one of the smallest steamers that ever crossed the Pacific Ocean."[8] Arriving safely in Yokohama after an unpleasant sea voyage, they were met by Fujimori's family. Wagner said of Fujimori, "Almost eight years ago Bro. Fujimori had left [Japan] a worshiper of idols, and now he comes back as a regenerated child of God, a soldier of the Cross, a banner bearer of the blessed gospel so dear to him." What were Wagner's feelings when he first saw the lights of Yokohama? "The panorama of my life in Europe and America passed before my inner vision. Here I was, on my way to the islands of a new continent, of Asia, a stranger among a strange people, the language of which I never can learn, now being too old for linguistic experiments. But I had no right to be melancholy. Were not my many tearful prayers graciously answered by a kind Father in heaven? Did I not bring two, instead of only one missionary to Japan?"[9]

Soon after their arrival in Japan, Wagner and Fujimori made a trip to Shimousa in the prefecture of Chiba, about sixty miles from Tokyo. Accompanied by J. M. McCaleb, they visited Yoshikawa, a convert to Christianity in 1893 at the Chicago World's Fair.[10] They spent the night in Yoshikawa's very primitive house.[11] Their host had attempted to form a Christian colony in Chiba but failed. Regardless of the circumstance, Wagner and Fujimori believed that with God's help, they could achieve this goal and spread salvation to their brothers in Christ on sometimes hostile shores.

A few days later, Fujimori returned to Shimousa to purchase twelve acres of government land and a "second-hand house" to be dismantled and rebuilt on the new location. Wagner chose to base their mission in the humble countryside, believing the cities had become so corrupted that the people would not hear the gospel message, "Hence we turn to the plain people in the country. To make them read, understand and love that the Bible is the Alpha and Omega of Bro. Fujimori's missionary work."[12]

Prior to their departure from Yokohama, two young Presbyterian ladies, acquaintances of Imamura, visited the small group of Christians gathered to hear Fujimori. One of the young ladies, O'kin Toyama, became interested in the message she heard from the preacher. As a result, on October 12, 1897, Oto immersed O'kin in McCaleb's chapel in Tokyo. Ten days later, F. A. Wagner performed the marriage vows of Oto and O'kin in the presence of Mr. and Mrs. John M. McCaleb, Mrs. Eugene Snodgrass, the family of the bride, and Oto's father and two older brothers. Now the colony could become a reality.[13]

The commitment F. A. Wagner made to Oto Fujimori in Detroit remained firm and even more so on the wedding day of Oto and O'kin. "Over three years ago, one evening I opened my house door to let in young Jap whom Bro. Campbell had baptized." At that moment, it seems, Wagner bonded with Fujimori through their love and commitment to Christ and spreading the gospel: "Divine Providence placed him near me, and he became my son in the faith, in the full sense of its Scriptural meaning."[14] Oto became more than a "Jap" on that day. Against all odds, through their love of God and dedication to the spreading the love of Christ, Wagner and Fujimori formed an unlikely family bond.

The Mission on the Frontier: Settling in Shimousa

Oto left his bride in Tokyo while he and Wagner traveled the sixty miles to their primitive farm in Shimousa—a place Wagner called the "frontier." The only housing available was a warehouse with no amenities. "Our mission home is still an unfinished house. There are no doors, no windows, no ceiling in it. But it was and is dear unto us."[15] Their first mission was to prepare a special place for O'kin in the corner of a room designated as living quarters. With winter approaching, they kept a fire burning in the middle of the room, in a hibachi, but it was not enough. They kept only partially warm by clustering closely around the open fire.[16]

Finally at home, with Christian joy, Wagner said of their first week in Shimousa, "Last Lord's day we were five [Brothers Takaoka and Sato, Oto and O'kin Fujimori, and Frederick A. Wagner], worshiping God in the midst of deep-dyed heathen!!" He added, "A great responsibility is resting on our Bro. Fujimori, and may God grant him strength to bear the burden of his duties with perseverance and spiritual joy. . . . Brethren, we beseech you to pray earnestly and often for us."[17]

During the winter months, the warehouse became an eight-room combination Japanese–Western style house. The structure measured twenty-seven feet by thirty-six feet. Wagner had his room equipped especially for his writing, something he did very well. The largest room in the house was the meeting place for the church. Inside the entrance was a sign in Japanese boldly proclaiming "Church of Christ." Adjoining rooms, with sliding paper doors, provided space for overflow crowds. The only addition to the original skeleton of a building was the lodging for Brother Sato's family.[18]

At the end of 1897 and early into 1898, the home and church were beginning to take final form. The last days of the old year saw O'kin recover from an illness likely caused by the living conditions in the makeshift house: "It was the loving hand of a living Father in heaven, who graciously heard the fervent prayers, rising like a sweet incense of faith, from the altar in the agonized heart of her husband."[19] On January 1, 1898, Oto and O'kin gave presents to everyone in the mission house family. On the first Sunday of the new year, the church—all nine Christians —gathered for worship where they sang hymns of praise and gathered around the Lord's table. Then Oto Fujimori spoke, "after which I [Wagner] addressed the little congregation [by interpretation]. . . . We remembered in a special manner all the dear friends of our humble mission work."[20]

While enjoying a rather late dinner, they began hearing noises. Looking outside, they saw several people approaching the house. They "had come to hear preaching, and, mark you, uninvited people. Our house is not fit yet for holding a meeting—that's what we thought. But the Lord thought otherwise!" Oto Fujimori and a Christian friend from Yokohama, Brother Harada, spoke on such basic topics such as the existence of one God. Oto invited the visitors, who came on their own initiative, to return next Sunday to hear him discuss "the creation of the world and man."[21] Wagner remained amazed at the happenings of the day. "It is the Lord's opening. It is He who brought this uninvited people into our yet unfinished house!"[22] On the second Sunday, twenty-five persons came to hear Oto Fujimori speak on the creation of the world. Looking forward to the next Lord's Day, Oto announced he would discuss the creation of man. Wagner saw in the faces of the listeners "the surprise and astonishment of an awakening mind, touched by the fullness of some never-thought-of light."[23]

"Colonizing, Civilizing, Christianizing": The Birth of a Mission Settlement

The dream was becoming clearer. The preaching ministry had begun; now to establish the colony: "Several people have asked [Oto] for land to rent and build a house on." But a concern continued creeping into Wagner's articles: "Brethren, I am now in my 63d year. Please do pray for me that our heavenly Father may protect and sustain me till I am as old as dear Bro. John F. Rowe [editor and publisher of the *Christian Leader*] was when he fell asleep in Jesus."[24] Still, Wagner continued his work, carrying out his duty to spread the love of the gospel despite his circumstances.

In April 1898, the Wagner-Fujimori mission team celebrated one year in Japan. "It was a time full of sunshine and darkness. We remember only the sunshine and try to forget the darkness. Ten had been baptized. Our little congregation, worshiping in the house God has built by the hands of his children, dedicating it on the first Lord's Day in this year, numbers eight souls."[25]

Spring finally arrived! Fujimori planted several cherry trees around the house. Wagner, looking to the future, saw the house surrounded by five hundred pine trees—such would be the progress of civilizing the wilderness of their mission. The planting of trees and building a bathhouse were important in the three steps Fujimori outlined for the Japan mission: "colonizing, civilizing, Christianizing."[26] But beyond these three goals, the mission overall was on a quest for brotherhood, as Wagner and Fujimori continued their work to educate and enrich the people around them, both with literacy and the love of Christ.

Colonizing began in 1898 when Brother Sato constructed a residence on the mission's land. And it must have thrilled Wagner and Fujimori as they witnessed the breaking of the deeply bamboo-rooted soil in preparation for planting vegetables, including American potatoes. And there was the possibility of a chicken farm.[27] In May, Wagner reported a chicken house with "fifty-two scratchers" and more to be added. Corn, potatoes (both sweet and common), lettuce, and beets were planted. And soon they would plant cabbage and set tomato plants.[28]

The new year also saw an addition to the Fujimori family. A few minutes past midnight, on July 21, 1898, Oto and O'kin became parents when she gave birth to a son, Toyowa, meaning "rich in peace." Following the birth of their son, Wagner observed "the young father kneeling by the side of his first-born, the eyes bathed in tears, the lips moving in a silent prayer, till the overflowing heart burst out in praising the goodness of God." Wagner, the child's honorary "grandfather," wrote happily, "The mission-house in Shimousa is now the home of a 'complete' Christian family. Husband and wife advanced to the higher dignity of father and motherhood."[29]

The colony continued to grow. On July 10, 1898, a young man, a former Greek Catholic, responded for Christian baptism. He lived seven miles from the mission but wanted to become a colonist. Then on January 31, 1899, two other men accepted baptism. They, as well, became colonists. The church now had ten members, and five were colonists on the mission's land.[30]

During 1898, as the mission continued to grow, a number of missionary brethren from Tokyo visited the mission. As reported in a letter dated July 2, Eugene Snodgrass, along with a Christian church friend, came to visit Wagner and Fujimori. Then in July, J. M. McCaleb shared with Fujimori his Tennessee knowledge on raising corn. He extended "his brotherly kindness as far as to tell a Jap blacksmith how to make a plow for the Christian colony."[31]

August brought a large container of "homeopathic medicine" from the Vinewood and Plum Street churches in Detroit. These churches kept the mission supplied with medications. Wagner was the mission's doctor. The month also had increased attendance at preaching services, with a high attendance of twenty-five. The colony, from the very first, served the people both spiritually and physically, tending to the Lord's sheep through an overarching vision of brotherhood and unity.[32] Early in September, a community some eight miles from Shimousa called for Oto to come share

Christ with them. Heretofore, the preacher would invite the people to come to a preaching service, but now he was invited to visit interested hearers—a major happening in Japan.[33]

F. A. Wagner's health concerns were becoming so serious that he accepted an invitation from J. M. McCaleb and Eugene Snodgrass to come to Tokyo for a "change of air and diet, and by the grace of God the invalid was able to gain a much improved condition, which, he hopes, will enable him to overcome the hardships of another winter in the highlands of Shimousa." On returning home, Wagner reported the colony's progress. The first harvest was modest, but now there were three colony houses in addition to the larger residence. Two hogs were added to the animal population. Fujimori planted six acres of winter wheat. Outsiders could see something special happening. They likely were saying: "That is a Christian village! And the people living there worship only one God; they believe in Jesus, the Christ, and follow a book's teaching called the Bible." Wagner believed the colony would be a success: "The seed has been sown, thank God, now let our friends do the watering, and God will give the increase."[34]

Just over a year before, Fujimori and Wagner had "found a dreary, monotonous, melancholy wilderness." Now in a new year, "the 'home,' although still unfinished, had become the 'sacred home' of worship and gospel preaching. Spiritual and physical work prospered. The plowshares of saving truth went deep into the souls of several persons who once bowed down in worship before heathen idols."[35] To his American brethren, Wagner offered thanks for the offerings so the Christian colony could become a reality: "In a few years [it] will become a center-point of successful mission work in this part of the 'country.'"[36] Here a man of German descent and a young Japanese man worked together to build their dream to uplift a rural and illiterate area of Japan. Their dedication to brotherhood formed in Christ can be considered a model for modern times.

The Continued Expansion of Helping Hands Mission

At times during 1899 as many as sixteen persons lived in the mission house. In part, this was the result of inaugurating what they called Helping Hands Mission. Wagner asserted: "The 'love of Christ' was the germ out of which it [Helping Hands Mission] developed."[37] A free school was the first inaugural part of the mission. Although the students did not live in the house, they came each day to a *free* school. The school became an important part of the Christian mission. For the most part, the ability to read was nonexistent among the adults, but Wagner and Fujimori believed in the importance of educating the young to civilize the prefecture.

As an added result, the youngsters who attended the school also came to the Bible school on Sundays. The first teacher was a young man by the name of Taketa, a student in his own right.[38] At some point during 1900, Brother Hono, a more qualified teacher, took over the classroom. He was described as "a modest, unassuming young man . . . a credit to himself. He loves to teach and to study."[39]

The two remaining parts of the Helping Hands Mission came to fruition in 1899 and 1900, an orphanage and an older folks' residence, respectively. The first child brought in as an orphan was incorrigible—he soon ran away from the mission.[40] A mother, abused by a drunken husband, with three children became residents.[41] As 1900 continued, one or two "old folks" came to the mission home.

The dream of Wagner and Fujimori was to have a separate building for the Helping Hands Mission. It would be a well-built structure, not like the buildings constructed during the first two years. This new building would include a much-needed hospital room. During the first three years of the mission, the need for an emergency hospital room for all who lived in the colony and in the surrounding area became evident. Wagner's medicines were what he called "homeopathic." He read medical books to determine the needs of those who came for healing. In August 1899 he pleaded for someone to send him an up-to-date copy of *Materia Medica*.[42]

And in the spring of 1900, the colony did prove to be desperately in need of updated medical resources, the emergency hospital room, and even more, God's healing. The woman who came to the Christian Colony with her children also brought illness with her. The sickness spread throughout the colony, especially attacking the Fujimori's youngest son, Otoji, who at the time was teething. Night and day, "Doctor" Wagner lovingly cared for all those who suffered.

Otoji, however, did not respond to the medicines. Wagner and the boy's parents thought he was near dying. Oto and Wagner kneeled next to the youngster in prayer earnestly praying, not for healing but to "be able to bear the cross with due submission to the ways of Divine Providence." Concluding their prayer, expecting the child to have died, they found him asleep—the crisis was past! But there was a new concern. "Doctor" Wagner became ill. "So bye and bye one patient after the other got well again, with the exception of myself, who had no time to handle my own case of la grippe."[43]

By the end of 1899, the Christian colony was two years old. They had begun colonizing families and had planted two crops. A church was meeting in the multipurpose house they had remodeled on the property. During the past year, nine persons had been baptized.[44] A free school was meeting. McCaleb and Snodgrass, sharing in the success of the colony, came from Tokyo on several occasions to preach. One of the largest crowds, forty-five persons, gathered on July 22 to hear the two American missionaries.[45] What a great time it was for the mission in the wilderness!

Yet amongst the clear skies of success came occasional storms. A devastating typhoon struck Japan in September, killing 694 people, injuring 1,336, and destroying 33,560 houses. The Christian colony was, for the most part, spared. But the storm played havoc with the crops, although there remained sufficient rice for the winter.[46] Truly the colony became a testament to the power of unity and brotherhood against all odds.

In the December 26, 1899, edition of the *Christian Leader*, editor James Bell included a poem by F. A. Wagner, again showing the elderly missionary a superb wordsmith. It describes well the mission in the wilderness of Chiba.

JAPAN'S GREETING.

On the distant heathen shore,
Far beyond the ocean's roar,
God has opened wide a door
    Over the sea.

And you Christians, true and brave,
Sent your bread along the wave,
Some poor heathen Jap to save
    Over the sea.

You help us hear the joyful sound,
That a Savior has been found,
To the souls in error bound
    Over the sea.

That the glorious gospel bright,
By its saving power and might,
May dispel the sin and night,
    Over the sea.
      —F. A. Wagner[47]

The year 1900 continued the work of the Wagner-Fujimori Japan Mission with more success than had been enjoyed during the two previous years. Wagner, writing about Oto with compassion, stated: "During two years of faithful mission work among a class of people which I call semi-barbarian, [Oto] has succeeded in opening the eyes of even some enemies of Christianity who, now are compelled to acknowledge the superiority of a religion opposed to the abominations of idolatry and heathenish immorality."[48]

Two weeks later, Wagner lovingly wrote, "It is a good thing that the heart be established with grace! Hence our Oto, whose religion is truly a heartfelt one . . . endeavors to educate the hearts of his countrymen in advance of the head, because 'with the heart man believeth unto righteousness.'"[49] In July, the elder missionary recorded that on May 18, they celebrated Oto's spiritual birthday. His young friend had not missed one Lord's Day worship time. In those six years, Fujimori had baptized more than fifteen persons.

"In This Grievous Loss": Tragedy Strikes the Mission

Although Wagner had been somewhat ill from the first months in Japan, only in early 1901 did someone in the United States take notice of his health issues. Editor Bell noted Wagner's concerns of a week earlier: "What will become of our Japan mission when the hand that is writing this letter has become cold and stiff in death?" Bell, although noticing Wagner's concerns, believed Oto Fujimori would be able to carry on—the only thing needed was the continued support of his American brethren. Bell recalled that

Wagner's "son Oto was a welcome guest in our home, and his speech and conduct left the impression deep on my heart that he had in truth become a disciple of the Lord Jesus. . . . He will fully preach the gospel of Christ to his own countrymen."[50] The editor added a word to the readers at the end of the editorial: "Redeem your pledges to Bro. Wagner's heroic work."[50]

However, not everything was positive in Shimousa. Illness and even death were often present at the Christian colony. On March 15, 1901, Oto and O'kin Fujimori buried their third son. It touched Wagner's heart: "The tender blossom of life dropped in the grave without opening its petals, and Death, in its mildest form, for the first time, came to us. . . . [I]t was a short season of beautiful Hope, a true parable of the frailty and uncertainty of human life."[51] A week later, Wagner noted, "We have decided to make the Coming of the Lord the banner motto of our gospel preaching and teaching, and to continue faithfully in the strict observance of our duties as laborers in the Lord's vineyard."[52]

The financial reports, always prepared by Wagner, were often late in 1901. Writing about himself, he indicated, "Wagner had another severe attack of inflammation of the kidneys, which is the reason why this report comes out behind. He is hoping and praying our friends will have patience with an old, sick man." And in June, he wrote, "Wagner has been quite sick for several weeks, confined to his bed. He is now slowly recovering, thank God."[53]

During the previous year, Wagner, in private letters, had been telling friends "that his remaining days would be few." On September 3, 1901, William J. Bishop, a missionary in Tokyo, wrote with sorrow to the *Christian Leader* that "Bro. Wagner" was dead. Editor Bell responded: "It doesn't seem possible that our faithful brother and the 'father in the Gospel' of our young brother Oto has laid his armor by, but it is not a dream; it is stern reality." He added, "May the grace of our heavenly Father abundantly sustain our Japanese colony in this grievous loss."[54]

Not until October 21 were the particulars of F. A. Wagner's death and burial fully known. Wagner had died on September 2 following a recurrence of illness. He had written in his diary on August 24, "I got very sick. Kidney trouble and chills." The next day he penned: "Sick in bed; very sick." But on August 27, he wrote, "Better, thank God." On August 28 he was up until noon hanging flags in celebration of Otoji's birthday. Visitors came to celebrate the youngster's birth. But at noon, after eating a bit, Wagner went to bed, saying, "I'm very tired." For five days he was quite ill. But even Wagner did not think he was near death. Before noon on September 2, the family came to their "father's" room—Brother Wagner was dying. Oto came close to the bed. Wagner clasped Oto's hand and said, "Oto, to you precious faith." Shortly afterward, he weakly spoke: "My end is coming." Oto, his brother in Christ and adopted "son," called to him time after time. The only answer was a faint "yes." "At half past one o'clock he peacefully fell asleep in Jesus."[55]

The death of his mentor was almost more than Fujimori could fathom. Writing the monthly report on October 15, 1901, he related how he had been in bed most of the time since Wagner's death. He had sore eyes and influenza, followed by a high fever. He lamented, "You know how sad it is for me to live without my dear Bro. Wagner! My heart is aching in every day and hour when I think of him. I try very much to forget for a while, but I cannot. He was more than my father to me, how can I forget him?"[56]

"Free from All Darkness": Oto Fujimori Carries On, Alone

For a short while, there were only three missionaries representing Churches of Christ in Japan: William Bishop, Oto Fujimori, and Frederick A. Wagner. Now there were only two. J. M. McCaleb was en route back to Japan when Wagner died on September 2, and McCaleb arrived in Yokohama on September 13. Once in Japan and hearing of Wagner's death, McCaleb soon traveled to Shimousa. Arriving on September 26, he remained until the following Monday. Entering the house, McCaleb recalled, "I could but feel that he [Wagner] ought to be there, and with both hands stretched out toward me, as was his custom." On Friday and Saturday, McCaleb instructed Fujimori on the working of a steel plow he had brought from Kentucky. On Sunday he preached to the mission church. He noted that some forty persons had been baptized since the founding of the colony, but many had moved away and others had fallen by the wayside. The church had twelve or thirteen members who met regularly.[57]

The mission continued to flourish as Christians in the United States contributed increased funds to support the mission. But this did not cause Fujimori to miss his "father in the gospel" any less. On December 24, 1901, Otake Masuda, only fifteen years old, was baptized. She had attended the

Helping Hand School for two years. She was one of "the first fruits of [the] Sunday school class," said Fujimori. "Bro. Wagner and I were longing and waiting for this blessing. If our dear old Bro. Wagner were living now how glad he would be! How he would rejoice!"[58] In May 1902, Fujimori, writing to America, noted that Wagner would have been pleased with the progress of the Japan mission. "How he would enjoy to report unto you the glad tidings! To draw the ideas, it makes my heart ache, and how lonely I feel!"[59]

Despite his sorrow at the loss of his friend, it seems that Wagner's death may have spurred Fujimori to become more involved in his preaching ministry. Most of his early teaching was at the Christian colony, but in 1902 and 1903 he reached out to communities surrounding the colony and as far away as Tokyo. One of Wagner's final reports detailed Fujimori's preaching in Kayada, a lovely village some twenty miles from the colony. Fujimori first preached there on August 6, before Wagner's death on September 2, 1901. On April 28, 1902, Fujimori returned to Kayada where he preached several times over three days. Encouraged by Brother Ishida, the first baptized believer in the village, three men were baptized in the Pacific Ocean. Brothers from the Takahagi church, the name given to the colony church, came to aid Fujimori with the baptisms. They also brought a communion set as a gift from Takahagi. Later they provided hymnals for the new church.[60]

The church at Takahagi had grown by forty persons by baptism since its beginning in 1897, a number McCaleb thought rather exceptional. Moreover, increased preaching at a number of distant locations led to additional baptisms. Fujimori mentioned that one year after "my father in the faith went to his reward," he had baptized twenty-two persons, with a large number of them at Kayada.[61] In May 1903, he reported thirteen additional baptisms, "the best and most successful month we have had since we commenced our work in this backwoods of Shimousa."[62]

The Christian Colony continued to flourish. Fujimori increased the size of the colony by twenty-five acres at a cost of $800; he had only $550 in the bank. He turned to his brothers and sisters in the United States, asking for help purchasing the additional land.[63] Noting the progress, J. M. McCaleb assessed the Wagner-Fujimori Japan Mission one year following Wagner's death: "The Wagner-Fujimori work was never so helpful as now. The church meets regularly to break bread, to edify one another and to teach the children. There is also a day school of ten children. Prayer meetings are held in the homes of neighbors in the community round about, and new mission points are being opened in the adjoining villages."[64]

In the midst of major destruction by a typhoon on September 28, 1902, Oto Fujimori reported successes in his preaching ministry. Four years later, he gave all credit to his Detroit brothers and sisters in Christ. He rejoiced that the Christian Colony was out of debt—all because of Plum Street and Christians across the United States. "I can assure you that we are all happy as you are, because we are free from all darkness."

Every year the Fujimoris held a celebration of the New Year. They invited all the poor people in the neighborhood to the colony—feeding them for three days and providing clothing to the needy. During the celebration of 1906, Oto baptized a young man "who walked eighteen miles to obey the Lord." For the first time, Fujimori mentioned that the Takahagi church needed a new building. This would be a concern for the next two years.[65]

Although in 1905 Fujimori had baptized one person and officiated at a Christian wedding, he was somewhat discouraged because of factors beyond his control. Japan had been involved in the Russo-Japanese War. The Japanese defeated the Russians, surprising European nations. Fujimori felt that once the war was over, interest in both church and preaching would improve. But he was wrong. Because the government encouraged Buddhist and Shinto priests to worship the soldiers who had died in the war—they were now considered gods—it had been difficult to get people to focus on Jesus Christ. And there was another problem—the horses that had pulled the plows in the colony were getting old, both eight years of age. As a result he had to purchase two new horses, at a cost of $59. He had only $17 to buy them. The remainder would be paid over time. Again, he mentioned the need to construct a new house for worship in Takahagi.[66]

By the middle of 1906, O'kin, Oto's wife, delivered another baby. O'kin had never been well, and the birth process left her especially weak. When her only brother passed away and was in need of a Christian burial, Fujimori traveled alone to Tokyo to perform the service. He had baptized him on July 30, 1900, but before he could reach Tokyo, a Buddhist priest had presided over the funeral ceremony. At that same time, the Takahagi church had to dismiss a few persons from the congregation because of disorderly conduct. It was not a good three months.

However, 1907 brought a more encouraging report. There had been six baptisms in the first quarter. Fujimori was especially elated with the baptism of a young man sixteen years of age. He was the son of the oldest member of the Takahagi church. Manzo had been attending Sunday school since 1897: "He is our Sunday-school boy ever since we came to this place and settled."[67]

On New Year's Day, 1907, J. M. McCaleb arrived and preached to about eighty persons and then taught the Sunday school children. On the morning of the third day, McCaleb, scheduled to return home to Tokyo, awakened to see the ground covered with snow. Oto reported, "Brother McCaleb said he had never seen such nice snow scenery since he has been in Japan." But the snow did not deter Fujimori's preaching—he had an engagement that night. The prospect of a new meetinghouse ever remained on his mind. He reminded his American friends that he needed $200 to begin the new building for worship.[68]

The second quarter of 1907 brought more good news. Fujimori received $300 from "our dear Brother Byers. We now have money enough to build a nice meetinghouse." In fact, the construction had already begun. The structure would be twenty-four feet by forty-five feet with a nine-foot-square entrance. He estimated the final cost would be $650. However, even with Byers's gift, it was necessary to borrow money to continue construction. When finished, it would be the first freestanding church building for the Wagner-Fujimori Japan Mission.[69] Disappointed, three months later, Fujimori reported that only the foundation had been laid. He had hoped to finish the house by November, but the Japanese carpenters cared nothing for contracts. "We have to bear the cross and faint not."[70]

Good Times and Hard Times for the Christian Mission

The entire year of 1908 would be a trying time. O'kin Fujimori was ill much of the year. She was in bed for three months. The children were also sick because their mother could not care for them. And Oto did not sleep for three weeks: "It was weakness of my body and nerves." Writing early in 1909, Fujimori said that O'kin seemed to be out of danger, but "the doctors think that it was rather a miracle that she got well. We believe so ourselves."[71]

There was more good news. The carpenters finally completed the new meetinghouse. November 23, 1908, was the grand opening. Every missionary and native preacher in Tokyo came to help celebrate the opening of what McCaleb called the finest building among Churches of Christ in Japan. Besides McCaleb, others who came were William Bishop and his wife, George A. Klingman, Yunosuke Hiratsuka, and Yoko, a deacon in the Kamitomizaka church.[72] Some 150 persons attended the dedication service. McCaleb and Hiratsuka remained five days, sharing preaching opportunities every night. It was a great time for the Wagner-Fujimori Japan Mission, but Fujimori reported a debt of over $500. It "makes us trouble and worry. . . . Now, I come to you, my dear brethren, would you sympathize with us in this time of sorrow and trouble?"[73]

McCaleb described the meeting with the Takahagi church in some detail with a critical note about the debt Fujimori had incurred. The meetinghouse was "a plain, substantial building, weather-boarded on the outside, plastered within." He estimated it would last a hundred years. He told Americans about Fujimori's work in the colony. The farm now had fifty acres—the original colony had only twelve. In the eleventh year of the Christian colony, there were ten families and thirteen Christians—sufficient to provide some income for Fujimori from rents charged.[74]

The year 1909, however, was not a good year for the Wagner-Fujimori Japan Mission. George A. Klingman, a relatively new missionary in Japan, enthusiastically described Fujimori's work in Shimousa. He had preached to thousands of his countrymen. He had baptized at least two hundred people. Several churches were meeting because of his ministry. Twelve families lived on the farm. And countless hundreds of poor, both old and young, had enjoyed his hospitality. But amid such a glowing report, Klingman noted the death of O'kin Fujimori. She had been ill on and off from the time she came to the Christian colony. Now in 1909, Oto Fujimori was a single father with seven children, one of whom had died since O'kin's death. Besides his six children, Oto was caring for five of his brother's children. Adding two orphans, he was responsible for thirteen children and his aged mother and a cook. What a daunting task! Said Klingman, "Imagine our brother's sorrow."[75]

The last of 1909 and months into 1910 were difficult times for Oto Fujimori. He searched for a housekeeper, but finding someone willing to care for a dozen children, an aged mother, and a preacher who was often away from home was impossible.

Yet, among the six persons he baptized in 1910, one was a Methodist woman named Ono. On November 29, 1910, they married and received the blessings of G. A. Klingman and Hiratasuka, who had come from Tokyo for the Christian ceremony. Oto, relieved and happy, stated, "Our home is now more like home and just [like] spring had come into my house. My motherless children are happy as can be." To repair the house for the ceremony and to buy nice things for Ono, he went into debt, having a deficit of $127.74 at the end of the year.[76]

All the while, the Takahagi church was progressing: Sunday school attendance had grown from sixty to seventy-three. Those partaking of the Lord's Supper increased from forty-three to fifty-six. The afternoon meeting increased from thirty to thirty-six, the evening meeting from twenty to thirty, and the prayer meeting from eighteen to twenty-five. But the best attended were the "magic lantern" meetings—increasing from 200 to 250. (Magic lanterns were early slide projectors using illumination from natural light or candles to project pictures on a wall. The slides were painted glass.) The Helping Hand School continued to grow, enrolling thirty-six students in 1912.[77]

There was a good working relationship between Oto Fujimori and J. M. McCaleb and the churches and preachers in Tokyo. In 1913, Fujimori's colony had been in existence for sixteen years, recognized by all American missionaries as being among the most successful mission efforts in Japan. With the exception of McCaleb's work in Tokyo, it was the oldest mission effort among Churches of Christ.

On January 18, 1913, Oto visited McCaleb in his Tokyo home. The following morning, the two men discussed a number of things important to their work. But the one thing that impressed McCaleb most was Fujimori's description of the week-long prayer meeting conducted on the first day of the year. The meetings began at 4 a.m. and lasted for two hours. To make sure everyone in the community would attend, two Christian men went among their neighbors, awakening them and urging them to attend the early morning prayer sessions. Among those who urged their father to allow them to lead a prayer were Oto's children—Toyowa, Otoji, and his little girl. Toyowa prayed with tears in his eyes. His father asked him why he was crying. "Well, I have done many bad things during the year, and I wanted the Lord to make me good." The youngest son prayed: "O Lord, make me a good Christian and a preacher. Amen." Oto told McCaleb, "When the older members heard these little children, they said, 'My! Can little children pray like that, and we can't pray?'" Then during those early hours of prayer, everyone prayed, both young and old.[78]

The year 1916 had to be a highlight year in the ministry of Oto Fujimori. The evangelist preached in Shimousa at the Katori Festival. Here he distributed tracts and preached in the afternoons along with his Tokyo brethren. He also baptized one person.[79] A month later, he reported eight baptisms at Takahagi, the most at any one time since he returned from America.[80] Preaching at Sawara, he baptized three young men. He reported improvement in the Sunday school since his niece Okei began working there, with seventeen present.[81] A loving son, Fujimori had also brought his aged mother to live with him in the Christian mission home, and for twenty years he had prayed that she would accept Christ and Christian baptism. With enthusiasm on October 31, 1916, Oto announced with humble pride that he had baptized his mother. What a tremendous answer to unrelenting prayer![82] That year he baptized fifteen persons.

Christian Missions Respond to a Destructive Earthquake

In 1923, Tokyo and Yokohama, along with Chiba, the home of the Fujimoris, were devastated by a horrific earthquake. Christened the Kanto earthquake, according to the *Guinness Book of Records*, it remains the most destructive earthquake of all time. It struck on September 1 at 11:58 a.m., measuring 7.9 on the Richter scale. Soon the region was inundated by forty-foot tsunami waves. Thousands of people were swept away. Areas not covered by floods were destroyed by fire, probably caused by overturned charcoal or coal stoves. These fires and the floods destroyed 80 percent of the houses in Yokohama and 60 percent in Tokyo. In the end, 143,000 people lost their lives.[83]

The missionaries quickly moved to help the suffering and homeless people. Sarah Andrews, returning to Japan after her furlough, arrived in Tokyo to assist with the efforts. A number of missionaries and Japanese Christians became involved in relief work in a small area of Tokyo. They distributed 125 blankets. Out of her meager income, Sarah Andrews provided lunch for the Japanese workers.

The missionaries involved in the relief efforts used the opportunity to preach Christ to as many as 10,000 persons. The lead preachers were Yunosuka Hiratsuka and Oto Fujimori. Andrews, speaking for everyone involved, hoped a church could be organized in the area of Tokyo where the relief work and preaching was taking place. Takagi San, taught by Oto, would possibly be the evangelist.[84]

As the years passed, Fujimori's preaching engagements increased outside the Chiba district. In 1925, he traveled once each month to Okitsu, the original missionary point for Sarah Andrews, for preaching appointments. On each visit, he preached three times. In response to Oto's work in Okitsu, Robert S. King in Nashville noted in the *Gospel Advocate* that "Brother Fujimori had baptized about forty-five or fifty of the approximately sixty members [at Okitsu]. Sister Andrews often went to Brother Fujimori for counsel and advice, and he gladly assisted her in her work [whether in Okitsu or Shizuoka]."[85]

As early as 1909, the year Fujimori's wife O'kin died, Oto had been contemplating a trip to America to visit his Christian friends in Detroit. But ensuing events caused him to cancel any thought of leaving his large family at Takahagi. The opportunity finally came in 1926, thirty years from the time he and F. A. Wagner had made plans to go to Japan. In October of 1926, F. L. Rowe, publisher of the *Christian Leader*, announced that "Bro. Oto may visit us." The Plum Street church needed $800 to ensure his passage across the Pacific Ocean both ways. Rowe added, "It will do the missionary cause good to have a native worker visit the American brethren." Two weeks later, the *Christian Leader* noted that the old Plum Street church, now the Hamilton Boulevard church, had decided to bring their Japanese missionary "home" for an extended visit.[86]

"Love Speaks One to Another": Oto Fujimori in America

Oto Fujimori left Japan on April 8, 1927; on April 17 he boarded a train for Detroit with a stopover in Chicago to visit his oldest son, Toyowa, who was a student at the University of Chicago. Later on the same day, he arrived at his destination, where thirty persons were gathered at the train station to welcome him: "Some cried out, 'Here comes Oto! Oh, here comes Oto! Hello, Oto! Hello, Oto!' Many hands were extended. It was a rather great treat for me, indeed. . . . I knew many of them in the crowd—among them some of my friends of thirty years ago. I just felt their brotherly love and kindness. My heart was filled with joy and happiness. I felt as though I were coming home."

The welcome continued at the Claude Witty home, where twenty of his American brothers and sisters greeted him. "O, how they welcomed me!" In the evening, the Wittys hosted a reception for Oto. "About 100 were present and certainly they all welcomed me again with true hearts. . . . I enjoyed talking with them in my poor English. Nevertheless they understood me quite well. Yes, love speaks one to another!"[87] They were not Americans and Japanese. They were brothers and sisters in Christ.

Vernon C. Fry, a leader in the Hamilton Boulevard church, covered the "homecoming" of Fujimori for the *Gospel Advocate*. Fry wrote exultingly: "The Fujimori of to-day is the 'Oto' of yesterday, with thirty years of 'walking with God' in between—years of wholly trusting God amid persecution and hardship, and too often disappointment when we almost failed him." He quoted from a recent letter from Oto: "Thanking you and my mother church for the love message and for bringing me once more to my second-birth country of America." Commending Fujimori to churches across the United States, Fry said of his Christian friend: "He is one of God's heroes of faith, a very energetic worker, and a man of prayer."[88]

Oto Fujimori's year's stay in the United States began with a month's visit with the churches in Detroit. Every Church of Christ in Detroit participated in Fujimori's visit and cooperated in the preparations for his travel among churches in the Midwest, South, Southwest, and Canada. The *Christian Leader* applauded the "hearty cooperation" of the churches in welcoming their "missionary" from Japan.

The first visit outside Detroit was the "June Meeting" at Selkirk, Ontario, where hundreds gathered to hear their friend whom they had not seen and heard for thirty years. H. M. Evans told the readers of the *Leader* that "the brethren in Canada have pledged themselves to unite in his support in the future." Describing his friend who spent time in the Evans' home thirty years earlier and now in June 1927, he stated, "He is certainly one of God's true noblemen."[89]

In August, Fujimori visited Nashville, Tennessee, for an extended stay. His last week in Nashville he spent in the home of Samuel H. Hall, the minister of the Russell Street church. The two preachers discussed at length how best to reach the Japanese people with the gospel. (Hall was mainly responsible for beginning a mission among the Japanese in Los Angeles in 1923. The founding and work of the church are presented in Chapter 5.) They agreed that native preachers could reach their countrymen much better than foreign missionaries. "Every American missionary should never be without such help. Sister Andrews has depended largely on such help, and her work . . . is among the best work that has been done in that field."[90] Oto's travels took him throughout the South as far as Valdosta, Georgia, with a stop in Atlanta.

He then traveled to Kansas, Oklahoma, Nebraska, and Iowa. Homer E. Moore, editor of the *Christian Worker,* chronicled Oto's visit to Wichita, Kansas, where he presented the lesson all wished to hear: "How I Became a Christian and a Missionary." He spoke in Albion, Nebraska, where a reporter said of Fujimori's visit, "I never heard a more appealing thing than the story of his conversion. . . . To hear his story fires the hearts of all true Christians to help him in his almost lone efforts among his people."

During the last days of October, Fujimori spent four days in the Davis City, Iowa, area. Because the building of the Church of Christ could not accommodate the crowd, the attendees moved to the Methodist Episcopal Chapel where nearly four hundred persons gathered. "What a wonderful commentary on Christ's reason for praying that all believers might be one— 'That the world might believe that thou didest send me.'" In November, Oto visited Elk City, Oklahoma, where people from almost every denomination came to hear the visitor from Japan. Fujimori's welcome by Christians in America certainly went counter to the majority view of Americans toward

Asians, especially on the West Coast. They found fellowship in the oneness of Christ.[91]

After one year in the United States and Canada, Fujimori was ready to return to Japan. Churches in Canada and Detroit held farewell meetings for their Japanese Christian friend. The Niagara peninsula churches honored him with a wristwatch. Sisters in numerous congregations presented him with watches for his wife Ono and daughter Tarusa.[92] A very special gift for Oto was a motorcycle given to him by the Vernon Frys—transportation for his scattered preaching appointments.[93]

Early in 1928, on his way home, Fujimori spent three days with the Japanese church in Los Angeles. Said Ishiguro, the preacher for the Japanese church, "These meetings gave to the people great Christian influences." The two evangelists traveled into the countryside for teaching engagements. Ishiguro stated, "By this effort we got several seekers after the truth in the country."[94]

Prior to returning to Japan on March 29, 1928, Fujimori wrote glowingly of his visit to America: "I have enjoyed very much the spirit of love, hospitality, and mutual fellowship in Christ Jesus that has been extended to me. Not only that, but they have shown me Christ's love, notwithstanding I was born in a heathen country and converted from the national Japanese religion." He estimated he had visited two hundred churches in fifteen states, "and in my visits I never saw anything bad or the dark side, but good and bright, and I was always blessed with good health." He added, "I am about ready to leave this beautiful country for my homeland, where my loved ones are waiting and longing, and many souls call for their rescue and salvation."[95]

Fujimori Returns to Japan

Soon after returning to Japan, Oto Fujimori visited J. M. McCaleb and continued to praise his American friends. However, he discovered things that disturbed him. In Japan, teachers had to begin with basic Christian themes themes, but in the United States, he heard about divisions among Churches of Christ. McCaleb relayed to his American brothers Fujimori's comments:"'Why,' he said, 'there are five parties in the churches,' and he proceeded to name them.'" He told his friend that he had no idea such divisions existed before he went to America. McCaleb told him that it was worse than he had discovered: "'That is not half of them,' I said; 'there are at least a dozen.'" McCaleb challenged his American brothers and sisters: "I hope that our brother will entirely forget that he ever discovered such divisions and will avoid lining up with anyone of them, but leave such things to the carnal-minded, while we in Japan go on preaching the gospel just as we find it written, as nearly as we can."[96]

Fujimori, partly because of age but also because of his need to be closer to transportation, told his Detroit friends that he would soon move from the Christian colony and, because of the move, be more involved in a wider ministry. By 1931, at age fifty-nine, he moved to Sawara, eight miles from Tarakawa. This would be his family home for the remainder of his life.

In 1931, Fujimori and Churches of Christ in Japan experienced a great loss when he was called to Sapporo, Hokkaido, in October to be with a young Japanese Christian, Kinji Tashiro, who had contracted typhoid fever some six weeks prior. Tashiro had become a Christian at Okitsu about two years after Sarah Andrews began the mission. Fujimori had baptized him. Andrews said of Tashiro, "He understood the plea [of Churches of Christ] better than any other person besides Bro. Fujimori in Japan." She further stated, "I have heard Fujimori say that if he died he felt the Church in Japan would be safe with Tashiro so well grounded."[97] Reporting Tashiro's death, Fujimori wrote, "We are all made sad over his death, especially Bro. Etter and his wife. And, of course Sister Ewing feels it very much. She does not know what to do at present. . . . I baptized Bro. Tashiro's parents in Okitsu. It was the faith of Bro. Tashiro that convinced them."[98] (A more detailed discussion of Ewing and Tashiro is found in Chapter 1.)

Oto Fujimori, always a picture of health, faced grief on several occasions during the decade of the 1930s. The loss of Tashiro was difficult—he was such a young man with unlimited promise. However, it was nothing compared with the tragic loss he faced with the death of his daughter, Tarusa. She was only eighteen years of age in 1932 when she took her own life by drowning in the local river. She had just finished high school, and her entire future was ahead of her. She left a letter telling of her intent. For twenty days the family grieved while men searched the river for her body.[99] Tarusa's death was extremely difficult for her father to overcome.

For the remainder of the 1930s, Fujimori preached widely throughout Chiba and southward among the churches established by Sarah Andrews and Hettie Lee Ewing. The decade, however, was a time of heightened nationalism in Japan. In 1937, Fujimori wrote, "We are having war with China. It is not very nice to have such trouble, that is killing one another. I hope it will soon be over and restore peace again."[100] His preaching engagements became limited, and there were few converts to Christianity. Likely his association with Americans caused concern among his neighbors who lived under a heightened outpouring of nationalism.

In 1937, Fujimori was sixty-five years of age, "I do not feel old. I am quite strong and healthy. I am still taking a cold bath every morning and exercise by the radio every morning."[101] In 1938, the Fujimori family united in Sawara. Oto moved the family's house from Takahagi, locating it on a hill overlooking Sawara and the Tone River: "The scenery is very fine and beautiful." However in Sawara, his children fell sick with tuberculosis and were confined to bed: "The T.B. takes a long time to heal."[102]

In the April 1941 edition of *Missionary Messenger,* a letter appeared in which Oto Fujimori communicated his final words before World War II to the religious journals in the United States. He saw no hope for a daughter recovering from TB, yet he added, "But we trusting the Lord's help, [she] might recover." Specifically, he stated, "our work is not progressing since the war." Having sold the colony, his family was financially secure for the foreseeable future.[103]

Oto Fujimori was a young man when he first chose to return to Japan with his older German Christian friend Fredrick A. Wagner to share the message of Jesus Christ with the Japanese people. The two unlikely brothers in Christ were successful in establishing a Christian colony in rural Japan. During the 1920s and 1930s, Oto faced a rising tide of Japanese nationalism, yet he maintained his relationships with his friends in American churches across the Pacific Ocean—bonds that remained strong, even in the wake of World War II. He must have felt extremely alone and isolated in a land that would now be at war with his adopted country. Now as an old man, he would await the outcome of the great battle, separated from his Christian friends in America. During this dark time, he would find comfort in memories of his mentor in the gospel and in recalling his close friendship with Sarah Andrews and his fellowship with Detroit's Plum Street church.

Endnotes

[1] J. M. McCaleb, *Christ the Light of the World* (Nashville: McQuiddy Printing Company, 1911), 142, 142.

[2] F. L. Rowe, "Otoshige Fugimory [*sic*]," *Christian Leader*, February 11, 1896, 5. The Cincinnati-based *Christian Leader*, edited by F. L. Rowe, gave extensive space to the Wagner-Fujimori Japan Mission. Wagner, an excellent wordsmith, often had weekly reports in the paper. Rarely did two weeks pass without a lengthy article by Frederick August Wagner.

[3] F. A. Wagner, "Japan Letter," *Christian Leader*, October 24, 1899, 9.

[4] Ibid.

[5] F. A. Wagner, "Otishige Fujimory [*sic*] and Naozo Imamura," *Christian Leader*, October 6, 1896, 5. The article includes a photograph of the two men who returned to Japan.

[6] F. A. Wagner, "Our Japan Mission," *Christian Leader*, January 28, 1897, 4.

[7] F. A. Wagner, "On Our Winding Way," *Christian Leader*, March 9, 1897, 9.

[8] Ibid.

[9] F. A. Wagner, "Japan Letter," *Christian Leader*, May 25, 1897, 9.

[10] J. M. McCaleb, *Christ the Light*, 170, 171.

[11] J. M. McCaleb, *Once Traveled Roads* (Nashville: Gospel Advocate Company, 1934), 90, 91.

[12] F. A. Wagner, "Japan Letter," *Christian Leader*, October 12, 1897, 9.

[13] Ibid.

[14] F. A. Wagner, "Japan Letter," *Christian Leader*, October 27, 1897, 9.

[15] F. A. Wagner, "Japan Letter," *Christian Leader*, January 25, 1898, 3.

[16] Ibid.

[17] Ibid.

[18] F. A. Wagner, "Japan Letter," *Christian Leader*, December, 27, 1898, 3.

[19] F. A. Wagner, "Japan Letter, 1897–1898," *Christian Leader*, February 22, 1898, 2.

[20] Ibid.

[21] Ibid.

[22] Ibid., 3

[23] F. A. Wagner, "Japan Letter," *Christian Leader*, March 8, 1898, 9.

[24] F. A. Wagner, "Japan Letter," *Christian Leader*, May 17, 1898, 2

[25] F. A. Wagner, "Japan Letter," *Christian Leader*, April 19, 1898, 9.

[26] F. A. Wagner, "Japan Letter," *Christian Leader*, June 28, 1898, 9.

[27] F. A. Wagner, "Japan Letter," *Christian Leader*, June 7, 1898, 4.

[28] F. A. Wagner, "Japan Letter," *Christian Leader*, July 26, 1898, 9.

[29] F. A. Wagner, "Japan Letter," *Christian Leader*, August 16, 1898, 9.

[30] F. A. Wagner, "Japan Mission," *Christian Leader*, October 4, 1898, 4.

[31] Ibid.

[32] Ibid.

[33] F. A. Wagner, "Japan Letter," *Christian Leader*, November 15, 1898, 9.

[34] F. A. Wagner, "Japan Letter," *Christian Leader*, December 20, 1898, 4.

[35] F. A. Wagner, "Japan Letter," *Christian Leader*, January 31, 1899, 4.

[36] Ibid.

[37] F. A. Wagner, "Japan Letter," *Christian Leader*, March 6, 1900, 2.

[38] Ibid.

[39] F. A. Wagner, "Japan Letter," *Christian Leader*, November 27, 1900, 9.

[40] F. A. Wagner, "Japan Letter," *Christian Leader*, August 1, 1899, 8.

[41] F. A. Wagner, "Japan Letter," *Christian Leader*, June 5, 1900, 2.

[42] F. A. Wagner, "Japan Letter," *Christian Leader*, September 12, 1899, 5.

[43] F. A. Wagner, "Japan Letter," *Christian Leader*, June 19, 1900, 4.

[44] F. A. Wagner, "Japan Letter, 1899–1900," *Christian Leader*, January 16, 1900, 2.

[45] F. A. Wagner, "Japan Letter," *Christian Leader*, September 12, 1999, 5.

[46] F. A. Wagner, "Japan Letter," *Christian Leader*, November 21, 1999, 4; F. A. Wagner, "Japan Letter," *Christian Leader*, January 23, 1900, 2.

[47] F. A. Wagner, "Japan's Greeting," *Christian Leader*, December, 26, 1999, 3.

[48] F. A. Wagner, "Japan Letter," *Christian Leader*, March 13, 1900, 4.

[49] F. A. Wagner, "Japan Letter," *Christian Leader*, March 27, 1900, 8, 9.

[50] John F. Rowe, "Japan Mission," *Christian Leader*, January 8, 1901, 8, 9.

[51] F. A. Wagner, "Japan Letter," *Christian Leader*, April 16, 1901, 9.

[52] F. A. Wagner, "Japan Letter," *Christian Leader*, April 23, 1901, 4.

[53] Otoshige Fujimori and F. A. Wagner, "Japan Mission," August 20, 1901, 9.

[54] John F. Rowe, "Bro. Wagner Is Dead," *Christian Leader*, October 1, 1901, 9.

[55] William J. Bishop, "Frederick August Wagner," *Christian Leader*, October 22, 1901, 9.

[56] Otoshigo Fujimori, "Wagner-Fujimori Japan Mission," *Christian Leader*, November 19, 1901, 8.

[57] J. M. McCaleb, "Bro. Fujimori and His Work," *Christian Leader*, November 5, 1901, 9.

[58] Otoshigo Fujimori, "Wagner-Fujimori Japan Mission," *Christian Leader*, February 25, 1902, 9.

[59] Otoshigo Fujimori, "Wagner-Fujimori Japan Mission," *Christian Leader*, July 15, 1902, 9.

[60] Otoshigo Fujimori, "Wagner-Fujimori Japan Mission," *Christian Leader*, June 10, 1902, 9.

[61] Otoshigo Fujimori, "Wagner-Fujimori Japan Mission," *Christian Leader*, October 21, 1902, 4.

[62] Otoshigo Fujimori, "Wagner-Fujimori Japan Mission," *Christian Leader*, August 4, 1903, 9.

[63] Ibid.

[64] Otoshigo Fujimori, "Wagner-Fujimori Japan Mission," *Christian Leader*, December 30, 1902, 4.

[65] Otoshigo Fujimori, "Wagner-Fujimori Mission: Report for November, December, and January," *Gospel Advocate*, April 19, 1906, 244.

[66] Otoshigo Fujimori, "Wagner-Fujimori Mission: Report for February, March, and April," *Gospel Advocate*, June 26, 1906, 470.

[67] Otoshigo Fujimori, "Wagner-Fujimori Mission: Report for May, June, and July," *Gospel Advocate*, November 1, 1906, 694.

[68] Otoshigo Fujimori, "Wagner-Fujimori Japan Mission: Report for First Quarter, 1907," *Gospel Advocate*, June 20, 1907, 390.

[69] Otoshigo Fujimori, "Wagner-Fujimori Japan Mission," *Gospel Advocate*, October 31, 1907, 694.

[70] Otoshigo Fujimori, "Wagner-Fujimori Japan Mission: Report for Third Quarter, 1907," *Gospel Advocate*, December 26, 1907, 823.

[71] Otoshigo Fujimori, "Wagner-Fujimori Japan Mission: Report for April to December, 1908," *Gospel Advocate*, August 12, 1909, 1011.

[72] There are many discrepancies in spelling the name Yunosuke Hiratsuka in primary sources. In 1947, the Gospel Advocate printed a brief personal history, reportedly written by Hiratsuka, in which his first name is spelled Yonnosuke. Clara Bishop and other co-workers, however, spelled his name Yunosuke in their correspondence with American churches. This more conventional spelling is used throughout this book.

[73] Ibid.

[74] J. M. McCaleb, "The Work in Shimosa," *Gospel Advocate*, March 18, 1909, 339.

[75] G. A. Klingman, "A New Year's Gift for Brother Fujimori," *Gospel Advocate*, December 16, 1909, 1586.

[76] Otoshigo Fujimori, "Wagner-Fujimori Japan Mission: Report for 1910," *Gospel Advocate*, May 25, 1911, 589.

[77] Ibid.

[78] J. M. McCaleb, "A Visit from Fujimori," *Gospel Advocate*, March 13, 1913, 246.

[79] Otoshige Fujimori, "Japan News," *Christian Leader*, June 13, 1916, 13.

[80] Otoshige Fujimori, "Japan News," *Christian Leader*, July 4, 1916, 13.

[81] Otoshige Fujimori, "Japan News," *Christian Leader*, October 3, 1916, 13.

[82] Otoshige Fujimori, "No Topic," *Christian Leader*, October 31, 1916, 13.

[83] Joshua Hammer, "The Great Japan Earthquake of 1923," accessed December 23, 2016, http://www.smithsonianmag.com/history/the-great-japan-earthquake-of-1923-1764539/.

[84] Sarah Andrews, "Letter from Japan," *Gospel Advocate*, January 31, 1924, 100, 101.

[85] Robert S. King, "News from Sarah Andrews," *Gospel Advocate*, August 13, 1925, 782, 783; Robert S. King, "The Sarah Andrews Mission," *Gospel Advocate*, August 25, 1927, 799.

[86] F. L. Rowe, "Bro Oto May Visit U.S.," *Christian Leader*, October 12, 1926, 10; No author, "Bro. Fujimori to Visit U.S.," *Christian Leader*, October 26, 1926, 10.

[87] Otoshige Fujimori, "My Trip to America," *Christian Leader*, May 10, 1927, 10.

[88] Vernon C. Fry, "Thirty Years without a Furlough," *Gospel Advocate*, May 19, 1927, 471.

[89] H. M. Evans, "Our Japanese Missionary," *Christian Leader*, November 8, 1927, 7.

[90] F. L. Rowe, "Bro. Fujimori Makes Good," *Christian Leader*, September 6, 1927, 10.

[91] David. J. Poynter, "Fujimori Came to Albion, Neb.," *Christian Leader*, October 25, 1927, 10; W. K. Manchester, "Bro. Fujimori in Iowa," *Christian Leader*, November 1, 1927, 10; article by Homer E. Moore, in *Christian Worker*, reprinted in *Christian Leader*, November 22, 1927, 10.

[92] Reprinted from the Detroit *Christian News*, "Brother Fujimori Returns Home," *Gospel Advocate*, April 12, 1928, 343.

[93] Otoshige Fujimori, "At Home Again in Japan," *Gospel Advocate*, August 9, 1928, 758.

[94] H. Ishiguro, "Japanese Mission in Los Angeles, Calif.," *Gospel Advocate*, March 29, 1928, 307.

[95] Otoshigo Fujimori, "My Trip to America," *Gospel Advocate*, March 29, 1928, 290.

[96] J. M. McCaleb, "News from Japan," *Gospel Advocate*, June 28, 1928, 605.

[97] I. B. Bradley, "Sister Sarah Andrews' Work," *Gospel Advocate*, January 7, 1932, 12, 13.

[98] Otoshige Fujimori, "A Death in Japan," *Christian Leader*, December 31, 1931, 10.

[99] No author, "Fujimori's Sorrow," *Gospel Advocate*, October 20, 1932, 1149.

[100] Otoshigo Fujimori, "From Brother Fujimori," *Christian Leader*, November 9, 1937, 22.

[101] Ibid.

[102] Otoshigo Fujimori, "Brother Fujimori—Japan," *Christian Leader*, January 18, 1938, 10, 11.

[103] Otoshige Fujimori, "A Letter from Japan," *Missionary Messenger*, April 1941, 968.

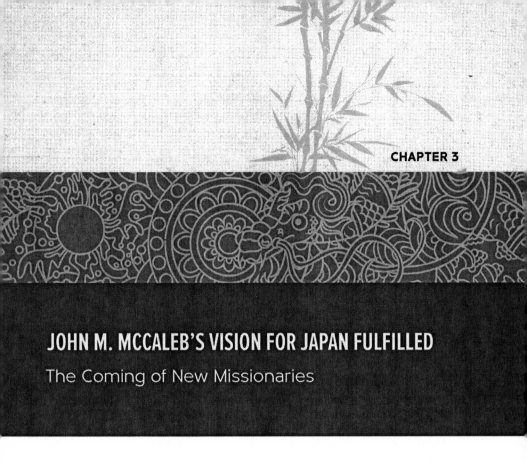

CHAPTER 3

JOHN M. MCCALEB'S VISION FOR JAPAN FULFILLED

The Coming of New Missionaries

While war still raged around the world, various writers for the religious journals among Churches of Christ began proposing the need for preparations for mission work in both Europe and the Pacific region. Grover C. Brewer, minister for the Broadway Church of Christ in Lubbock, Texas, sent one basic article to the major papers, including the *Gospel Advocate* and the *Firm Foundation*. In February 1943, believing then that the Allied powers would be victorious, he encouraged the evangelizing of the world after World War II: "Christianity offers to the world the only remedy for its ruin and the only panacea for its ills." He added, "Even the people of Germany and Italy and Japan should be ready to receive kindness and Christian treatment from those who have been the conquerors, if these victors demonstrate the proper spirit and attitude toward the vanquished."[1] In response to the call for missionaries, three missionaries who had been in Japan before World War II returned in late 1945 and 1946. They found a nation totally destroyed but open to Christianity.

"Gazing upon the Shambles": Post–World War II Ministries of Fox, Bixler, and Rhodes

Even though most all prewar missionaries left prior to the outbreak of the conflict, these same missionaries—Harry R. Fox, Sr., Orville D. Bixler, and Erroll Rhodes—remained interested in the Japanese people. John M. McCaleb was beyond his prime when the war ended in 1945. However, his vision for Japan was not lost on some of the younger prewar missionaries and certainly on the younger families who would come after the war's conclusion.

Although it would still be two years before full-time missionaries could return to Japan, one of the pre–World War II missionaries, Harry R. Fox, Sr., was chosen by the military to aid in interviewing the survivors of Hiroshima and Nagasaki.[2] Dressed in an army uniform, he returned to war-ravaged Japan late in 1945. Overwhelmed by what he saw, which was far from what he remembered when he left Japan in 1935, he told Americans, "The Japanese nation has suffered a terrible retribution: Most of Tokyo and Yokohama and a score of other large cities lie prostrate, victims of the worst which incendiary and atomic bombs could inflict." He found it difficult to even look at the two cities destroyed by the nuclear bombs. "As I gazed upon the shambles that used to be Hiroshima and Nagasaki I saw stark evidence of the truth that 'crime never pays.'"[3]

Visiting the two cities, only one word described the destruction caused by the bombs: "Disintegration. All physical matter within the central or inner zone of the bombed sites has been reduced to the original elements. 'Ashes to ashes, dust to dust.'" It was difficult for Fox to describe the human destruction: "A grisly pile of human bones here, a family of five orphaned children there, a lad whose face had been charred black, another instantaneously and permanently blinded, hospitals full of people, slowly but surely dying—all spoke eloquently in proving that 'war is hell.'"[4]

Speaking on the need for ministry and Christian brotherhood in the face of such incredible loss and tragedy, Fox indicated, "I am certain that if we really want to reclaim the Japanese people we can never do so by kicking them while they are down or continuing to condemn them as international [*sic*] outcasts." He continued, "There are two chief means or methods whereby we, as Christians, can proclaim the love and goodness of God that leads men to repentance toward God and faith toward the Lord Jesus Christ." The first of these two means was to share the teachings of Jesus with the people by every avenue possible—through Christian businessmen, teachers, diplomats, chemists, engineers, and certainly proclaimers of the gospel. The second was to "show the love of God toward our erstwhile enemies [by] help[ing] feed and clothe some of their millions of destitute war-victims." He noted that MacArthur and his military associates estimated that "upwards of four million will probably starve or freeze to death this winter unless heroic measures are taken soon." In a call to respond to the needs of Japan, he quoted both Jesus and Paul: "Love your enemies, bless them and do good to them" (Matthew 5:44, KJV). Paul added to Jesus' admonition, "Therefore if thine enemy hunger, feed him ... for in so doing, thou shalt heap coals of fire on his head. Be not overcome of evil, but overcome evil with good" (Romans 12:20, 21, KJV).[5]

However, despite the great need of the people, Japan was not yet open for Christian missionaries to freely enter so soon after the war. The MacArthur administration required every religious group that desired to send missionaries to appoint a recognized person who could recommend appropriate candidates. Of special concern was acquiring the necessary financial resources to live in a destitute Japan and the assurance of a sponsoring organization or church.

When Fox returned to Chicago's Cornell Avenue Church of Christ, he encouraged Orville D. Bixler, a missionary to Japan prior to the war, to serve as a go-between for Churches of Christ and the military authorities. Bixler became the second missionary person from Churches of Christ to return to Japan. Before the war, he had served twenty years as a missionary among the Japanese. With his arrival on December 16, 1946, he found the country ready for Christianity, even more so than pre–World War II Japan.

Bixler was overwhelmed by the reception the governmental officials afforded him. The people in the communities where he and other missionaries had served before World War II welcomed him with open arms. He was offered land for two Bible schools—an idea approved by the occupational authorities. MacArthur himself predicted that American missionaries would be widely accepted and embraced by a defeated and disillusioned people. It was reported that the general would call for a thousand American missionaries for Japan.[6]

While in Japan, Bixler visited churches that had met before the conflict. Wherever he went he was welcomed by large, enthusiastic crowds: he estimated the turnout to have been in the thousands. At one location, Bixler baptized fifteen persons. This would never have happened before the war. So pleased with the reception, he remarked, "Never in the history of missions has God placed so great opportunities and obligations on us." The only thing that dampened Bixler's enthusiasm was the news that his wife, Anna, who was never well, had died in his absence.[7]

The grieving Bixler went home but did not remain long in America. He returned to Japan in late 1947. Almost immediately, the Japanese Christians, led by Dr. Takashi Hiratsuka, a physician who was the nephew of Yonosuka Hiratsuka, a longtime native evangelist, held a special service in honor of Anna Bixler in Ibaraki Prefecture. They proposed building a memorial for her. Following the memorial service, Bixler, along with a Brother Takamatsu, made a five-day tour visiting towns he had not seen in eighteen years. Following his preaching in Daigo, the city where Herman Fox ministered, Bixler announced that seventy-nine persons had been baptized during his preaching tour in 1947.[8] Bixler exclaimed, "None of us realized that such a great awakening, such open doors, would come in our life-time."[9]

A third pre–World War II missionary family returned to Japan before any new workers were allowed to come. Erroll and Bess Rhodes returned early to Japan and their church in Yokohama because their son, Captain Robert Rhodes, was stationed there with the army. In late 1945, Robert had visited his birthplace in Omiya where he discovered Christians still carrying on the work his parents had begun.[10] On their second time in Japan, the Rhodeses found a ready reception. In early 1947, he reported 24 persons gathered for worship.[11] They would spend their entire time in Japan following World War II in Yokohama.

The coming of Harry R. Fox, Sr., Orville D. Bixler, Erroll Rhodes, and Herman Fox and their families was an answer to the prayers of John M. McCaleb. Even though McCaleb was from Tennessee, most of his associates lived in Louisville, Kentucky. By 1819, McCaleb's immediate family had left Japan for Louisville when McCaleb's oldest child was ready for school. McCaleb's trips back to the United States always led to Louisville. Therefore, when the new missionaries arrived in Japan, it was only natural for them to settle first in Tokyo, the focus of the earliest missionaries in Japan. The new missionaries fit perfectly into the vision McCaleb had for long-term missions in the nation across the Pacific Ocean.

A Legacy of Compassion: McCaleb's Vision for Japan

In 1908, J. M. McCaleb had a vision of his work in missions in Japan—some thirty years prior to World War II. He longed to build up a bustling and successful mission in Zoshigaya. He prayed for its success and flourishing. He envisioned welcoming, over time, many missionaries to Zoshigaya. There would be at least three residences in the Zoshigaya compound. There would be a boys' home. There would be a large hall suitable for all types of meetings. A school with a curriculum would be in place. Perhaps later in life, his own children with their mother, then in the United States for education, would return as missionaries. He could retire there, and his wife could join him by his side, "then serene and happy in a well-spent life, having stood by her husband's side in the trials of missionary life for fifty years." At that golden point in life, they would make one last visit to their home in the United States before returning to Japan to "spend the sunset of life and meet the dawn of the glorious morn in the 'land of the rising sun.'"[12]

But alas, the vision would not come true. God, in His providence, never doubted by McCaleb, had other plans. Lamenting, McCaleb wrote, "Not one of my family has ever seen Zoshigaya." In 1918, after twenty-six years in Japan, McCaleb mentioned that only four missionaries representing Churches of Christ continued in Japan: Sarah Andrews, Lillie Cypert, Alice Miller, and himself. Many of the first wave of workers were now dead: Eugene Snodgrass, William Bishop, and Frederick Wagner. Others had gone back to America, many for health reasons, including Charles Klingman, C. G. Vincent, B. W. Hon, and their families. W. K. Azbill, Lucia Scott, and Carme Hostetter, who had come with McCaleb in 1892, did not remain in Japan for long. It seemed that McCaleb's vision of a successful and flourishing mission was not meant to be.

Yet the providence of God still held a vision and a plan for the missions in Japan. Soon four young families were called to serve in Japan between 1918 and 1920. Orville and Anna Bixler arrived in 1918. Harry and Mary Pauline Fox and Bess and Erroll A. Rhodes came to Japan in 1919 to begin long years of mission work in their chosen field. In 1920, Herman and Sarah Fox became the second Fox family in Japan.

This was the largest single contingent of missionaries from Churches of Christ to arrive in Japan at that point in time. These young couples all came to Japan from the vicinity of Louisville, Kentucky, where they had come under the influence of Robert H. Boll at the Portland Avenue Church of Christ and Don Carlos Janes of the Highland Avenue church, two strong advocates of foreign missions whose influence would be felt throughout Japan and the Far East for many years.[13]

Almost without exception, the American missionaries would first find their church home with McCaleb at Tokyo's Zoshigaya church. This was done, for the most part, to facilitate language study. Furthermore, this long-term missionary, now fifty-six years of age, was a father figure to the young men and women who came to a foreign, even strange, culture. Thus it was only natural that all would first come to Tokyo. Only later would they move to other places, mainly to the Ibaraki Prefecture, north of Tokyo. This area would become the foundation for the major missionary activity in Japan after World War II. Beginning with these four couples, upward of eighteen missionaries worked in Ibaraki from 1918 until the outbreak of war in 1941. According to O. D. Bixler, "Perhaps more effort, at least longer years of effort, have been spent in Japan before the war than in any other country in the world as far as Churches of Christ mission work is concerned."[14]

Before going to Japan, Bixler was told by a teacher at Kansas State Normal School (later Emporia State) that he should be crossing the Atlantic Ocean to the war in Europe instead of the Pacific Ocean to Japan. For the same reason, he had difficulty getting his release from the draft board to leave the United States for Japan. Born in Albion, Nebraska, on May 12, 1896, he attended Western Bible and Literary College in Odessa, Missouri, for three years. He then spent a semester at Cordell Christian College in Oklahoma where he came under the influence of J. N. Armstrong, who encouraged Christians to be conscientious objectors to war. Later he enrolled in the University of Louisville. But most importantly, while in Louisville, he studied under Robert H. Boll at the Portland Avenue Church of Christ, who was influential in his decision to pursue mission work.[15]

Among the most unique stories of the 1918–1920 coming of missionaries to Japan was that of twin brothers Harry and Herman Fox. Harry R. Fox arrived in 1919 and Herman came in 1920. From Louisville, Kentucky, they, too, had come under the influence of Robert Boll. Boll's emphasis of God's grace and his focus on Jesus rather than on the church impacted both brothers. In addition, Herman accepted Boll's views on premillennialism—the literal reign of Jesus on the earth for one thousand years. Both men had attended the Highland church in Louisville.[16]

Erroll and Bess Rhodes were from Louisville, where Erroll was also a student of Robert Boll. The couple associated themselves with the Otsuka church in Tokyo where Hirosuke Ishiguro was then ministering.[17] (Later Ishiguro would go to America to attend Abilene Christian College. Then in 1923, he would establish the Westside Church of Christ in Los Angeles. His story is told in detail in Chapter 5.) Rhodes continued with this church until he relocated in Hatachi Omiya, Ibaraki Prefecture.

With a nod to God's continuing providence, McCaleb recalled how all the missionaries had first come to Tokyo and then located elsewhere. The most recent arrivals were no different from earlier missionaries. "The Bixlers arrived in 1918, and after about two years hopped off to Ibaraki province, some ninety miles northeast. The Rhodes and Fox families arrived in 1919. Mr. and Mrs. Rhodes came down to Omiya, seven miles from the Bixlers. Harry Fox and family sailed on some forty miles further to Tanakura, in the adjoining province. His brother, Herman, arrived in 1920, and after a brief stay with us, found himself located at Daigo, between his brother's place and the Bixlers."[18]

In addition to the four families who arrived between 1918 and 1920, after 1925, Barney Morehead and his wife Nellie would come to live in Ota, only ten miles on the Kuji River from the Pacific Ocean. In all, these five families were responsible for establishing six churches.[19] Although the missionaries did not remain in Tokyo, they did set the stage in the Kuji River Valley for McCaleb's vision to come to fruition.

Four Families Move to Ibaraki

When the four families began searching for a region where they could minister, the logical person to give them advice was Yunosuke Hiratsuka. (Hiratsuka is discussed in detail in Chapter 4.) He was from Ibaraki and had preached there when he returned to his birth area. He had baptized several people, including his mother, in this rather rural region.

In 1938, after the Rhodes family moved to Yokohama to place their sons in an international school, Erroll reported the history of the Omiya church for Barney Morehead's *World Vision* magazine. Omiya was a small farming town of three thousand people. When the Rhodeses first arrived in the 1920s, they perceived the people to be rather backward compared with those who lived in the urban centers of Japan. They did not respond well to Western ways, content to instead adhere to the ways of their ancestors.

The Rhodeses claimed a major advantage over other missionaries in the Kuji River Valley. Yunosuke Hiratsuka, a preacher and an elder of the Kamitomizaka Church of Christ in Tokyo, became widely known before the arrival of the Americans in the vicinity of Omija. He had baptized a young man shortly before the Rhodeses arrived. Under the Rhodes's tutelage, by 1928, he became a full-time evangelist. Ten years later this native preacher, who became known as Brother Chinone, was widely honored and respected for his preaching among his people; he tragically died in 1932 at an early age. Four months after Chinone's death, Rhodes baptized Chinone's father.[20] In the meantime, the Rhodeses did the best they could through personal work and holding public assemblies on Sunday evenings. Few adults attended, but the couple stood strong and held faith. To eventually reach adults, Bess Rhodes began a kindergarten in the fall of 1924. A Sunday school, organized to attract young people, also began meeting in 1924 and was fortunately met with good attendance.

In 1928, an event came about that brought heightened excitement among the mission families. Entrepreneur and Christian philanthropist George Pepperdine, of Los Angeles, while on an around-the-world trip with his mother, visited the American missionaries in Japan. His visit certainly provided a morale boost. Fourteen American missionaries and five Japanese workers met with him in Omiya. Among other things, he called for a thousand American missionaries to come to Japan to be joined by five thousand native workers.[21] One of the positive outcomes of the visit was the completion of a building for the Omiya church.[22]

From 1923 to 1938, when the family left Japan, Rhodes reported in Omiya and Yokohama a total of 135 baptisms. Of this number, ten had died and only eight remained faithful Christians. Because of family-required marriages, the majority no longer attended worship. Yet the involvement of native workers, preachers, and persons of faith is considered essential to the health and success of any mission. The Rhodeses considered the Japanese faithful among them "a light in this darkened community." Faced with a heightened war frenzy in the 1930s, there were few responses to Christian outreach, and the number of native participants in the mission dwindled.[23]

O. D. Bixler recalled those times when he and his wife first moved to Nagasawa in 1921. They chose to build a house 2.5 miles outside the town: "There were only two Christians besides my wife and me and one of them was an immoral backslider." They happily reported that after three or four years, the man, penitent, returned to Christ. Because of Hiratsuka, a small group of Christians was meeting across the hills, but a leading member ran off with a "bad girl." The little church faced difficult times. Possibly because of the immoral relations within the church, a young baptized believer with potential to serve within the church, evidently discouraged, was toying with returning to the Salvation Army. Bixler and Oto Fujimori went to the Salvation Army to explain their interest in the young man. Hearing their concern, the Salvation Army no longer pursued the young Christian. The young man, whom Bixler never mentioned by name, became Erroll Rhodes's native worker.[24]

The Bixlers, and the Rhodes, from the time they moved to Ibaraki, were interested in reaching out to the community with physical help, especially with prepared food. For instance, needy people, many being young children, knew the Bixlers would feed them if they stopped by their home. It was widely known that both the Rhodes and Bixlers served rice and gravy to the poor.[25] Over many years, the Bixlers estimated that thousands had come to their home seeking something to eat.[26] The Bixlers believed that missions serving the everyday needs of the people were far more effective than evangelism. They believed it was easier to reach people with the gospel by first caring for their physical needs.

Anna Bixler recalled in 1932 that young children came to their house to see the foreigners. One young boy, needing motherly friendship, often came to visit. She would feed him; then Mr. Bixler would talk to him about his soul. Without a stable home, the young boy ran away. But he kept coming back to the Bixler home. It was a safe haven for the boy. Bixler would say to him, "I must talk to you about your soul every time you come." Without pause, the young boy responded, "You see I keep on coming, don't you?" It took ten years, but in the spring of 1932, as a young adult, he accepted Christ in baptism.[27]

The Fox brothers and their families moved to the Kuji River Valley early in 1923. Whether in Tanakura, the Fukushima Prefecture, near the headwaters of the Kuji River, or in Daigo, ten miles downriver, Harry and Herman faced daunting tasks: How could they attract a rural people, many of whom were illiterate and steeped in Japanese traditions, to the Christian message? Since both families were Western foreigners, their rural neighbors needed to know they were not "fly-by-night" religious predators.

Therefore, with help from the Missions Home Building Fund, administered by J. M. McCaleb and Don Carlos Janes, the brothers in 1924 constructed precut homes in their respective towns. Their homes were comparable to the one constructed by Sarah Andrews in Shizuoka—designed by the Aladdin Company in Portland, Oregon. Every piece was precut, with directions for construction included. These Western houses were quite an attraction to the people in both Tanakura and Daigo.[28]

Early in 1926, the brothers devised unique methods to attract local people to venues for preaching the gospel. In a long letter to J. M. McCaleb, Herman Fox related his efforts to provide a meeting place in Daigo. Without a permanent place to meet, Herman erected a tent to attract the people to preaching meetings. Since all the people worked in their fields during the day, it was necessary to provide meeting times at night. At first he thought about hanging lanterns in the tent, but he determined it best to have electric lights. He faced quite a task and had no idea about the problems he would face. The electric company agreed to string the lights, but they did not have the required heavy wiring. Ever industrious, Fox learned that an electric company several miles away had the wiring he needed. So he mounted his motorcycle, which he called "Indian," and retrieved the wire. But the electricians could not string the lights until Sunday morning—and the first meeting was scheduled for that night. Miraculously, by the afternoon the lights were in place. Then it began to rain, and as the meeting time drew closer, the rain came down in a flood. Fox did not cancel the meeting, but few persons showed up.

It was a great disappointment. Undaunted, he made plans for Monday night. He posted announcements around town. He was not disappointed. When the time came for the 7:30 p.m. preaching service, some 125 people showed up to hear preaching by this American missionary. He preached from 7:30 to 9:00 p.m. with good attention. He told McCaleb, "I give all the praise, honor and thanksgiving to him whom it is all due."[29] However, the outreach in Daigo was never very successful. Only twelve persons were baptized between 1924 and 1933.[30]

Upriver in Tanakura, the new house was an incentive to get the people to listen to a Japanese preacher share the Christian message. Harry and Pauline Fox chose to have preaching services on their front lawn. Across the street, Tanakura was holding its annual horse sale. Buyers and sellers came in great numbers from throughout the region. As the visitors came to the horse sale, they admired the house of the foreigners. To get the visitors to hear a Christian message, the Foxes offered tours of their home. The people "came in swarms to see the house," reported Pauline Fox. The tours were given only after the people listened to Yonosuke Hiratsuka preach Christ.

For a full week, crowds came from forty different villages to visit the horse sale and to tour the house. According to Pauline, "The crowds started gathering about 10 o'clock in the morning and continued until four or five in the afternoon." They estimated that at least 200 people listened to preaching during the day. Each night Hiratsuka again preached. In all, he spoke between four and five hours each day. By the end of the week, three persons had been baptized. Hiratsuka, according to Pauline Fox, was pleased with his week's preaching: "He was certainly enthusiastic over the meetings and said he considers last week the most blessed week of all his twenty years' evangelistic experience." Hiratsuka said of those who heard his preaching, "They had tears when they listened about the cross or the love of God."[31]

As a point of interest, a second Japanese preacher, Brother Ebine, was scheduled to share in the preaching. However, he suffered a heart attack on the second day of the meeting. Herman Fox, acting quickly, seated Ebine in the sidecar of his motorcycle and took him home. Ebine thought he was at the point of death. He made an oral will in the presence of Hiratsuka.[32] However, he did recover and became one of the outstanding native preachers both before and after World War II.

The Families Travel Back to America

During the fall of 1926, Harry Fox, Orville Bixler, and Erroll Rhodes took furlough and returned with their families back to America. All three returned to the churches in Louisville that supported them in Japan. On a Sunday night in September, the three missionaries led worship at the Highland church in the Japanese language. The presence of these brave followers of Christ and their families must have inspired the Louisville churches. They gave liberally on this and other occasions to foreign missions. The Highland church—sponsor of the Fox families—contributed $2,543 for missions in 1925. Don Carlos Janes, a member of Highland, raised $7,512 for missionaries during the last half of 1926.

An interesting insight was made by six-year-old Harry Robert Fox, Jr., when he observed Christian men in Louisville smoking cigarettes: "Why Momma, they're in America. They know about God and ought to know better."[33] By October 1927, the Fox, Rhodes, and Bixler families had returned to Japan. Herman Fox, who indicated being lonesome with his fellow missionaries on furlough, left Japan in 1928 for a furlough trip to the United States.[34] He and his family had been in Japan eight years without a vacation from what he called a difficult work at Daigo-Machi.

The Fifth Family: Barney and Nellie Morehead Arrive in Japan

At this juncture, it is wise to introduce a very important family who came in 1925 to join other American missionaries in the Kuji River Valley. Barney and Nellie Morehead, 1924 graduates of David Lipscomb College, went to Japan specifically to establish a school in Ota. The school would focus on educating Japanese men to become Christian workers.[35] Supported by the Waverly-Belmont Church of Christ, they left Nashville around July 1, 1925, with plans to stop in Los Angeles to study Japanese with Ishiguro, the preacher for the Westside Church of Christ. They would sail for Japan around September 1.[36]

As was true of all American missionaries, the Moreheads remained for a year in Tokyo in language school. Knowing generally where they wished to settle, the young missionaries visited both the Fox, the Bixler, and the Rhodes families during a long Thanksgiving weekend. In the meantime, Barney and Nellie were teaching six Bible classes in English each week. In April, Barney reported baptizing his Korean student.[37]

Robert S. King, one of the most mission-minded men among Churches of Christ before World War II, called for churches to construct the Moreheads a Western-style house when they relocated in Ota. The David Lipscomb College church, where King attended, raised the money for the house. King believed it would take $4,000 for the entire Morehead building project.[38] But in the meantime, the Moreheads lived in the Rhodes's house in Omiya while they were on furlough. Finally, late in 1926, the time came for the Moreheads to move to Ota, "a town of 10,000 to 12,000 where no other missionary has preached."[39]

In an article entitled "A Word to the Nashville Churches," Morehead announced, "We have selected a location near a large boys' school and in easy reach of all our mission points, where we want to erect a small school in which to teach Japanese young men the Bible."Morehead believed that native teachers could reach their own people much better than foreign missionaries. He would use Hiratsuka and Fujimori, experienced native preachers, to teach short terms each year. In addition, he would employ one full-time teacher. Nellie Morehead desired to begin a kindergarten. The dream for a school was becoming a reality. In May 1927, a three-room build-ing for the school was under construction. Robert King and the Lipscomb church made a call for $2,000 more to finish the project.[40] The King Bible School was near reality.

In early 1927, Barney Morehead hinted at his inability to learn the Japanese language. He feared that the language, customs, and habits could not be learned in the relatively short span of a few years. He then related the experience of J. M. McCaleb, a missionary in Japan for thirty-two years. Every day, for an hour, he had a teacher read Japanese to him and teach him to write in the language. Morehead added, "I believe every missionary should have a few Japanese young men in training all the time."[41] Yet by February 1928, he reported that while he and Nellie came to Ota alone eight months before, now eight Christians were worshiping together.[42]

The year 1928 was a year of transition for Barney and Nellie Morehead. On Sunday, May 20, they left for America to be with his dying sister. While in the United States, the Moreheads were intensively involved in a campaign for foreign missions. In the United States for 202 days, they were involved for 180 days in active work. Barney spoke to one hundred churches. Of these churches, sixty-six gave $2,621.73 for missions. And "Sister Morehead collected funds for her special work." As a bonus, they recruited two new missionaries. Edith Lankford returned with them to Japan early in 1929. She would work closely with Nellie Morehead in the kindergarten and classes for women. Homer Winnett, a student at Lipscomb, would come to Japan after the spring session.[43] Morehead, on this trip home, may have found his talent for foreign missions—raising funds for other missionaries.

New Faces and New Trials for the Japanese Mission

The death of a long-term missionary and the coming of another family to Japan were events of 1928. On March 5, Alice Miller, once a coworker with J. M. McCaleb, passed away. For McCaleb, the last twenty years or so were somewhat disappointing. At some point, probably near 1910, William Dayton Cunningham, Miller's coworker, had introduced an organ into worship at the Yotsuya Mission in Tokyo. In deference to McCaleb, who strongly opposed the use of instrumental music, it was never used when he visited their worship times. McCaleb, however, remained in relationship with Miller and visited her while she was in St. Luke's International Hospital, reaching the hospital only a few minutes prior to her death. She had served in Japan since 1896, only four years less than McCaleb.[44]

A different type of missionary arrived in Japan in 1928. Carl L. Etter's family had been scheduled to arrive in Japan in 1927, but he deferred for a year because he desired to earn a master's degree at the University of Southern California. In the meantime, his wife gave birth to a baby. Arriving late in 1928, they spent a few weeks in Tokyo and then moved to Sapporo on the northern island of Hokkaido. Here he had a contract to teach at the University of Sapporo for three years. Etter did what he could to share Christ, but a mission was not established there until 1931 when Hettie Lee Ewing and a young Japanese preacher, Kinji Tashiro, came to Sapporo. Soon thereafter, Tashiro contracted typhoid fever and died. (Further information on the Sapporo mission can be located in Chapters 1 and 2.) The Etters returned to the United States in July 1932 when Carl's teaching contract expired.[45]

By that time, the three missionary families who had been on furlough were again in Japan. The Rhodes family was busy in Omiya, the Bixlers in Nagasawa, and Harry Fox and his family were in Tanakura. The year would not be kind to Bixler and several members of Harry Fox's family. During the winter seasons of both 1928 and 1929, Harry Fox's family lived in Sarah Andrews's house in Shizuoka while she was on a three-year sick leave to America. Harry would provide ministry leadership to native preachers while members of the family, because of illness, enjoyed the warmer weather as opposed to the colder climate of Tanakura. For some time, Harry Sr. had been suffering from sciatica, a nerve pain in the lower back and pelvic region, and in 1928, several family members had diphtheria. While the Foxes were away from Tanakura, the capable Brother Ebine carried on the work. Young Harry Fox said of his two years down south, "I like Shizuoka best but *my home* is in Tanakura."[46]

Orville Bixler, as did Herman Fox, owned an auto cycle—a motorcycle with a sidecar. These vehicles provided cheap and efficient transportation for the missionaries. In October 1928, Bixler and Ryohachi Shigekuni, recently returned from California to preach among his people, were traveling in Bixler's vehicle when it overturned, crushing one of Bixler's legs under the cart. The large bone was broken in two places and the small bone in one. Treated in four hospitals, only one month after the accident, he visited McCaleb's Zoshigaya church in Tokyo. Later he would trade the auto cycle for a small French sedan, which was much safer. While in the hospitals, Bixler, ever the evangelist, converted a number of people, including several nurses in training.[47]

McCaleb's Trip around the World

The year 1929, the year of the Great Depression, was an eventful year for American missionaries in Japan. In January, McCaleb began his trip around the world to visit missionaries of Churches of Christ. The last meeting he attended at the Zoshigaya church, six young people, educated in the Sunday school, were baptized. Bixler spent the night with him before he left on his journey. At the train station, some fifty people gathered to say goodbye. These included Bixler, Lillie Cypert, and a number of Japanese brothers and sisters. McCaleb would board his ship at Kobe, but since he had an extra day, he visited and spent the night with Harry Fox and his family in Shizuoka, at the home of Sarah Andrews. He also passed through Okitsu, where he saw the little church building Andrews had constructed.

Among those in Tokyo who came to wish him a good trip was Clara Kennedy, a missionary in Japan since 1924. From Portland, Maine, she had worked closely with McCaleb and Lillie Cypert. Soon after she bid farewell to McCaleb, she left for America for her first visit home since coming to Japan. Near the end of his trip, McCaleb, the world traveler, stopped in Portland where he spent two days, one with the Portland church and the second day meeting with the church in Unity. It pleased him to visit with Kennedy's family and her home church. "I was pleased to find that the brethren there who have known her from childhood speak well of her." During the meetings at the two churches, McCaleb and Kennedy together sang a song in Japanese. Clara Kennedy would spend six more years in Japan, leaving that country amid war fever on September 25, 1936.[48]

A second highlight of 1929 was the coming of two men from David Lipscomb College. One, Homer Winnett, came as a missionary, committed to working with Barney and Nellie Morehead in Ota. The other was Samuel Pittman, a teacher at Lipscomb. After a short visit in Ota, Winnett quickly went to Tokyo for language study. He lived in McCaleb's home while in Tokyo and worked with the Zoshigaya church. However, Winnett did not long remain in Japan. He returned to the United States in 1931 to marry a woman he had never met. J. M. McCaleb was evidently the matchmaker.[49]

Pittman came to Japan at the invitation of Barney Morehead to lead a summer Bible study. Most of the missionaries and a number of the Japanese workers—some forty-five individuals—attended the Bible drills. The Ota church building, completed in June 1929, made Ota an excellent meeting place for Pittman's Bible drills. Pittman preached in the morning and held round-table discussions in the afternoon; at night, the attendees were divided into five groups, preaching in different parts of the town. Before scattering to their preaching locations, everyone "met at one place and marched from there through the town singing God's praise."[50] Morehead often said this was the first week-long campaign held among Churches of Christ.[51]

In the July 31, 1930, issue of the *Gospel Advocate*, Barney Morehead announced that he, Nellie, and Lankford were leaving their work in Ota and the King Bible School to return to America. He wanted everyone to know that his enthusiasm for missions had not diminished: "God knows my reason for coming home. If it be God's will, I expect to return to Japan at the best time, but not as a located missionary. My talent is not suited for located work." At the urging of Morehead, Harry Fox and his family moved to Ota to operate the King Bible School and to work in all church activities in the community.[52]

Orville D. Bixler's Dream

Orville D. Bixler, after completing his furlough in 1927, told his Christian friends in the United States why he and his family were returning to Japan. "We are going because we believe it is God's will for the Japanese to have a chance to know of the Christ—for he is not willing that any should perish— there is no distinction—and there is no other name given under heaven wherein man must be saved." Bixler had in mind the story of the Good Samaritan: "There are multitudes of people to be helped, and in helping them their hearts are opened to hear the Gospel."[53] Nellie Morehead told of how "the Japanese have learned to resort to the Bixler home for medical aid, for food and clothing, some having been brought into the kingdom through their kindness and sympathetic welcome."[54] Indicating that six thousand to eight thousand people, from beggars to statesmen, had come to their door in Nagasawa, they said, "We can now begin to see the sprouting seed sown helter-skelter as it seemed.... I know it would be almost impossible to live in any place where we could come in contact with more people than we do right here at these crossroads several miles from a town of any size."[55]

Before and after World War II, O. D. Bixler was interested in establishing a hospital to serve the high percentage of tubercular victims in Japan. Recalling his accident in 1928 that caused a broken leg and several days in hospitals, he told his Japanese friends that his accident was by the providence of God—"for my own good and for the good of others." Why did he feel this way? The stay in the hospital resulted in the conversion of two nurses in training, leading to the opportunity to teach between fifty and one hundred others at the hospital. Developing from these contacts was the opportunity to work in the tuberculosis ward. He concluded, "The greatest possibilities to relieve suffering in Japan is in the tuberculosis work."[56]

Bixler's experiences as a patient in hospitals caused him to propose the formation of a Christian hospital, reminiscent of the work of the Good Samaritan. He outlined a hospital plan "for the salvation of suffering souls." In June 1931, he had already located four doctors, a nurse, and a pharmacist who were interested in the hospital. The nurse was Emma Beech, who recently in 1930 came from Chattanooga, Tennessee. With eighteen years of experience, she was the perfect fit for Bixler's dream. However, she did not remain long in Japan, resigning in 1934. She even refused free passage to the United States.[57]

Most of all, Bixler needed a hospital facility. A Japanese brother, Iskikawa, had a site he could provide free of charge for the hospital. Iskikawa was once a sufferer from tuberculosis. Bixler, however, did not think large. He needed only a house for a resident doctor and two or three cabins for patients. He believed he could begin the facilities for only $1,000. At first, the hospital would only be able to care for ten patients.[58] The hospital remained only a dream, a dream Bixler resurrected following World War II.

The Bixlers used their rural location to create a home industry. They produced what they called "health foods." To manufacture cereals, they used grains grown by their Japanese neighbors, thus giving them an outlet for their surplus rice and wheat. The Bixlers made puffed rice and puffed wheat, not unlike the cereals developed by the Kellogg and Post companies in the United States. McCaleb, a customer of the Bixlers' home industry, often had breakfasts that included Bixler cereals. In 1933, Bixler began producing American-style molasses. He grew his own cane on two acres of his land. He had his own sorghum mill using horses to power the mill. "We are encouraged to see our industry growing nicely whereby men are able to be self-supporting in the work."[59] Bixler provided work for four employees, all Christians. Thus, by providing their own income, they could preach without salaries from churches.[60]

When Barney and Nellie returned to the United States, Harry Fox was the choice to replace him at the King Bible School and various other enterprises in Ota. The Fox family had been in Tanakaya since early 1923. They had reached a number of people with the gospel but had not constructed a separate meeting place for a church. They met in the Fox home. Thus the move to Ota seemed a plus for the family. They enjoyed a good house, a new meetinghouse constructed in 1929, and a building housing the King Bible School. And Ryohachi Shigekuni joined the Ota work. (Shigekuni's story is discussed further in Chapter 4.)

All the missionaries along the Kuji River had small children. Barney Morehead had indicated a need for a school where the children of the missionaries might be educated. However, when the Moreheads left for America, the proposed school did not yet have a college-trained teacher. Likely through correspondence between Harry Fox and Morehead, the missionaries soon located a teacher. Christine Jones from Barren County, Kentucky, had just finished at David Lipscomb College. She arrived in 1931 to a class of ten students at various levels of learning. When the Rhodeses returned from furlough, she had twelve students. Unfortunately, because of fatigue (for which she spent three weeks in a sanitarium), doctors recommended in 1932 that she return to the United States.[61] Schooling for missionary children was still not available.

In the meantime, Harry Fox and Shigekuni were engaged in many activities in and around Ota. Fox mentioned setting out 1,500 tomato plants, but because of unfavorable weather, the crop was almost a failure. "From now on," stated Fox, "we plan to specialize on canning chicken and broth, all of these are good sellers during the winter months." The church was doing well, with about thirty members. They were involved in street preaching, conducting Sunday schools, and a kindergarten. And they began reaching out to surrounding villages by distributing circulars and portions of the Bible—especially the Gospels.[62]

Harry Fox's Family Returns to America and David Lipscomb College

The lack of a trained teacher for the King Bible School may have been part of the reason Fox in 1932 returned to America. This time, however, they came to Nashville, where Harry Sr. would attend David Lipscomb College.

This move was at the urging of Barney and Nellie Morehead, but there were also other concerns.[63] Earlier in 1932, Pauline Fox had spent time in a sanitarium. Although it was only an iodine infection, the Japanese doctors feared scarlet fever. Furthermore, her husband believed, "It seems she cannot get entirely healed as long as she remains here." About himself, Fox revealed, "My nerves are all on edge ... and [I] can't sleep well at night." They left the work at Ota under the directions of the Rhodeses, who also were responsible as well for the efforts in Owiya. Featuring the Fox family on the cover of *Missionary Messenger* for December 1932, Don Carlos Janes noted that Harry Fox had baptized seventy-five persons in his tenure in Japan.[64]

With his brother away in America, Herman Fox reported the best results he had had since he first located in Daigo. In 1933, although church attendance was sparse, a Sunday school was begun and a meeting hall had been constructed. He also established a church in Kami Osaka in the same year, with fifteen baptisms and very good attendance. However, they needed a place to meet.[65]

The two years Harry Fox's family spent in Nashville were an introduction to an experience totally new to them—attending a Christian school. The Fox children were enrolled in Lipscomb's campus school while the father attended the college. After two years, the Fox family felt prepared and eager to return to Japan. The Lipscomb college church assumed the sponsorship of the Foxes in Japan. Their return to Japan would cost $800; already by February 1934, the campus community had raised $100. Robert S. King, the treasurer of the church, would oversee the Fox Japan funds.[66] On May 20, the faculty and students wished them bon voyage in a special meeting of Lipscomb's chapel as they prepared to leave Nashville.[67]

In the pages of the *Oriental Christian*, Harry Fox told about the family's desires on their return to Japan: "The door is open; the field is ripe unto harvest." He added, "The purposes of our coming to America accomplished, we are now ready and eager to get back to our post 'over there.'" Affirming that evangelism remained the primary task of the missionary, he underlined the need for a Bible training school. If he were not convinced of the importance of a Christian school before attending Lipscomb, he was after his family's experience at Lipscomb, from elementary school through two years of college. The Christian school was a means of instructing disciples following their conversion to Christ: "This was the apostolic practice." The King Bible School, modeled on David Lipscomb College, was established for this very reason: "Already, a few young Timothys have received training here and are now preaching." In early August, Harry preached for the Long Beach, California, church before the family boarded the *Komaki Maru* on August 6, 1934, for their trip back to Japan.[68]

Their time in Japan, however, would be short-lived. While in Nashville, Harry Fox, Sr., fell from a hammock, injuring his already pained back. He thought it was "a recurrent attack of what was supposed to be ordinary 'sciatica.'" But as the cold of winter increased, his condition worsened. Finally, an x-ray image revealed a fractured vertebrae and "an abnormality of bone structure in the lumbar region." Doctors in Tokyo advised him to enter a hot springs resort in southern Japan, where he spent several weeks. Although away from home, he conversed with a number of inactive Christians. Others with whom he talked made little response, although they did accept the offered literature.[69]

Probably the most important activity he conducted while away from home was to develop a list of negative reactions of Japanese people to the Christian message:

1. Japan has her own religions and gods; hence as Japanese citizens, we must be loyal to them.
2. My family would not approve of my accepting a "foreign" religion.
3. Christianity does not fit in with our Japanese form of government (i.e., "the emperor is divine, sacred, and inviolate").
4. Christianity would oblige me to violate national customs.
5. It would interfere with my business and cause me to lose money or fail.
6. It would involve my forsaking my ancestors (i.e., ancestor worship).
7. Christianity has failed to purify society in America and other Christian countries.
8. The Christian delegates at the London Conference were as selfish and intolerant as others.

9. Christian countries discriminate against the Japanese (e.g., the Immigration Act and Arizona "outrage").

10. Christianity is impracticable in a non-Christian land like this.[70]

It was a list that could have helped the missionaries, had not the volatile issue of war been present in Japan.

By mid-summer of 1935, both Fox brothers had decided to return to America because of health reasons.[71] Harry Fox stated sadly, "[I]t has been decided that we must return to America for expert medical attention for my persistent back trouble. . . . This does not mean that we are abandoning 'missionary work' among the Japanese, even though a change of location is necessary just now."[72]

Harry Fox's family moved to Southern California, where he received treatment from Dr. C. H. Carpenter, an endocrinologist and a member of the Church of Christ. While the missionary family was in Los Angeles for two years, George Pepperdine supported them and paid for the doctor's care. Recovering from his back problems, Harry and his family moved back to Nashville where Harry Sr. became the minister for the David Lipscomb College church. The children enrolled in the elementary and high schools of Lipscomb. By 1938, the Fox family considered returning to Japan, but they were advised not to return because of anti-American sentiment—Americans were no longer welcome in that country.[73] Not until after World War II would Harry Fox and his sons, Harry Robert, Jr., and Logan, return to Japan as missionaries.

The Death of a Vision: Japanese Missions in the Wake of the Great War

The Bixlers reached Japan on November 14, 1936, after spending two years in America. For Anna Bixler, it was a bittersweet return to their "home:" "We are glad to be back and are thankful for the welcome we received." But, on the other hand, they had left their two daughters in the States "where they can study and prepare for future work for the Lord."[74] Although they were again in Nagasawa, they were aware of the war between Japan and China. Japan was under the influence of extreme nationalistic excitement. Yet, said Anna, "The people are very kind to us and very considerate of us."[75]

The Bixlers would not long remain in Japan. Anna became quite ill; thus she had to leave Japan for Kansas City, Missouri, where she would receive medical care. Because of worsening conditions in Japan due to wartime conflicts, Orville Bixler decided it best to join his family in America. On November 29, 1938, Bixler arrived in Los Angeles from Japan. He was welcomed by Harry Fox's family. Like Harry Fox, Bixler would not return to Japan until after World War II.[76]

Yet, even in the face of missionary families leaving Japan because of war fever, two families decided to go to Japan in 1937—one new family and one returning. On August 19, 1937, Elbridge B. Linn and his wife sailed for Japan. They were graduates of Abilene Christian College and were sponsored by the Cornell Avenue Church of Christ in Chicago. Met at the dock by Bixler, they were shown around Tokyo. Linn said of his introduction to Japan, "I had read a number of books about Japan, had talked with several people and thought I was prepared for this 'new world' to which we were coming, yet many customs, attitudes and conditions are new to me, and some are almost startling at first." He noted that they had arrived at a critical time—even people on the street were suspicious of all foreigners. This was especially true if they suspected the foreigners "frowned upon Japan's actions in China." The wartime conflict proved too harsh to establish a successful ministry, and less than a year later, the Linns announced they would be leaving Japan in the summer of 1938.[77]

Herman Fox, against the advice of family and friends, was determined to return to Japan. His brother Harry, Orville Bixler, and Erroll Rhodes discouraged his going. Under the present conditions, it would be "exceedingly difficult to reach the people's ears with the message."[78] By June 1938, the Fox family was back in Japan. The situation, however, had changed dramatically since 1935. Herman was limited as to what he could do. He was even deprived of the use of his automobile. Thus by October 1941, he and his family returned to America, only three months prior to the attack on Pearl Harbor.[79] In addition, Hettie Lee Ewing (1940) and Erroll and Bess Rhodes and their two sons (1940) felt the pressures building in Japan against Americans; thus they also returned to the United States prior to the attack on Pearl Harbor.

With his vision shattered in the wake of the horrors of war, McCaleb, who had come to Japan in almost fifty years prior, left on October 22, 1941, never to return again. As late as the summer of 1940, McCaleb had not planned to leave Japan, but he realized, "The gospel cannot be forced on people. They must have a receptive state of mind or one's efforts are in vain."[80] All hope was seemingly lost for McCaleb's once great vision. It seemed the love of Christ would not survive the plague of a world at war.

But there was a glimmer of hope. Two solitary woman missionaries, Lillie Cypert in Tokyo and Sarah Andrews in Shizuoka, remained when the Japanese attacked Pearl Harbor on December 7, 1941, their strong faith guiding them, a testament to the power of Christ's resurrection. Perhaps one day, there would be the dawn of a new era after the trials and death endured in the war. Perhaps one day the missions would return to the land of the rising sun, fulfilling McCaleb's vision of brotherhood in Christ.

Then, in 1945, Harry Fox, Sr., set foot on Japanese soil to begin that healing process. There was still hope.

Endnotes

[1] G. C. Brewer, "Evangelizing the World in the Postwar Period," *Gospel Advocate*, February 18, 1943, 154.

[2] Correspondence with Harry Robert Fox, Jr., May 23, 2013.

[3] Harry Robert Fox, Sr., "Reflections from Nagasaki," *World Vision*, March, April 1946, 5.

[4] Ibid., 5, 6.

[5] Ibid., 7.

[6] George Benson, "Open Doors in Japan," *World Vision*, March 1947, 10.

[7] O. D. Bixler, "Dear Ones of World Vision, Office and Readers," *World Vision*, March 1947, 13, 14.

[8] O. D. Bixler, "A Five Day Trip," *World Vision*, March 1948, 9, 15.

[9] Ibid.; O. D. Bixler, "Ripe Harvest in Japan," *World Vision*, November 1948, 8.

[10] Charles R. Brewer, "Editorial Notes," *World Vision*, January, February 1946, 3.

[11] O. D. Bixler, "Brother Bixler's Letter," *World Vision*, March 1947, 3.

[12] J. M. McCaleb, *Once Traveled Roads* (Nashville: Gospel Advocate Company, 1934), 364–66.

[13] For more on the work of Don Carlos Janes, see Jeremy Heigi, "One-Man Missionary Society: The Indefatigable Work of Don Carlos Janes," *Restoration Quarterly*, 58.4 (2016), 211–27.

[14] McCaleb, *Once Traveled Roads*, 364–66.

[15] No author, "Regarding a New Missionary," *Christian Leader*, July 1, 1919, 16.

[16] O. D. Bixler, "A Beautiful Decision and What It Meant," *Oriental Christian*, December 1932, 8, 9.

[17] B. D. Morehead, "A Missionary on the Field," *Gospel Advocate*, February 10, 1927, 127.

[18] J. M. McCaleb, *Once Traveled Roads*, 366, 367.

[19] Correspondence with Harry Robert Fox, Jr., August 12, 2012. All correspondence with Fox is deposited in the Beaman Library of Lipscomb University.

[20] B. D. Morehead, "Foreign Missionary Activity of Nashville Tenn.," *Oriental Christian*, August 1932, 11, 12. (Includes a letter from Harry Robert and Pauline Fox.)

[21] J. M. McCaleb, "Notes from Japan," *Gospel Advocate*, June 28, 1928, 605; George Pepperdine, "Mission Work in Japan," *Gospel Advocate*, August 9, 1928, 746–48.

[22] Erroll Rhodes, "Hitachi Omiya," *World Vision*, January 1938, 16.

[23] Ibid.

[24] O. D. Bixler, "A Continued Story," *Oriental Christian*, February 1933, 9.

[25] Conversation with Harry Robert Fox, Jr., summer 2013.

[26] O. D. Bixler, "Scattering Precious Seed by the Wayside," *Oriental Christian*, July 1932, 10.

[27] Erroll Rhodes, "Hitachi Omiya," *Oriental Christian*, November 1932, 8, 9.

[28] Don Carlos Janes, "Greater Things for God," *Boosters' Bulletin*, April 1924, 7, 8. This monthly bulletin was the predecessor of *Missionary Messenger*, edited by Don Carlos Janes of Louisville, Kentucky. Janes had raised $2,752 for the construction of the Fox homes. Information also from conversation with Harry Robert Fox, Jr., on July 23, 2013.

[29] Pauline Fox, "Good Results in Japan," *Christian Leader*, June 15, 1926, 10.

[30] J. M. McCaleb, *Once Traveled Roads*, 533, 534.

[31] Pauline Fox, "Good Results," *Christian Leader*, June 15, 1926, 10.

[32] O. D. Bixler, "A Continued Story," *Oriental Christian*, February 1933, 9, 10.

[33] Don Carlos Janes, note in *Boosters' Bulletin*, March 1927, 9.

[34] Herman J. Fox, "Appreciates Gospel Advocate," *Gospel Advocate*, December 2, 1926, 1145; Orville D. Bixler, "Notes from Japan," *Gospel Advocate*, August 9, 1928, 758.

[35] B. D. Morehead, "What the Church Needs in Japan," *Gospel Advocate*, January 7, 1926, 33.

[36] Robert S. King, "More Missionaries for Foreign Service," *Gospel Advocate*, June 25, 1925, 604.

[37] B. D. Morehead, no title, *Gospel Advocate*, March 4, 1926, 216; B. D. Morehead, no title, *Gospel Advocate*, April 15, 1926, 344.

[38] I. B. Bradley, "Japan Mission Work," *Gospel Advocate*, March 25, 1926, 269.

[39] Robert S. King, "The Consolations and Joys of a Missionary," January 6, 1927, 6, 7.

[40] Robert S. King, "The Morehead Mission," *Gospel Advocate*, May 5, 1927, 415.

[41] B. D. Morehead, "Missionary on Field," *Gospel Advocate*, February 10, 1927, 127.

[42] Don Carlos Janes, "Missionary Medley," *Boosters' Bulletin*, March 1928, 77.

[43] J. M. McCaleb, "Moving Pictures," *Gospel Advocate*, June 21, 1928, 591; J. M. McCaleb, "Our Messages," *Gospel Advocate*, July 12, 1928, 657; Don Carlos Janes, "A Fine Accomplishment," *Missionary Messenger*, April 1929, 181.

[44] Bonnie Miller, *Messengers of the Risen Son in the Land of the Rising Sun: Single Women Missionaries in Japan* (Abilene, TX: Leafwood Publishers, 2008), 27–34.

[45] J. M. McCaleb, *Once Traveled Roads*, 367; Robert S. King, "The Moreheads Start Westward," *Gospel Advocate*, December 6, 1928, 1158.

[46] Don Carlos Janes, "Missionary Medley," *Boosters' Bulletin*, March 1928, 75; Don Carlos Janes, "Missionary Medley," *Missionary Messenger*, June 1929, 195; Correspondence with Harry Robert Fox, Jr., August 12, 2012.

[47] J. M. McCaleb, "News from Japan," *Gospel Advocate*, January 10, 1929, 39; O. D. Bixler, "Information from Bro. Bixler," *Missionary Messenger*, August 1929, 214.

[48] J. M. McCaleb, *On the Trail of the Missionaries* (Nashville: Gospel Advocate Company, 1930), 9–11, 260, 262.

[49] C. Philip Slate, *Lest We Forget: Mini-Biographies of Missionaries from a Bygone Generation* (Winona, MS: J. C. Choate Publications, 2010), 108.

[50] B. D. Morehead, "Letter from Japan," *Gospel Advocate*, November 28, 1929, 1040.

[51] C. Philip Slate, *Lest We Forget*, 108.

[52] B. D. Morehead, "King Bible School, Ota, Ibaraki Ken, Japan," *Gospel Advocate*, July 31, 1930, 734, 735.

[53] Orville D. Bixler, "On Our Way Back to Japan," *Christian Leader*, October 11, 1927, 10.

[54] B. D. Morehead, "A Year's Work," *Christian Leader*, February 23, 1932, 11.

[55] O. D. Bixler, "Scattering Precious Seed by the Wayside," *Oriental Christian*, July 1932, 10.

[56] O. D. Bixler, "In Pastures Green, in Deserts Drear," *Oriental Christian*, April 1931, 11.

[57] J. M. McCaleb, "Sister Beach, of Chattanooga, Wanted in Japan at Once," *Gospel Advocate*, September 25, 1930, 928, 929; Emma Beach, "First Experiences in Japan," *Christian Leader*, December 30, 1930, 11; J. M. McCaleb, "Missionary Quits," *Gospel Advocate*, July 26, 1934, 720.

[58] O. D. Bixler, "The Good Samaritan," *Oriental Christian*, June 1931, 10.

[59] O. D. Bixler, "A Continued Story," *Oriental Christian*, February 1933, 9; O. D. Bixler, "Letter to J. M. McCaleb," *Oriental Christian*, November 1933, 10.

[60] O. D. Bixler, "Home Letter from Bro. Bixler," *Christian Leader*, February 19, 1935, 14.

[61] Bonnie Miller, *Messengers of the Risen Son*, 170, 171; Christine Jones, "A Personal Letter," *Oriental Christian*, August 1932, 12.

[62] Harry R. Fox, Sr., "King Bible School," *Christian Leader*, November 3, 1931, 10, 11.

[63] Correspondence with Harry Robert Fox, Jr., on March 8, 2013; Mrs. Harry R. Fox, "The Peace of God: An Experience," *Oriental Christian*, June 1932, 9, 10; Harry and Pauline Fox, "Dear Ones in the Homeland, Greetings," *Oriental Christian*, August 1932, 11, 12.

[64] Don Carlos Janes, "Missionary Medley," *Missionary Messenger*, May 1932, 423; Don Carlos Janes, "The Harry R. Fox Family," *Missionary Messenger*, June 1932, 449; Don Carlos Janes, "The Morehead-Fox Work in Ota, Japan," *Missionary Messenger*, September 1932, 437.

[65] Howard L. Schug and Jesse P. Sewell (eds.), *The Harvest Field* (Athens, AL: Bible School Bookstore, 1947), 251.

[66] Harry R. Fox, "Japan Is Calling," *Oriental Christian*, March 1934, 10; B. D. Morehead, "An Opportunity Given," *Oriental Christian*, March 1934, 10.

[67] W. E. Brightwell, "To Bid Foxes Farewell," *Gospel Advocate*, May 10, 1934, 461.

[68] Stewart Hanson, "Fox Leaves for Japan," *Gospel Advocate*, August 30, 1934, 843.

[69] Harry R. Fox, "Japan Health and Home," Oriental Christian, May 1935, 7.

[70] Ibid, 7.

[71] Don Carlos Janes, "News and Notes," *Missionary Messenger*, October 1935, 233.

[72] Harry R. Fox, "Harry Fox Returns to America," *Oriental Christian*, September 1935, 8.

[73]Correspondence with Harry Robert Fox, Jr., March 8, 2013.

[74]Anna Bixler, "Dear Cousin Jennie," *Christian Leader*, February 16, 1937, 16.

[75]Otoshige Fujimori, "Brother Fujimori's Report," *Christian Leader*, February 16, 1937, 10.

[76]Don Carlos Janes, "News and Notes," *Missionary Messenger*, November 1938, 444; O. D. Bixler, "After Twenty Years," *World Vision*, April, May, June 1939, 20.

[77]J. M. McCaleb, "Two Missionaries to Japan," *Gospel Advocate*, May 6, 1937, 431; from *World Vision*, "Cornell Commended," *Missionary Messenger*, August 1937, 368; Don Carlos Janes, "News and Notes," *Missionary Messenger*, April 1938, 416; Elbridge B. Linn, "First Impressions of Japan," *World Vision*, January, February, March 1938, 17.

[78]Don Carlos Janes, "Missionaries Speak for Themselves," *Missionary Messenger*, December 1937, 392.

[79]Don Carlos Janes, "News and Notes," *Missionary Messenger*, February 1941, 946; Don Carlos Janes, "Herman J. Fox Returning from Japan," *Missionary Messenger*, October 1941, 1081.

[80]J. M. McCaleb, "Some Things That Happened in 1941,) World Vision April, May, June 1941, 12.

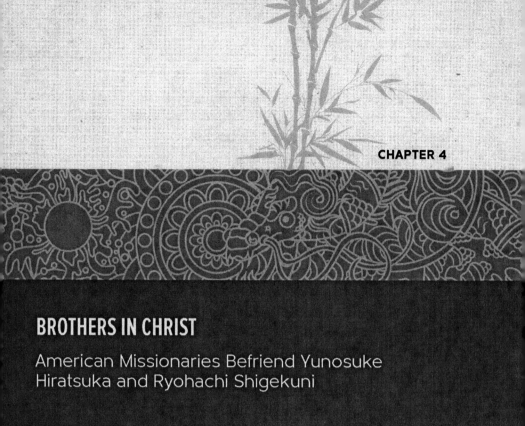

CHAPTER 4

BROTHERS IN CHRIST

American Missionaries Befriend Yunosuke Hiratsuka and Ryohachi Shigekuni

Most American missionaries connected with Churches of Christ, with the exception of Sarah Andrews and Lillie Cypert, chose to follow the United States government's urging in 1940 and 1941 to leave Japan as war imminently loomed. Yet these American missionaries had brave Japanese allies who worked closely with them and supported them up until their last hours, defying the mandates of their government and the fever of war that had stricken the world over, pitting brother against brother. One of these brave allies was Yunosuke Hiratsuka, who worked closely with American missionaries before they left Japan prior to World War II. Another was Ryohachi Shigekuni, a preacher in Ibaraki who had worked closely with American missionaries since the 1920s and inherited responsibility for six churches when the American missionaries had no choice but to flee in the face of the impending war.

Just imagine the pressure placed upon these two men as they struggled to fight for their faith in Jesus Christ. Both Hiratsuka and Shigekuni had lived through the turbulent 1930s as the Japanese government pursued war with China. Now they faced war with the United States. The two men were Japanese nationals, both influenced by American Christians. Where would their allegiance now lie? Would it be with Japan and its pagan Shinto religion or with Christianity?

It was not an easy time for Japanese Christians, especially those who would not accept Japan's nationalization of Christianity. Neither Hiratsuka nor Shigekuni surrendered their churches to the *Kyodan*—the Japanese United Church of Christ. It must have been a difficult decision for these men to oppose a dictate of their government. Although not bodily persecuted, they were under close surveillance by the government and their neighbors. They were suspected of spying for the United States.

The stories of Yunosuka Hiratsuka and Ryohachi Shigekuni offer a unique insight into the introduction of Christianity to Japan. Both men and their families lived through World War II, bravely continuing their work in the Americans' absence. They would welcome the American missionaries back to Japan in 1945 when Harry Robert Fox, Sr., and O. D. Bixler called on them. Their commitment to Jesus Christ had not wavered. In the face of a world at war, they were truly brothers in Christ.

Yunosuke Hiratsuka: Nothing but Faith in Jesus Christ

Hiratsuka was born on October 27, 1872, in Shioda Mura, Naka Gun, Ibaraki ken, Japan. He first came to Tokyo in 1888 as a sixteen-year-old to study bookkeeping. He returned home in 1890, but in 1893, he returned to Tokyo to work as a policeman at the Imperial Palace.[1]

Eager to study the English language with a native speaker, in 1895, he began to study with J. M. McCaleb in the Kanda district of Tokyo. He soon began to attend church and Bible class with McCaleb. In 1895, he asked McCaleb to baptize him, perhaps unaware that he was destined to have a great impact on his people as a preacher among Churches of Christ.[2]

Like many other Japanese young men at the time, Hiratsuka was not satisfied with job opportunities in his home country, and in 1897 he made his way across the Pacific Ocean in search of his fortune. Speaking of his decision, he said, "The new borned [*sic*] young man did not [was not] satisfied with anything at all to live in Japan." He sold his rice field, purchased his ship ticket, and left for the United States. In America he found "many good and beautiful things, materially and spiritually."[3]

He arrived in San Francisco during the Christmas season. At age twenty-five, this new world impressed him. "The young man was wondered [overwhelmed] at first, and soon was felt in his heart with the true enjoyment that comes from Heaven. And he started his new life." He found a place to live "in a good pastor's family of Dr. F. B. Cherington." Here he remained three years, studying in a grammar school and attending a high school for two years. Attending school by day, he studied the Bible at a Japanese YMCA at night. On Sundays he attended a Japanese church, helping in any way he could.

Hiratsuka earned his stay in the Cherington home by cleaning their house. Telling of his experiences in the American home, he said, "the family treated him as if [I am] a . . . [son] in that family. And [I] learned many good things in that family." Then one day, Mrs. Cherington asked Hiratsuka, "So you [wish to] become a minister?" This conversation remained with him until he returned to Japan. She planted a seed that grew to a major harvest in Japan.[4]

Attending school, studying the Bible at night, and cleaning house were too much for him, and he became sick. Yet ever faithful, even at that young age, Hiratsuka believed this was in accordance with God's plan: "By the guidance of the Lord, he could go to a Japanese Mission at Sarinas [Salinas] Town, California, and worked there for three years . . . as an assistant of a Japanese Pastor, Mr. K. Inagawa." There, Hiratsuka ministered to young Japanese boys, an experience that would help him in forty years of ministry in Japan.[5]

Not unlike the prodigal son, "he thought [to] himself, one day, that he [had] spent six years since he came to America, in rather, *vain* [ways]." He decided in August 1903 to return to Japan, "leaving those dear friends who came there [to the ship] to see me [off]." Describing his return to Tokyo, the young man stated, "He returned to Japan without anything at all but 'the faith in Jesus Christ.'"[6]

He had not forgotten the man who had introduced him to Jesus. Immediately on returning to Japan, he went to 12 Tsukiji Street and knocked on the door. McCaleb answered the knock but failed to recognize the man standing before him. Then the young man said, "I am Hiratsuka." He had grown a mustache since McCaleb saw him last, and certainly he was not expecting to see his long-lost friend at his door. He "welcomed him very heartily." It was a happy meeting of a father and son in the gospel. He had gone away, but now he had returned, a young man ready to spend the rest of his life proclaiming the good news of Jesus Christ.[7]

McCaleb wasted little time in introducing Hiratsuka to William J. Bishop, the American missionary associated with the Kamitomizaka church in Tokyo. This was the oldest Church of Christ in Japan. Specifically, Bishop had come to Japan to oversee the printing of materials in the Japanese language. McCaleb recognized in Hiratsuka the ideal person to work as a translator of English materials into Japanese. Bishop wrote pamphlets on biblical topics, and Hiratsuka translated them into his native language. One important full-length book he translated was Hurlbut's *Studies in the Four Gospels*.[8] Bishop also had McGarvey's *Commentary on Acts of the Apostles* translated as well. McCaleb, assisted by Hiratsuka, read the proofs of the books.[9]

As noted in Chapter 1, Eugene Snodgrass had to return to the United States in 1903, the year Hiratsuka returned to Japan. Besides the printing and translating, Bishop now replaced Snodgrass as the overseer of the Kamitomizaka church. His new friend Yunosuke became his valued associate, thus beginning his ministry with the church. His relationship with the church would continue until the middle of World War II. When Bishop went on furlough in 1909, it was Hiratsuka who conducted and carried on the work at Kamitomizaka.

Another important event of August 1903 was Hiratsuka's marriage to Hana, who became the mother of his six children, all of whom became devoted Christians. Hana was not a Christian when she married Hiratsuka, but Bishop baptized her in August 1908 before leaving in 1909 on his trip to America.[10]

As discussed in Chapter 3, in the early 1920s, four American missionary families chose to go to the Ibaraki and Fukushima Prefectures. While studying Japanese in Tokyo, they came into contact with Hiratsuka. He was from Ibaraki and thus had a deep interest in his rural family and friends in the prefecture, some one hundred miles north of Tokyo. In 1932, O. D. Bixler paid tribute to Hiratsuka when he wrote, "Brother Hiratsuka is responsible for the opening of the work in this part of the country. He made regular preaching trips out here for years." Hiratsuka said himself that he made trips north every other month for ten years until the American missionaries relocated to his home prefecture.[11]

When the four American families arrived in Ibaraki, they found two groups of baptized believers.[12] Among those baptized on Hiratsuka's visits to Ibaraki were Brother Ebine, who would become one of the most outstanding native preachers, and Dr. T. Hiratsuka, Yunosuka's nephew. Most impressive, however, was the baptism of his mother in 1909. The son remembered from his youth a hope his mother voiced while watching the setting sun one day: "Surely there is a great God somewhere." He recalled fondly baptizing his mother in the small stream that meandered in front of their old home place.[13]

Bishop returned to Japan in April 1911. While the Bishops were on furlough in America, C. C. Klingman and his wife worked with Hiratsuka at the Kamitomizaka church. They returned to America in 1912. Returning from furlough, Bishop's health began deteriorating rapidly, until in 1913 he had to leave Japan for America in search of medical help. He died of tuberculosis on April 4, 1913. This was devastating to Yunosuke Hiratsuka. He and Bishop, who were the same age, had worked together for ten years. Hiratsuka had lost his mentor and his brother in Christ. Almost the last thing Bishop did prior to leaving Japan was to appoint elders for the Kamitomizaka church. Three men—T. Yokoo, I. Kamikura, and Yunosuke Hiratsuka—met in Bishop's home, where he laid hands on the men and committed them to faithfully serve the church.[14]

Clara Bishop, with her three children, left Japan later in 1913 to be with her husband and their father. However, he died before their arrival in California. Although remaining in America, she did not lose interest in the Kamitomizaka church and her friends Yunosuke and Hana Hiratsuka. After mourning the loss of her husband, she wished to return to the Kamitomizaka church and carry on the legacy of their work alongside the Hiratsukas. However, McCaleb staunchly opposed the widow's return, going so far as forcing the sale of the Bishop family home in Japan and enlisting the editors of the *Gospel Advocate* to oppose Bishop's proposals. Sadly, as Jonathan Straker has shown, this was not an isolated incident. Single women like Sarah Andrews and Hettie Lee Ewing also experienced similar discouragement at the hands of McCaleb and male-dominated mission efforts in Japan.[15] After finding employment with Abilene Christian College and as a member of the college church, Bishop resigned to support her friends from afar and encouraged support of the work in Japan.

In the wake of these events, the C. G. Vincent family became the resident missionaries at the Kamitomizaka church. But their tenure would be short-lived—they returned to America in 1916 because of health reasons. They, however, continued to have a close long-distance relationship with Hiratsuka and his work in Japan. Other missionaries, including Sarah Andrews, who worshiped and worked with Hiratsuka from April 1917 until she moved to Okitsu in June 1918; Erroll Rhodes and his wife Bess; and Harry Robert and Pauline Fox, partnered with the church until they followed Hiratsuka's advice and moved to the rural areas north of Tokyo. Later in 1928, Clara Kennedy worked with the church.[16]

Preacher for the Nation of Japan

Hiratsuka, however, did not limit his work to the Kamitomizaka church. He preached for some time every second Sunday at Sawara, the railroad connection near Oto Fujimori's home. Of interest, in May 1927, while in Sawara, a man came for baptism. Describing the memorable event, he reported, "We went to a river and had the ceremony. It was a very beautiful evening, the sky was very clear and the stars were shining so beautifully—I thought myself that these same stars are the same which you look at in America." He also preached at the post office every Saturday. Often enquirers came to his home to ask about Christianity. On one occasion, he talked for an hour and a half with a soldier.[17]

Since the Kamitomizaka church was located in Tokyo, many converts, especially young college graduates, spread Christianity to other sections of Japan. In an article titled "What Kind of Christians Do the Japanese Make?," Clara Bishop, widow of William Bishop, quoted from a long letter from

Hiratsuka telling stories of men who had accepted Christ while in Tokyo. All of them referred to Kamitomizaka as the "Mother Church," even tracing their conversion back to the time of Bishop. He told of Brother Murashima, a student at Waseda University and a Sunday school teacher at the church, who recalled, "I remember very well our prayers to the Heavenly Father, with all the other brethren in the church. I am visiting many places in the world for our business, but wherever I go, I remember and am glad and thankful to be a Christian."

Hiratsuka's love of Christ seemed to spread all around him. A young man, an officer in government service, who was a supervisor of 130 officers and 2,000 men, visited Hiratsuka in 1927. He related to his mentor in the gospel, "To believe in the true God is the first thing of all. . . . I have two lectures every month for them [the men over whom he was the supervisor]. Their religious beliefs are different, but Christian love is the first need for them." Hiratsuka told lovingly about his son who was in school at Mito, Ibaraki Prefecture. He and six other students preached on the streets and taught those who came to their living quarters. Clara Bishop stated, "These young men live together while they are in school and call their house 'House of Friendship.' There is no telling what this young son of Bro. Hiratsuka may accomplish in God's service in Japan." Hiratsuka's two oldest sons, Michio and Masunori, were early involved in Christian teaching and service.[18]

In a letter appearing in the *Christian Leader* in 1927, Hiratsuka told of the work of a Brother Nameki, who, for some time, had taught a Bible class at the "Mother Church." Nameki returned to his hometown in Yokoshiba in Chiba'ken, some fifty miles from Tokyo. Hiratsuka encouraged him to begin a Sunday school in a town where the gospel had never been taught. The young man asked his mentor to send two teachers to Yokoshiba to help him in preparation for inviting the youngsters to a Bible school. Three teachers went, including Michio Hiratsuka. They held a prayer meeting among themselves, and then distributed invitations throughout the town.

Hiratsuka told of the results: "On the next Sunday morning the children came to Bro. Nameki's house, so many the house could not hold them." Some seventy children responded to the invitation. The three young men from Kamitomizaka returned to Tokyo excited about their experience: "These brothers came back to our church with feeling and great interest for the new work, and we thanked the Lord who has given us such new work." The next Sunday, Nameki attempted to teach the seventy children by himself, but realized he needed help. The young men from Tokyo traveled again to Chiba to help their brother in Yokoshiba.[19]

Efforts in Yokoshiba to establish a church took time, but by September 1930, Hiratsuka reported three baptisms. One was a young man named Kaiho, who wanted to hear about Christianity. He was especially interested in comparing it with Nichiren-shu, a sect of Buddhism. Hiratsuka shared with him the Bible's God and His Son, Jesus Christ. He told Hiratsuka, "Sometime I wish to become a Christian, after I have studied more." He went back to his native village and at a later date studied again with Hiratsuka: "He is converted now from Buddhism."

Hana Hiratsuka, during a two-week stay in Yokoshiba, studied with two young ladies, ages eighteen and twenty. On August 24, 1930, she reported, "We went to a river . . . which runs into the Pacific Ocean, a silent place, . . . where some pine trees made chorus by the wind with our songs, and they were baptized in the name of the Father, the Son and the Holy Spirit." These converts began attending the Yokoshiba church every Sunday and volunteered their help in the Sunday school.[20]

The Kamitomizaka church celebrated thirty years at its present location on November 3, 1928. On that day, they opened a new Sunday school building to celebrate the anniversary. It was also a day of thanksgiving for their blessings from God. Hiratsuka wrote and illustrated a booklet that gave the history of the church. It also included articles by Japanese and American Christians sending greetings even from across the Pacific Ocean. The very comprehensive booklet, gave the history of the church from its beginnings under Eugene Snodgrass.[21]

The thirty-year anniversary meeting was certainly a worthy celebration. Even though Hiratsuka reported 353 baptisms during the lifetime of the church, many of these men and women did not remain faithful to the church. Many others moved away, and some very important leaders of the church died, including one of the original elders.

On January 30, 1930, Isutaro Kamijura, suffering from tuberculosis for a number of years, passed away. Even though most converts in Japan were from the poorer classes of people, Kamijura was an educated man who oversaw a school with seven hundred students and thirty teachers. Honored on a number of occasions by the government for his work in education, at his memorial service, more than five hundred people came to honor him at the Kamitomizaka church. Hiratsuka said of him, "He was a peace lover and a peace maker." He often preached for the church, but his major work was superintending the teaching of children who came to the Sunday school. Said his elder friend, "The death of Bro. Kamijura brought sorrow to us 'over here,' for we admired and esteemed him highly."[22]

The death of Brother Kamijura must have been a deep loss for Yunosuke Hiratsuka. He had baptized Kamijura early in his connection with the church and met with him and the other elders often to plan the workings of the Kamitomizaka church. These meetings also focused on how they could reach out to the city of Tokyo and the nation of Japan. Discussions included such topics as how to keep faithful those who dropped out of their Christian walk. And of course, as true of all churches, the concerns for the needs of the church and the individual Christians who were looking to the elders for leadership and help, both spiritually and physically, were ever on their minds. Writing in third person in 1946, Hiratsuka said of himself, giving also the core of his beliefs:

During those long time [years], he never [became] discouraged for the noble work, but he continued it as a faithful servant to the Lord, Jesus Christ and the Heavenly Father. Sometimes there were very hard discussions between he and his friends or some others, but he told them always that "Are there the cross and the resurrection in other religions of the world?" [B]ut Christ was crucified on the cross for the sins of the people in this world, and resurrected himself after the three days. These facts are the wonderful acts of the Heavenly Father who did them, showing his righteousness and the [His] love. Therefore, the Christianity is the only one religion to be saved in this world.[23]

Because there were younger men who could preach in his absence, Hiratsuka reached out to other areas of Japan. Said Hiratsuka, "Our young men are growing spiritually, some of them can preach the Gospel," allowing him to preach at Yokoshiba, Sawara, Takaedo, and other places within traveling distances from Tokyo. However, he did not abandon his home church. Hiratsuka reported that Kamitomizaka had met 266 times "in the name of the Lord" during 1930. "These services or meetings were held to praise God, our Heavenly Father with most high spirit, to worship, to pray, to study His words and to do other religious things." The Sunday school was ever active, teaching "many thousand children into their pure hearts."

In those other places, especially Yokoshiba, Hiratsuka remained active. He was present when 250 children attended a Christmas-time meeting. "We had the children recite the Bible to those other people who never heard the Christ." In fact, the children's meeting was so popular in the community that a circus had to shut down, "because they [the children] were all going to the Christmas party."[24]

Yunosuke Hiratsuka, from reports of all American missionaries, was a dedicated Christian and of major importance in keeping alive the message of Christ taught by Churches of Christ. Harry Robert Fox, Jr., was a teenager in the years before World War II and a missionary who would return to Japan in 1947. His description of Hiratsuka suggests why he was successful in his forty years of preaching for the Kamitomizaka church. "His personality type was that of a mild, reserved, dignified gentleman—always kindly, warm and smiling."[25]

Hard Times for Yunosuke Hiratsuka

For all his kindness and warmth, Hiratsuka was met with some severe challenges and hardships over the course of his ministry, testing his faith. Throughout the 1930s, the preaching of Jesus Christ was not an easy matter in Japan. The nation was on the brink of war, and the state emphasized Buddhism, Shintoism, and the worship of the emperor. Thus by the middle of the decade, missionaries met discouragement on every side. It must have been especially difficult even for native preachers to preach Christ. After 1937, with Japan at war with China, the situation became worse. Both Tokuo Mazawa, who served with Sarah Andrews in Shizuoka, and Oto Fujimori indicated how difficult it was to reach the people with war fever so rampant. Mazawa stated in 1941, "Due to the present warfare the work of the churches has become quite difficult."[26] Fujimori wrote, "Our work is not progressing since the war."[27] Hiratsuka did not comment, but he must have had similar feelings.

The year 1939 was an exceedingly difficult time for the Hiratsuka family. In June, doctors diagnosed Hana Hiratsuka with brain cancer. Even though she was under the care of two good doctors, her life could not be saved. She died on August 21, 1939. Born July 4, 1879, at death she was sixty years of age. On August 20, the day before her passing, she shared the Lord's Supper for the last time with her family. Hiratsuka recalled that they sang a song, "gave thanks and gave it to her, and she herself also whispered her thanks and partook of the bread and the cup." The bereaved husband said of her, "She was a loyal, devoted Christian woman." He recalled the words of his beloved Hana: "The Lord's favor is very large upon me, so I thank to the Father and His Son, Jesus Christ." At her "Christian funeral ceremony," some four hundred people attended, mostly "strangers" to the Christian religion. They remembered fondly the service given to them by this servant of God, Hana Hiratsuka.[28]

World War II impacted Christians in Japan severely, testing their faith at every turn. How would they respond to the "Religious Control Bill" scheduled to go into effect on April 1, 1941? Throughout the 1930s, especially since the invasion of Manchuria in 1931, the military-controlled government required school children—and on special days, adults—to pay homage to the state Shinto shrines. To obtain an official charter for involvement in other religious activities, the government required homage to Shinto shrines. Americans in Japan met treatment somewhat like the Japanese met in America—they were looked at with suspicion. The missionaries had the option of leaving Japan, but Japanese Christians had to make a decision—comply or abstain.

Most Churches of Christ and their Japanese leaders refused to comply with the requirement of Christian churches to join the *Kyodan*—a United Church of Christ made up of all the different denominations registered with the government, thus losing their individual identity. The missionaries had no say in the churches; each church had to be overseen by Japanese nationals. The churches that chose not to join the super-church were under greater surveillance than the Kyodan churches. According to Harry Robert

Fox, Jr., only the Zoshigaya church in Tokyo joined the United Church of Christ. Therefore, Hiratsuka and the Kamitomizaka church remained separate from the organization.[29]

War came to the Japanese islands with a fury—especially when American bombers were within striking distance of Japan's cities. Low-flying planes dropped firebombs on the cities, including Tokyo, where buildings, for the most part, were constructed of flammable materials. Fortunately, the Zoshigaya building and the next-door parsonage escaped destruction, but the building of the Kamitomizaka church burned to the ground. The churches were never large, but the destruction scattered the Christians even more. The remnants of the Kamitomizaka church joined with the brothers and sisters at Zoshigaya to form one church. Yunosuke Hiratsuka was asked to preach for the combined church. But by October 1943, he asked to be relieved of his responsibilities. In his place, the church chose S. M. Saito, a graduate of Northwestern University and a longtime member of Zoshigaya, to replace the aging Hiratsuka.[30]

Writing in third person, Hiratsuka discussed his retirement from preaching: "In the October of 1943, the full time of the forty years' Christian work of the elder, Hiratsuka has just finished, so, he retired from the blessed and long work through his long life, and his age was just seventy years old, handing his work to S. Saito now." He continued his story: "His Christian work is not only to the church and his family, but it was into his many relations." In 1943, he counted thirty Christians in his family. Including those who had died over his long ministry, he counted forty relatives who "came into Jesus Christ and are living their happy Christian lives."[31]

In his retirement, Hiratsuka moved to a village outside Tokyo where he had a small plot for raising vegetables. "The neighbors looked at him curiously, saying 'Dear old man, are you not tired? You are a very curious old man, because when a man becomes old, he does not work but only rest[s], sitting in his house room, but you work all day.' Then the old man answers 'I am a Christian, therefore I work all the time.'" Possibly Hiratsuka also enjoyed his little farm because the family had been very limited in what they had for nourishment during the war. In 1946, he mentioned that he had eaten no meat of any kind except for two or three times since 1942.[32]

But the most insightful statement of all was his observation in 1946 of Japan's circumstances and the importance of Christianity to answer those conditions.

> Yes, that old man works in the field, not only, but he began to study the Bible again with his new spirit, because the New Japan must be born again in this great and wonderful historical period in Japan and the world, indeed. The old Japan was damaged now, all of Christian[s] believe that this is the will of God. And the new Japan should be born again by the will of God who has all-mighty power upon the people of this world.[33]

Yunosuke Hiratsuka, age eighty, died on December 15, 1953, at his home in Tokyo. He had served Jesus Christ and Churches of Christ for fifty years. In a letter to Clara Bishop in October 1953, he mentioned that four hundred people had been baptized at the Kamitomizaka church during a half century. But the most meaningful number shared with her was that between forty and fifty of his relatives had accepted Christ. The one-time co-worker with Hiratsuka wrote of her Christian friend and brother: "Yunosuke Hiratsuka was truly one of God's own, and as all who knew him have said, he had 'a most Christ-like character.'"[34]

Ryohachi Shigekuni: Called to Preach While in America

Coming to America was the goal of millions of Europeans during the nineteenth and early twentieth centuries. It was during this time that Ellis Island became an icon in the history of the United States, as immigrants flocked to the East Coast. On the West Coast, thousands of Asians began coming to the United States from the middle of the nineteenth century into the twentieth century. However, Asians were not as welcome in California and other western states as Europeans were on the Eastern Seaboard.

Not long after Asians came to San Francisco during the gold rush and the construction of the transcontinental railroad during the 1850s, legislation began to control the actions of Asians, especially the Chinese. During the 1890s, immigrants began to arrive from Japan, first settling in San Francisco. By 1906, the city passed a school law segregating Asian students, including the Japanese. The state followed in 1913 with the Alien

Land Law, stating that "aliens ineligible for citizenship" were also ineligible to own agricultural land. Oregon, Washington, and other western states followed California's leadership. In 1924, the US Congress passed a law denying immigration from Asian countries, mostly focused on Japan.

Four years before the passage of the Exclusion Act, Ryohachi Shigekuni arrived in Los Angeles from Japan. Not unlike most immigrants, whether European or Asian, Shigekuni came to America looking for economic prosperity. The Shigekuni family, natives of the Hiroshima Prefecture, had a difficult time earning a living in Japan. Thus in 1910 the father, Toraichiro, along with his ten-year-old son, Ryohachi, went to Korea looking for economic opportunities. After two unsuccessful years, Toraichiro died. Ryohachi returned to Japan to live with his mother and siblings. However, no work was to be found in Hiroshima.[35]

His only hope for economic success seemed to lie across the Pacific Ocean in America. He sailed for Long Beach, but his destination was Los Angeles because he had an uncle and aunt, Yonetaro and Shizuyo Shigekuni, living in that city. The Los Angeles family offered their nephew a place to live while he searched for work, oftentimes finding only lawn care.

Even though his American family showed no interest in Christianity, Ryohachi had one of those experiences that caused him to begin thinking about his spiritual well-being. One day while cutting grass, the young man felt something hit his chest—a pellet had hit his tie clasp and then lodged in the tie.[36] Ryohachi accepted the shooting as a call to consider a change in his life. He associated himself with a Methodist church in the neighborhood.[37] Thus began a journey that led to a totally changed direction for his life.

In 1923, Hirosuke Ishiguro established a Church of Christ in Los Angeles. The church became a major Christian presence in the Los Angeles Japanese community and baptized many (discussed further in Chapter 5). Shigekuni, finding steady work at the Alameda Salt Company,[38] quickly became involved in church work with Ishiguro. Even though he enjoyed his time in America, even purchasing a fine automobile, he desired to return to Japan, where he committed himself to sharing the Christian message with his own people.

Therefore, in 1927—after seven years in America and at the age of twenty-seven—he sailed for Japan. Amazingly, on the same ship was Erroll A.

Rhodes's family, returning to Japan after a furlough in America. At Yokohama, the Rhodeses went north to Omiya, and Shigekuni went the twenty miles to Tokyo, where he associated with J. M. McCaleb for one year. In 1928, he traveled north to work with O. D. Bixler in Nagasawa. In his native land, he spent the remainder of his life in faithful Christian service, preaching Christ and reaching out with Christianity to people with special needs.

In his association with Orville and Anna Bixler, because of his knowledge of the language, he served as the Japanese preacher in their ministry. He also worked in the food industries operated by the missionary family. Also working in the Bixler industries was a young Japanese Christian named Hurako Fukusawa, known as a woman of the Bible, who taught scripture predominantly to women and children. In 1929, Shigekuni and Hurako were married, beginning a life together that led to three or four generations of the Shigekuni family's involvement with Japanese Churches of Christ. Hurako was a favorite of the American missionary children, who fondly called her Fu-San.[39]

Working with Bixler had its interesting moments for Shigekuni. Because the Bixler s' land was about 2.5 miles from Nagasawa, Bixler had a motorcycle with a sidecar. In 1929, Shigekuni was traveling with Bixler when the vehicle overturned, the sidecar falling on Bixler's leg, breaking it in several places. From all indications, Shigekuni suffered no injury. As noted previously, Bixler used this event to teach a number of nurses-in-training the gospel of Christ while in the hospital. Ryohachi and Hurako began preaching services in the hospital.[40]

In 1929 or 1930, the Shigekunis moved from Nagasawa to Ota, where they began working with Barney and Nellie Morehead at the King Bible School. Much of their work at the school and the church in Ota was being the Japanese voice for the Moreheads. As with the Bixlers, they involved themselves in Morehead's various economic endeavors, including a dairy farm. The Moreheads left Japan and returned to Nashville in 1930 after five years as missionaries.[41] However, the Shigekuni family remained at the Bible School. Barney Morehead had invited Harry Fox, Sr., to move to Ota from the Fukushima Prefecture to operate the school and the dairy.

Ryohachi and his family became long-term fixtures at Ota, the church, and the King Bible School.

As an example of the hearts of both Ryohachi and Hurako, in 1930 they took two orphaned children into their home—one a two-month-old baby and a girl of thirteen years. Harry Fox, Sr., called this "true religion."[42] The Fox family went to America on a furlough in 1932, leaving King Bible School and the Ota church partially in the care of Ryohachi with aid from local missionaries, including Erroll Rhodes from Omiya.[43]

By 1930, a small number of Japanese men had converted to Christianity, who, in turn, became leaders in the various churches. One such Christian was Sumiaki Horiguchi, who wrote for *Michisilbe*, a monthly Christian magazine funded by George Pepperdine and edited by J. M. McCaleb. The Shigekunis and the Horiguchis, sharing the Christian faith, became the best of friends. Significantly important for Japanese Churches of Christ, Yoshiaki Shigekuni and Michiko Horiguchi, children of the Shigekunis and the Horiguchis, married and became leaders in the Ota church.[44]

Harry Fox's family returned to Japan in 1934, and he reclaimed the oversight of King Bible School and the Ota church. However, this would be of short duration, as the Fox family returned to the United States in 1935 and could not return to Japan because of acute war conditions in the Pacific region. This meant, with all American missionaries leaving Japan, the care of the churches became the responsibility of Japanese Christians. And Ryohachi Shigekuni took his church responsibilities seriously. He continued his evangelistic efforts in the rural areas around Ota, reporting in 1937 good meetings throughout the countryside.[45]

According to Harry Robert Fox, Jr., the churches in the Kuji River Valley had excellent leadership during the war years. Even though the number of attendees dwindled to very small numbers, the six churches had good leadership that transcended World War II. The Omiya church was led by Brother Goto, while the church at Urizura was under the direction of Brother Masaichi Kiruchi. The church that met at Tanakara was kept together by Brother Komine. Comparable to the leadership of the Shigekunis at Ota, the Hiratsuka family kept the church alive at Nagasawa. A Brother Akutsu kept the Christians in Akutsu from completely scattering.[46]

Ryohachi Shigekuni and his family did not hide their Christian commitment during the war in the face of constant suspicion on the part of their neighbors. They were thought to be spies for the Americans, based in part on their association with the missionaries prior to the war. They were constantly under scrutiny from their neighbors. When Hurako hung the family's bedding on outside clotheslines to air, neighbors believed this was a signal to American bombers flying overhead. Yet despite being constantly judged, throughout the war years, Ryohachi, from the King Bible School farm, delivered milk and grains ground in his grist mill to his neighbors. Regardless, the feelings in the community were so strong at times that Yoshiaki, Ryohachi's son, remembers not attending school for two years because of the taunting by his classmates for being Christian and an American sympathizer.[47]

With the end of the war in August 1945, Ryohachi Shigekuni became an extremely important figure in the Japanese Churches of Christ, with the return of Harry Fox, Sr., and O. D. Bixler. Both men visited the Shigekunis in the Morehead home in Ota. Although he had sent a message ahead, Fox appeared at the front door of the Shigekuni home at 8 o'clock p.m., unannounced, on December 15, 1945. They had not received Fox's message.

Ryohachi and Hurako came to the door from different parts of the house: "Their 'pop-eyed' expressions on their faces, as well as the excited tone of their voice in greeting, told their great astonishment at seeing me." Also at home was Jimilo San, the Shigekuni's sixteen-year-old daughter, who was "somewhat shy." Fox was impressed that Hurako Shigekuni had not aged, and her hands showed signs of much hard work during the years of war. Ryohachi had not "changed or aged at all." Fox remembered living in the house just ten years before, although with the war intervening, it must have seemed much longer. He went through the house, touching pieces of furniture so familiar to him. He noted, "My desk [was] exactly as I left it ten years ago with the bookcase on top, and even some of the very same books in the same place they used to be."[48]

After exploring the house, Fox and Shigekuni sat for two hours before the fireplace talking about the situation of their Christian friends and the condition of the churches in the Kuji River Valley. The Japanese brother told of the trials faced during the long war. The church's "evangelistic work was practically banned even before the war began . . . [It became] all but impossible to continue weekly worship." Shigekuni told Fox that the government ordered members of the church "into various kinds of war activity, which kept them occupied all day on Sundays and [they were] subjected to heavy pressure, both by government officials and by their suspicious neighbors."[49]

All but four members of the Ota church had moved away, but within a few weeks, Shigekuni's goal was to begin gathering the church for formal meetings. He walked with his American Christian brother Fox around the farm, showing him the equipment he had installed over the previous ten years. Shigekuni, concerned about his neighbors, had provided work and housing for four families in the farm industries. Even though the Shigekuni family had little income, they did have a good food supply during the war for themselves and other people in the community. Fox noted, "[Shigekuni] never ceases to express his gratitude to God for enabling him to carry on these activities during the war, instead of having to go and carry a gun against his American and Christian friends."[50]

Later that same day, Fox and Shigekuni found a taxi driver to drive them to the various locations where the churches had met before the war—and especially to visit with Christian friends. Thus they visited Omiya, Nagasawa, and Asada, where they had good visits with Dr. Hiratsuka and his family, the Ebines, and the Gotos. Said Fox, "It was indeed a mutual joy for all of us to meet again after so many years and to talk over some of the common experiences and problems pertaining to the re-establishment of the church in those areas." Every person believed, even though much was lost because of the war, that obstacles were evaporating "and the time was nearly ripe to march forward again . . . to recapture the old land-marks and to press on in the great task of building a new and better Japan."[51]

Returning to Ota, a large crowd of Christians and friends gathered in the Shigekunis' living room "for an evening of fellowship and worship." The evening began with a hot Japanese meal, then a long period of worship. They invited Harry Fox to speak: "I felt constrained to do so, on this rare occasion." He asked three brothers to read Psalm 113, Isaiah 35, and Hebrews 12. Then Fox spoke on "the kingdom of God, and how it differs from the kingdoms of this world." After a thorough discussion of the topic, the audience asked him to preach some more; his talk continued for twenty minutes. He called Japan the "Preacher's Paradise." The longer the sermon, the more they liked it. After Fox concluded his sermon, the Christian assembly continued talking until midnight. At that hour, the congregation went to its knees for prayer: "There was not a dry eye in the group as we knelt for a final prayer of thanksgiving for the wonderful privilege of sweet Christian communion." Fox received an urgent invitation to return to Japan with reinforcements from America.[52]

Later Bixler, who had come to Japan on the recommendation of Harry Fox, wrote Barney and Nellie Morehead while sitting in the sunroom of their Ota home. He told how "Brother Shigekuni has built a fire in the extravagant fire place, but I am wearing both my bath robe and overcoat."[53] No matter the circumstances, it certainly was a joyous occasion when the Brothers in Christ experienced their reunion. Describing Ryohachi Shigekuni, Bixler wrote, "Brother Shigekuni is one of the most energetic and efficient preachers, and worked satisfactorily with the Bixlers and Moreheads nearly twenty years ago."[54]

When the combatants signed the peace treaty on September 2, 1945, on board the USS *Missouri*, attitudes toward Ryohachi Shigekuni dramatically changed. Now Shigekuni was invited to speak throughout his home country on the needs of a new Japan. Governmental officials sought his advice.[55] Specifically, he accepted an invitation to be a speaker on a public forum discussing "Democracy in the New Japan."[56]

Of the three representative native preachers featured in Chapters 2 and 4, two of them were older men in 1945. Oto Fujimori and Yunosuka Hiratsuka, both born in 1872, were seventy-three years of age. The difficult years of war led to physical exhaustion. This was not true of Ryohachi Shigekuni. Born in 1900, he was still a young man in 1945. He became closely involved in the work of Churches of Christ after World War II. His story continues into the years of the rising of the new Japan.

Undoubtedly, the most impressive stories concerning mission work in Japan involved native preachers. Without men like Oto Fujimori, Yunosuka Hiratsuka, and Ryohachi Shigekuni, American missionaries could not have been successful, especially after World War II. These three men impacted three main areas of the great island of Japan: Fujimori focused his influence southward where he worked closely with Sarah Andrews and Hettie Lee

Ewing, his adopted American sisters. Hiratsuka, although he preached in Ibaraki Prefecture before Americans arrived in Japan, focused on the Tokyo area. Shigekuni, although he would preach in Yokohama later in his life, held the churches together during World War II. All three men had close relationships with American missionaries. These relationships were not lost because of conflict between the United States and Japan. Their relationships were sustained because they were brothers and sisters in Christ.

Endnotes

[1] Y. Hiratsuka, "A Personal History of Hiratsuka," *Gospel Advocate*, January 30, 1947, 82.
[2] Office of the Historian, "The United States and the Opening of Japan, 1853," accessed December 23, 2016, https://history.state.gov/milestones/1830-1860/opening-to-japan.
[3] Hiratsuka, "A Personal History."
[4] Ibid.
[5] Ibid.
[6] Ibid.
[7] J. M. McCaleb, *Once Traveled Roads* (Nashville: Gospel Advocate Company, 1934), 121; Y. Hiratsuka, "A Personal History," *Gospel Advocate*, January 30, 1947, 82.
[8] Gary Owen Turner, "Pioneer to Japan: A Biography of John M. McCaleb" (unpublished MA thesis, Abilene Christian College, 1972), 62, 63.
[9] W. J. Bishop, "Bishop-Hiratsuka Mission, Tokyo, No. 2," *Gospel Advocate*, May 19, 1910, 614.
[10] Y. Hiratsuka, "A Letter from Japan," *World Vision*, January, February, March 1940, 26; C. G. Vincent, "Hana Hiratsuka," *Christian Leader*, October 15, 1939, 18.
[11] Y. Hiratsuka, "A Personal History," *Gospel Advocate*, January 30, 1947, 82, 83.
[12] O. D. Bixler, "A Beautiful Decision and What It Meant," *Oriental Christian*, December 1932, 8, 9.
[13] C. G. Vincent, "Our Labor Not in Vain in the Lord," *Christian Leader*, April 30, 1929, 10.
[14] Hiratsuka, "A Personal History," *Gospel Advocate*, January 30, 1947, 83.
[15] Jonathan Straker, "Changing Hands: Clara Bishop and the Transfer of Oversight of the Koishikawa, Japan, Work in 1913," *Restoration Quarterly* 54:2 (2012), 91–104.
[16] C. G. Vincent, "Brief History of the Kamitomizaka Church of Christ, Tokyo, Japan," *Christian Leader*, January 1, 1929, 10, 11.
[17] Y. Hiratsuka, "Letter from Bro. Hiratsuka, Bishop-Vincent Mission, Tokyo, Japan," *Christian Leader*, July 12, 1927, 10.
[18] Clara Bishop, "What Kind of Christians Do the Japanese Make?" *Christian Leader*, August 23, 1927, 10.
[19] Y. Hiratsuka, "Letter from Hiratsuka," *Christian Leader*, July 12, 1927, 10.

[20] Y. Hiratsuka, "From Brother Hiratsuka," *Christian Leader*, November 4, 1930, 10.

[21] C. G. Vincent, "Brief History," *Christian Leader*, January 1, 1929, 10, 11.

[22] C. G. Vincent, "Brother Kamukura Is Dead," *Christian Leader*, March 4, 1930, 10.

[23] Y. Hiratsuka, "A Personal History," *Gospel Advocate*, January 30, 1947, 82, 83.

[24] Y. Hiratsuka, "From Brother Hiratsuka," *Christian Leader*, February 17, 1931, 10.

[25] Communication with Harry Robert Fox, Jr., May 23, 2013.

[26] T. Mazawa, Letter, *World Vision*, April, May, June 1941, 10.

[27] Otoshige Fujimori, "A Letter from Japan," *Missionary Messenger*, April 1941, 968.

[28] C. G. Vincent, "Hana Hiratsuka," *Christian Leader*, October 15, 1939, 18; Y. Hiratsuka, "A Letter from Japan," *World Vision*, January, February, March 1940, 26.

[29] Correspondence with Harry Robert Fox, Jr., March 8, 2013.

[30] Pryde E. Hinton, "The Opportunities of the Centuries in Japan," *Gospel Advocate*, April 25, 1946, 403.

[31] Y. Hiratsuka, "A Personal History," *Gospel Advocate*, January 30, 1947, 83.

[32] Ibid.

[33] Ibid.

[34] Clara Bishop, "Brother Hiratsuka," *Firm Foundation*, January 19, 1954, 7.

[35] Harris Ives, "Japan: An Odyssey of Faith—The Remarkable Story of Ryohachi Shigekuni," *Christian Chronicle*, March 2002, 17–19. This is the most complete story extant of Ryohachi Shigekuni. The author, Harris G. Ives, was a longtime teacher at Ibaraki Christian College. Much of the information for Shigekuni's story is based on this article.

[36] Hettie Lee Ewing, "Circumstantial Evidence," *Oriental Christian*, October 1931, 12, 13.

[37] Harris Ives, "Japan Odyssey," *Christian Chronicle*, March 2002, 17.

[38] Ibid.

[39] Communication with Harry Robert Fox, Jr., March 8, 2013.

[40] J. M. McCaleb, "News from Japan," *Gospel Advocate*, January 10, 1929, 39; O. D. Bixler, "Information from Bro. Bixler," *Missionary Messenger*, August 1929, 214.

[41] Communication with Harry Robert Fox, Jr., March 3, 2013.

[42] Don Carlos Janes, "Missionary Medley," *Missionary Messenger*, June 1931, 359.

[43] Harry R. Fox, Sr., Letter, *Oriental Christian*, December 1932, 11.

[44] Harris Ives, "Japan: An Odyssey," *Christian Chronicle*, March 2002, 18, 19.

[45] Don Carlos Janes, "Missionaries Speak for Themselves," *Missionary Messenger*, October 1937, 377.

[46] Ibid.

[47] Ibid.; Harris Ives, "Japan: An Odyssey," *Christian Chronicle*, March 2002, 19.

[48] Harry R. Fox, Sr., "Ibaraki Trip," *World Vision*, May, June 1946, 5–7.

[49] Ibid.

[50] Ibid.

[51] Ibid.

[52] Ibid., 7.

[53] O. D. Bixler, "Brother Bixler's Letter," *World Vision*, March 1947, 3.

[54] Ibid.

[55] Ibid.

[56] Harry R. Fox, Sr., "Ibaraki," *World Vision*, May, June 1946, 6.

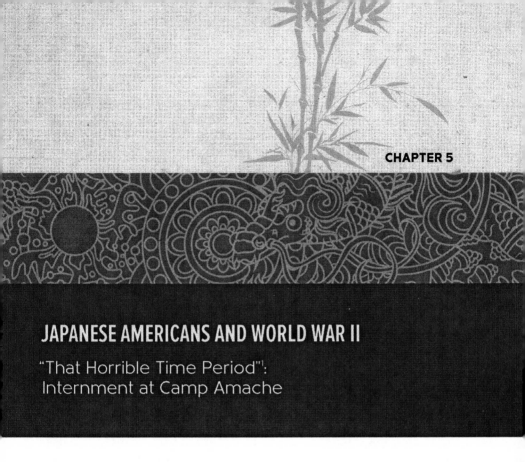

JAPANESE AMERICANS AND WORLD WAR II

"That Horrible Time Period":
Internment at Camp Amache

Traveling east on US Highway 50, one must watch closely when approaching Granada, Colorado, to see a small sign identifying directions to the site of Camp Amache. Driving approximately a half mile, visitors find an entrance into an unpaved parking area with several attractive displays with photographs and a short history of how the Japanese Americans arrived there in 1942. There are a few walking paths, one directing visitors to a large rock with a marker identifying the Granada Relocation Center (Amache) and naming the site as a National Historic Landmark. In both English and Japanese, the marker notes that 7,300 men, women, and children lived there against their will throughout the years of World War II.

On one of the displays is a grid showing the outlay of the camp. Anyone visiting in the twenty-first century must use their imagination to see the tar-paper covered barracks that provided housing for the internees—only the concrete outline of floors remain amid the waterless landscape of eastern Colorado. At a location marking the perimeter of the camp, a marker states,

Site of Guard Tower
Equipped with a machine gun and
searchlight, it was staffed by
US Army Military Police

The visitor leaves the camp site with more questions than answers.

Dark Days in 1942

It was August 27, 1942, when the first Japanese Americans were forced to set foot in Camp Amache by the United States government. Amache was one of ten camps established quickly to house Japanese Americans who lived in California, Oregon, Washington, and Arizona at the outbreak of World War II. Upon their arrival, the buildings were not finished as promised. Arriving by night, with little light and often only candles to show the way, some fell into open ditches. The new arrivals had to walk many blocks to bathhouses to get water—it had to be trucked in from Granada. The central water system was not yet operative. Because of the lack of water, the government had to provide wood privies. By October, even with all the problems, Camp Amache reached its peak population of 7,567 internees, two-thirds of whom were US citizens, born in America.[2] There was a total of approximately 110,000 Japanese Americans imprisoned in camps across the United States at this dark time in American history.

Constructed hastily for the relocation of the Japanese, the camps housed both older Issei (those born in Japan) and a larger number of Nesai (younger Japanese born in the United States and therefore citizens). While the camps were being completed, evacuees lived in horrible conditions. But it did not matter: they were thought to be a threat to the United States, at war with Japan.

Americans began fearing a Japanese invasion along the West Coast, especially those living in California, Oregon, and Washington. If the Japanese could attack the Hawaiian Islands, what would deter them from attacking the mainland United States? To add to their concern was the rather large population of Japanese people living in the Pacific Coast region, especially in Southern California. How many of those people were agents of Japan? As the war entered 1942, the reports from the South Pacific were not good. In mid-February 1942, Singapore surrendered unconditionally, forcing the Allies to withdraw to the Dutch East Indies. Winston Churchill called the surrender "the greatest disaster to British arms which history records."[3] In a frenzy, Caucasian Americans became even more concerned about Japanese living among them. But the seeds of discrimination were already planted deep in American culture, in a long history of hatred spanning back nearly a hundred long years.

A Long History of Discrimination

Harsh feelings against the Japanese and other residents from the Pacific regions had been present in the United States from the 1850s onward, when the Chinese arrived on American soil during the gold rush era. Asian immigrants were deemed the "yellow menace" in gold mining areas, including San Francisco, or wherever the Chinese "coolies" settled. Japanese migration to the United States began around 1880. In 1882, the United States denied citizenship to all Asians. But by 1900 there were thirty thousand Japanese in the United States, mostly in California, looking to start a new life.[4]

The world took notice of a new power in Asia when Japan defeated Russia in the Russo-Japanese War in 1905. When Japan invaded and then controlled the Korean Peninsula in 1910, Japan became a force in the Pacific world. After the war with Russia and the takeover of Korea, Japan began a supreme makeover of their country. They began a Westernization process that would culminate in World War II.

As a result of modernization, a number of Japanese, mostly truck farmers, found their livelihood in jeopardy. The only country to which they could migrate with the hope of finding the opportunity to practice their skills was the United States. What they had done so successfully in Japan they could replicate in America. Arriving in the United States in the early 1900s, Japanese immigrants began purchasing land unwanted by others—sandy soil, swamps, and land near power lines. Then in 1913 California passed the Alien Land Law, which made it illegal for Japanese immigrants to purchase land. Shortly thereafter, the state amended the act to deny the Japanese even the right to lease land.[5]

Despite these obstacles, Japanese farmers were able to take poor-quality land and produce excellent crops. In fact, by 1941 these Japanese farmers were producing approximately half the fruits and vegetables grown in California. They dominated the Los Angeles market, particularly for tomatoes. Caucasian farmers became concerned, even envious. This became a national topic. Soon, Congress passed the Oriental Exclusion Act of 1924—a special provision of the Johnson-Reed Act of the same year—denying citizenship to Japanese immigrants.[6] The US Supreme Court had ruled in 1922 that Japanese could not be citizens because they were not "white."[7] As a result, the United States denied citizenship to the first settlers—the Issei—until 1954.

Amid all this discrimination, a close Japanese American community began to form and thrive. In fact, of the more than 100,000 Japanese Americans on the West Coast at the outbreak of World War II, 75,000 lived in the Los Angeles area. Among those who settled in Los Angeles was Hirosuke Ishiguro, the minister of the Westside Church of Christ, whose story would become fully entwined with the horrors of discrimination endured by Japanese Americans in 1942.

A Light in the Darkness: The Japanese Church of Christ in Los Angeles

Since 1892, Churches of Christ had supported missionaries in Japan. However, up to that point, no one suggested evangelizing the Los Angeles Japanese community. The idea came to S. H. Hall while spending a year (1920–21) preaching for the Sichel Street Church of Christ in Los Angeles. He had read the papers with calls to send missionaries to Japan, and yet there were seventy-five thousand Japanese in Los Angeles County. "Why not make an effort to convert these people right here at our door, then send them back to their own people with the gospel?"[8]

During his year in California, Hall met Hirosuke Ishiguro, a young Japanese man on his way to Abilene, Texas, where he would enroll in Abilene Christian College. He had arrived in the United States with very little money. The Sichel Street church and two individuals provided his travel money to Abilene. After meeting his new friend, Hall became even more interested in ministering to the Japanese population in the United

States.[9] In 1922, Hall moved to Nashville where he became the minister for the large Russell Street Church of Christ. After graduating from Abilene Christian College, Ishiguro also migrated to Nashville.

In Japan, Ishiguro had been baptized by a Kansan missionary named B. W. Hon. But after only a year in the Tokyo area, Hon became ill and had to return to the United States. The remaining three American missionaries in the Tokyo area also soon returned to America, leaving Ishiguro the only person to serve his church in Otsuka. He diligently studied the Bible, talking about Christ to his Shinto and Buddhist friends and neighbors. In the meantime he married a Christian young lady who also helped teach the Bible among the Otsuka church population. Soon enough, the church associated with David Lipscomb College heard of Ishiguro and agreed to support him in his work. "During his ministry," reported Robert S. King, "more than one hundred souls left their idols to serve the living God."[10] Erroll Rhodes, who would stand with his friend Ishiguro during World War II, remembered favorably worshiping in 1919 with the church where Ishiguro preached before coming to America.[11]

Now in Nashville, Ishiguro visited with Robert King and the college church, and he became reacquainted with Hall. They discussed Ishiguro's dilemma. Should he return to Japan or remain in the United States? He had every reason to return to Japan. His wife and family were there. But the more they talked, the more they saw the need to go to the Japanese community in Los Angeles and share the gospel with Ishiguro's people in America. S. H. Hall had found the answer to his question.

Hall first suggested that Ishiguro should go to Los Angeles, get a job, and begin working within the Japanese community. Without telling the young Japanese minister, Hall approached the elders at Russell Street about supporting Ishiguro for a year in Los Angeles. They agreed to do so. If the year went well, the church would bring his wife and son to America, and the church would continue to supply a hundred dollars a month support. The year went extremely well, but they were meeting in rented quarters. They needed a building of their own.

Early in 1923, S. H. Hall submitted a long letter to the *Advocate* from W. Edgar Miller, an elder of the Sichel Street church in Los Angeles, describing the needs of Ishiguro in his new work. He needed a house for living and a meeting place to welcome people—and he needed to bring his family to the United States. Ishiguro needed his wife to help him minister among the Japanese. "And, of course," Miller wrote, "we know his mind will be in better condition to work with his home established here than it can possibly be with him here and his wife and child in Japan."[12]

Around this time, a Christian woman named Cora Brooks, unsolicited and unknown to him, sent S. H. Hall a check for $10,000 to use where he thought it would do the most good. What a godsend! With $7,500 of the gift, the Japanese church constructed a building. By 1930 it was too small—Ishiguro had done his work well. The church asked for support to obtain larger facilities. Ishiguro wrote the *Gospel Advocate* in the fall of 1930, relating the progress of the work in Los Angeles:

> We ordinarily have one hundred twenty [to] two hundred attendance of the Sunday school children. And these children [are] divided into twelve classes. . . .
>
> We have over [forty] memberships. On morning service many people come over to the meeting with faithfulness. . . .
>
> We had eight [baptisms] the other day, and we will have several people again pretty soon.[13]

The call by Hall for the Japanese church in Los Angeles to send missionaries to Japan became a reality soon after the church began meeting. But the call was not answered by a Japanese Issei or Nisei who had been in the United States for some time. Ryohachi Shigekuni came to America in 1920, the same year as Ishiguro, because his family could not make a living either in Japan or Korea. Knowing only an uncle in Los Angeles, Yonetaro Shigekuni, Ryohachi came to California. Here he lived with his uncle and aunt, and he became a missionary after an eye-opening experience, when he was struck by a pellet gun while doing yard work. He carried out a long and successful ministry, as detailed in Chapter 4.

The stories of faithful Christians associated with the Westside church are many. Consider the Shigekuni family, composed of Yonetaro Shigekuni and his wife, Shizuyo, along with their sons Tseneo (Tunny), Henry, and Thomas, who converted after the tragic death of their six-year-old daughter, Fumiko, a devout believer in Jesus even at such a young age. Fumiko attended the Sunday school of the Westside Church. She stepped on a rusty nail, causing tetanus to spread through her body. Before she died, Fumiko said to her mother, "Momma, we do not need to weep when people die. They go to God. There is a resurrection and eternal life, so do not weep." She then told her mother that she was going to live with Jesus. When Hirosuke Ishiguro spoke at Fumiko's funeral, the Shigekunis were so impressed that they invited Ishiguro to tell them more about this Jesus their daughter loved so much. After a while, the entire family accepted Christ. Yonetaro Shigekuni would, in time, become an elder of the Westside Church of Christ in Los Angeles. S. H. Hall's vision was becoming reality.

Another Ishiguro convert was Tokuo Mazawa. Following his baptism, he returned to Japan to minister to his people. However, he felt a need for education in the Bible. He returned to the United States where he enrolled in David Lipscomb College, graduating in 1935. He then returned to Japan to work with Sarah Andrews in Shizuoka. In a letter to *World Vision* on December 15, 1939, Mazawa said of his work in Shizuoka and Okitsu, "I confess this is 'work in hard places.'"[14] Sadly, on August 6, 1945, he died as a result of the nuclear bomb dropped on Hiroshima.[15]

In the midst of great darkness and discrimination, the Los Angeles church became a rallying place for missionaries on their way to and from Japan. Sarah Andrews, Barney and Nellie Morehead, and Hettie Lee Ewing all spent time with the church, either studying language or visiting when on furlough. In 1925, when the Moreheads were on their way to Japan for the first time, they spent forty days studying with Ishiguro. Ewing also studied at the Japanese church, with plans to go to Japan in 1926. S. H. Hall, ever interested in the Los Angeles mission, underlined the importance of Ishiguro's work:

> The Japanese mission affords an opportunity for the church
> of Christ to show its interest in the salvation of souls. Brother
> Ishiguro has baptized ten of his native people in the short time
> he has worked. I doubt very much if an American soldier of the
> cross could go from Nashville, Tenn., to a city like Los Angeles,
> where the church of Christ is not known, as among the Japanese
> the church was not known, and baptize ten in the same length

of time under the same circumstances as Brother Ishiguro has worked.[16]

By the end of 1932, the Westside church had developed to the point of appointing elders and deacons with over fifty baptized believers. The church continued steady growth during the 1930s, even reaching out to the farmers on the outskirts of Los Angeles. Erroll Rhodes, a recently returned missionary in Japan, and Ishiguro spent one night each week among the farming communities near Los Angeles late in the decade and early in the 1940s.[17] Because of this growth, toward the end of the decade, the church bought lots for the construction of a new building for worship. S. H. Hall must have been pleased with the response to his 1920 dream. But in the midst of such a victory for Christ, the troubling events of World War II would threaten to destroy this vision and the brotherly love of Christianity forever.

Hirosuke Ishiguro Arrested

The pent-up feelings along the Pacific Coast against the Japanese overflowed following the bombing of Pearl Harbor. On February 19, 1942, President Franklin D. Roosevelt issued Executive Order 9066, allowing military commanders to establish "military areas" with the ability to exclude any and all persons. The power given by the executive order required all persons of Japanese ancestry in California, Oregon, Washington, and Arizona to be held in internment camps. The Supreme Court upheld the executive order and the internment of Japanese people in ten camps, stretching from California to Arkansas; a total of approximately 110,000 Japanese Americans were relocated to these camps at this time.

Even before World War II, the Federal Bureau of Investigation had been investigating and cataloguing men and women who were leaders among the Japanese population. After Pearl Harbor, they rounded up five thousand men for interrogation before the Alien Enemy hearing boards. Most were freed. But over the next two or three months, under pressure from California officials and citizens, the government arrested two thousand Issei and sent them to FBI detention camps. Herbert V. Nicholson, a former Quaker missionary to Japan and a minister to a Japanese American church in Los Angeles, could not believe what was happening. He remembered:

"[They] picked up anybody that was the head of anything. . . . Because of public opinion and pressure, others were picked up later for all sorts of things. Buddhist priests and Japanese language school teachers were all picked up later."[18] Among those incarcerated and interrogated was Westside's own Hirosuke Ishiguro.

The church in Los Angeles was in turmoil. The government had arrested their preacher and carried him off to jail. The American prejudices against the Japanese that culminated in the Immigration Act in 1924 led to overt actions against leaders in the Japanese community with the outbreak of war. Ishiguro believed his arrest happened because in 1931 he had been asked by parents who had come to the United States before 1924 to teach their children the Japanese language. This was suspect by American authorities, and on the morning of March 13, 1942, the FBI arrested him. Ishiguro explained the situation: "Due to the declaration of war between the United States and Japan, any alien Japanese who were the leaders of schools, churches, and social organizations, affiliated with Japan in any way, were arrested by the FBI."[19]

Ishiguro's recollection of the events of 1942 was accurate. According to Jacobus ten Broek and his associates, "Increasingly severe restrictions— including exclusion of all enemy aliens from small coastal areas and the establishment of a curfew for those living in a larger zone—followed rapidly as demands for closer supervision arose from the War Department and the Western Defense Command (WDC). Before long, in response to what it deemed a serious threat to national security, the WDC sought and gained power to remove all enemy aliens whom it judged dangerous."[20] Some 40,000 of the 112,000 Japanese on the West Coast were aliens over fifty years of age. These persons were born in Japan and not eligible for United States citizenship. This was Ishiguro's dilemma.

The minister's first thought was to call Erroll Rhodes, a longtime missionary to Japan and a personal friend. Rhodes had returned from Japan before the war and was working with Ishiguro among the Japanese in Los Angeles. He would know what to do under the circumstances. The authorities would not allow their prisoner to call Rhodes; instead, they called for him. Ishiguro, taken to the police station, was later that evening transferred to the county jail. They photographed him, gave him a number, and questioned him until midnight. He recalled years later, "This was my first experience in jail, and it reminded me of the saints of old when they were imprisoned for the gospel's sake. Thinking on these things gave me courage, and I went off to sleep, feeling happy."[21] The next morning the jail officials gave the detainees two slices of stale bread. He refused to eat it, even though he had not eaten since breakfast the day before. "But," he added, "thinking of the Lord fasting, I thought I was fortunate."[22]

In the middle of the morning, in a downpour of rain, the authorities took the prisoners to an abandoned CCC camp where they retained a multitude of Japanese aliens. The hills surrounding the camp, covered with snow, caused Ishiguro to believe he was in an alien world. However, the government did provide Japanese cooks to prepare Japanese food for the detainees: "It was a treat." In the meantime, those in charge interrogated the Japanese prisoners several times a day. But Ishiguro was fortunate. His Christian friends, including Erroll Rhodes, came to visit him. The authorities, however, would not allow them to visit alone—they could only talk through an interpreter. These friends brought items Ishiguro would need while in guarded camps.[23]

What would happen to his son, Masaaki (also known as Robert), a student at Pepperdine College, was ever on Ishiguro's mind. His son would not be allowed to stay at Pepperdine since it was in a military zone. Again, Ishiguro's Christian friends came to his aid. He immediately asked J. M. McCaleb, the former missionary to Japan, to recommend Masaaki to Abilene Christian College (ACC) in Texas. Pepperdine's president, Hugh Tiner, initiated contact with the Texas school. The dean at ACC quickly admitted Masaaki Ishiguro.[24]

After three weeks in the California camp, the authorities sent Ishiguro to Santa Fe and then transferred him to a newly constructed prisoner-of-war camp in Lordsburg, New Mexico. According to the New Mexico Office of the State Historian, "The first internees arrived the first week of June 1942 by a special highball train from a war relocation camp in California." Historian Millie Pressler continued, "The Federal Bureau of Investigation had determined these civilian men were potentially dangerous enemy agents, and deemed their incarceration essential for national security." Once in the camp, the internees had to surrender all personal possessions, including their clothing. A green uniform with identifying numbers on the back was his new attire. Ishiguro was among two thousand Japanese men housed in the Lordsburg camp.[25]

In June 1943, Erroll Rhodes visited Ishiguro at Lordsburg. "It was indeed a great pleasure, for we talked about the church and tentative plans for the future." And Rhodes told his friend about visiting Masaaki in Abilene—"All of this was a real comfort to me." Following Rhodes's visit, those in charge transferred Ishiguro to Santa Fe. It was here that he heard good news. Through the influence of numerous Caucasian friends, including Hugh Tiner, J. M. McCaleb, Erroll Rhodes, and W. Ray Johnson, an official at the Amache internment camp in Colorado and a member of Churches of Christ, Ishiguro received parole and was transferred to Amache, where most of the Los Angeles Christians lived. It had been over a year since he had been taken prisoner and removed from his family and friends. Now they were together again.[26] It was a trying time for God's people. However, their brothers and sisters in Churches of Christ did not desert them.

The Mass Internment of Japanese Americans

In March and April 1942, Japanese aliens and those born in the United States began noticing posters tacked to telephone poles throughout California, Oregon, Washington, and southern Arizona, boldly proclaiming,

ALL PERSONS OF JAPANESE ANCESTRY, BOTH ALIEN AND NONALIEN, WILL BE EVACUATED FROM THE ABOVE DESIGNATED AREA BY 12:O'CLOCK NOON

President Roosevelt's Executive Order 9066 of February 19 was now in force.[27]

Up and down the Pacific Coast and in Arizona, the government instituted sixty-four civil control stations near heavy concentrations of Japanese Americans. Operated by the Wartime Civil Control Administration (WCCA), the army became the arm of government to set up and administer the relocation and internment camps. The Japanese, including those with as little as one-sixteenth blood relation, were required to register. (These regulations were later relaxed.) Individuals and families became numbers on tags. At registration, everyone received instructions, direct and explicit, from the army as to what they should do. Every person and all families were given a time and date to report voluntarily for internment. They were to bring only bedrolls and baggage, no more than could be carried by hand. The evacuees had a week to ten days to wrap up their business, including the disposal of their excess belongings.

The US government did little to aid these hapless people in preparation for going to camps where they would live for the duration of the war, except to offer warehouses for storage of their belongings.[28] However, few trusted their life accumulations to a government that would deny them citizenship or take their rights from them.

Given fewer than two weeks to dispose of years of hard work, what could they do? Bargain hunters descended on the defenseless evacuees. Junk dealers bought their possessions for almost nothing. The Japanese Americans had no other recourse. They had to turn their belongings into cash or lose everything. They were easy prey to swindlers who threatened the confiscation of their property if they did not sell for a small pittance of its worth. Others trusted Caucasian friends to care for their possessions, even offering them the opportunity to live in their houses without rent. Some even boarded up their property, hoping it would not be found ravaged when they returned after internment. It has been estimated that the evacuation cost the Japanese people $350,000,000 in income and lost property.[29] Michi Weglyn commented, "For the majority of the Issei who had helped to make the California desert bloom, the rewards of a lifetime of zealous perseverance evaporated within a frenzied fortnight."[30]

The Japanese Americans brought to the United States the learned quality of unquestioning obedience. There was fear, but because so much had happened in just a few days, they meekly went along with government orders. When the appointed day arrived, they came to the appointed places at the appointed times. According to Colonel Karl Bendetsen, the architect of the evacuation, the removal proceeded in such an orderly fashion that everything happened "without mischance, with minimum hardship, and almost without incident." From these control stations, the evacuees were taken by train or bus to "reception centers."[31]

There were twelve centers in California under the direction of the Works Progress Administration. However, the army had a decided presence in each camp, including guard towers with searchlights moving about the camps all night. In California, race tracks, such as Santa Anita, became detention facilities, including stables for "apartments." As many as five persons, oftentimes including grandparents, lived in rooms measuring twenty feet by twenty feet. The beds were so close there was no room to walk.[32] South of San Francisco, the Tanforan Race Track housed four hundred bachelors in one large room under the grandstands, without partitions to provide privacy. The Portland Livestock Pavilion was the only center in Oregon.

The camps were much more than "assembly centers." Pinedale, some ten miles outside Fresno, California, was a hastily constructed small city of tar-paper-covered barracks. Barbed wire enclosed the entire camp, with army sentries guarding the perimeter.[33] According to the authorities, the "assembly centers" were not concentration camps and the evacuees were not prisoners. It was difficult for the internees to know the difference. The food initially consisted of canned goods: lots of beans, pork, hash, and canned wieners. There were no fresh vegetables, and the dining arrangements—massive mess halls—had little family orientation.[34]

The members of the Westside Church of Christ were taken to the Santa Anita Race Track along with over 19,000 other persons while the ten internment camps were under construction. Tom Shigekuni, then twelve years of age, described the conditions at Santa Anita: "We were sent to the Santa Anita Assembly Center which was a true concentration camp with guard towers and armed guards. The US Army had searchlights on all night long."[35] And the odor of horses was ever present. While in the Assembly Center, the internees, loyal to their overseers and to the United States, produced 27,011 camouflage nets for the army.

After several months, the internees transferred to camps in Heart Mountain, Wyoming; Granada (Amache), Colorado; Rohwer and Jerome, Arkansas; and Poston and Gila River, Arizona.[36] The camps, operated by the War Relocation Authority (WRA; established by Executive Order 9102), were part of a civilian organization at first under the direction of Milton Eisenhower.[37] The civilian organization, however, did not lessen the importance of the army in the camps.

The Internment of the Shigekuni Family in Camp Amache

The story of the Westside Church of Christ, closed by the internment of its minister and all of its members in 1942, can be followed in one family who spent the duration of World War II in the Amache, Colorado, internment camp. The Shigekuni family—Yonetaro, the father; Shizuyo, the mother; and their three sons—left California in August 1942 by train to Colorado to the camp on the high plains near the Kansas border. The camp sat in the midst of 10,500 once privately owned acres of windswept, arid land. The Arkansas River, offering irrigation to the region, flowed only 2.5 miles to the north. However, only 640 acres were used for the camp.[38] The remainder would be used for agricultural enterprises, with the internees as workers. Many now living in Amache had been connected with agriculture or horticulture—farmers, nursery men, and gardeners—in California. The Shigekuni family owned and operated a wholesale and retail nursery in Los Angeles.[39]

It must have been an intimidating experience for the Shigekunis when they stepped off the train, probably at night, after several days en route, the many miles from California to Colorado shielded from their view by curtained windows. All they had were pieces of luggage and bedding they could carry. Where were they? What would they do? How would they live? The morning after their arrival, they viewed a large expanse of unfinished barracks. Deep ditches crisscrossed between the hundreds of barracks, lined up row upon row, surrounded by a fence topped by barbed wire. Guard towers at intervals around the perimeter of the camp had soldiers with guns and high-powered searching spotlights.

The authorities directed the Shigekunis to a nondescript tar-paper-covered barrack, their living quarters—only one room, possibly sixteen feet by twenty feet. Entering the room, they noticed an open ceiling with one electric light hanging from a rafter. There were five army beds and a coal heating stove in the middle of the room. The Shigekuni family, however, was fortunate—there were only five of them. Other families, much larger, had to live in similar spaces. And it must have been disconcerting to learn they had to leave their room to go to a bathhouse and their meals would be served in large mess halls. They no longer had their coveted privacy. For all these reasons, Michi Weglyn used the words "concentration camp" in the subtitle of her study of the Japanese internment.[40]

Despite all this hardship, the larger Christian community across America did not abandon their fellow Christians detained in the camps. Members of the Christian community responded negatively to the evacuation of Japanese aliens and Japanese Americans from the Pacific states. This was especially true among the historical peace churches—those holding pacifist views. The Society of Friends—known as Quakers—were among the first to oppose the internment of the Japanese. Immediately when a camp began operation, the Quakers were there to provide for the needs of the evacuees. Most of all, they brought assurance that not all Caucasians were anti–Japanese American. Equally, the Friends openly criticized the army's abuse of power. From the very beginning, they spoke out against the housing of humans in stables and shacks at Santa Anita and Tonfron.[41]

The Amache camp was no exception, also receiving love and support from Christian organizations in the spirit of brotherhood, transcending all notions of race and nationalism. Tom Shigekuni, remembered, "The town of Granada had a Church of Christ whose members welcomed us royally despite the general hostility of the people of the region to us prisoners."[42] The churches "met with us and brought us many things that made life more comfortable and greatly encouraged us," recalled Ishiguro.[43] According to Tom Shigekuni, the Granada church met with the Japanese Church of Christ at least once a month: "They were very friendly."[44]

The commitment to religious responsibilities did not completely come from outside the camp. A large number of Christian churches, as well as Buddhists, had adherents in Amache. The majority of Protestant Christians joined each Sunday in a single worship service. However, the Los Angeles Japanese Church of Christ met separately every Sunday morning to partake of the Lord's Supper. A young man, Michio Nagai, years later a professor of religion at Pepperdine College, helped gather members of the church for communion prior to leaving to attend Abilene Christian College.[45] Then in 1943, Hirosuke Ishiguro, released from Lordsburg, gave leadership to members of his congregation. He approached Ray Johnson about the possibility of providing the church a larger meeting place each Sunday. Ishiguro reasoned, "I desired this because I wanted to follow the principles of the church of Christ as it is written."[46] Tom Shigekuni recalled, "Our members didn't really mix with other denominations. They didn't believe the others were true Christians." Johnson found the church a larger space for meeting.

But the most inspiring stories to emerge from Amache were from the evangelistic endeavors of Shizuyo Shigekuni. She shared her faith with those incarcerated with her. She was a strong and powerful force for Christ amid harsh circumstances. Tom fondly recalled his mother's religious convictions: "Shizuyo became an ardent evangelist for Christ [while in Los Angeles], and when she was incarcerated in the WW2 camp . . . at Amache, Colorado, for three and one half years, she took this opportunity to evangelize every Japanese person she met."

In many ways, Shizuyo "must have considered this imprisonment a 'gift of God' for the evangelistic opportunities presented." Since the women of the camp had little to do, Shizuyo found a ready reception for discussing Christ.[47] According to Tom, "She was able to convert many to Christianity during the . . . years of imprisonment." Buddhist husbands of the women converted to Christ often objected to their wives becoming Christians. The husbands "hated my mother for her preaching to their wives." But the more they objected, the more she attempted to convert the women to Christ.[48]

Tom observed the men's objections to his mother teaching their wives. On one occasion, he admonished her to "lay off the women if their husbands objected to Jesus's message of salvation." After lecturing his mother on numerous occasions, Tom was taken aback: "[O]ne day after one of my 'lay off' speeches to her, she turned on me and told me that I lacked faith, that I needed to accept the Lord and I must be baptized to show my faith." After that, Tom kept quiet, never again interfering with his mother's evangelizing efforts.[49]

Tom's father, Yonetaro, was responsible for mopping the mess hall in Block 12-G every night. Such a chore did not keep him from serving his fellow internees. As a service to his block, the elder Shigekuni, on his own initiative, supplied one hundred pounds of rice each week for his neighbors. Other enterprising detainees had fish shipped to the camp every day. Although the Japanese Americans were under close control of the US government, they made the best of a difficult situation, even establishing a Japanese "tea house" in the camp.[50]

The Japanese students did not attend Granada schools; Amache had its own school system, not unlike the other internment camps. The WRA had the responsibility for the schools in all ten camps. Initially, the school buildings were little different from the living accommodations—the federal government provided little special preparation for education. The teacher-to-student ratio was much higher than the public schools across the nation—48 to 1 in elementary schools and 35 to 1 in high schools. The vast majority of the teachers were Caucasian, and a total of six hundred instructors served all ten camps. There were only fifty certified Japanese teachers, with four hundred Japanese assistant teachers among the internees.[51] The most difficult subjects for teachers in all camps were ones involving government. In a class discussion at Amache High School, provocative questions were common: "If we are citizens, why are we in concentration camps?" Or, as another student asked: "Is the United States a real democracy?"[52] It was here that Tom Shigekuni received his education during his formative years.

Evidently, the Amache camp had better relations with the outside community than other camps—a beacon for the hope amid the plight of war pitting brother against brother. The *Densho Encyclopedia* states that the camp was unique among the ten camps in several ways. For instance, a number of teachers in the Amache schools petitioned to live in the camp, which they felt would give them more influence over students. Possibly a reason for this attitude was the acceptance by the internees of Amache administrator James G. Lindley. They "felt he was an able administrator with a deep regard for fairness."[53]

Granada was not a large town, with only a few hundred people; it was a predominately agricultural community. On the other hand, Camp Amache, at its greatest population, was Colorado's tenth largest city. Although the internees did not have lots of money, they did have enough to help the economy of Granada. Tom Shigekuni remembers with pleasure shopping "in town." Speaking generally for the internees, he said, "[The Caucasians in Granada] were pleased with us—unlike the Caucasians in Los Angeles."[54] By 1945, local businesses advertised in the Amache High School annual. Newman Drug Store even employed Japanese internees.[55] Among the leading retail stores in town, one was owned by Arley Bever, a leader in the Granada Church of Christ.[56] This church embraced the Japanese members of the Church of Christ. Perhaps there was a bond that ran deeper than the pledge to nationalism that was so heavily influential in such a time of war. Perhaps, in these small ways, the love of Christ shined through the darkness—there was hope for brotherhood in even these trying circumstances.

However, lest the wrong impression be left, Amache was not fully accepted throughout Colorado. When the Amache school board formed a PTA, the state organization would not accept their membership. Amache High School scheduled a football game with the Wiley, Colorado, high school. And as the date for the game approached, the Wiley administration canceled the game due to protests.

In 1943, after less than one year in the camp, a young woman by the name of Marion Konishi gave a very positive and insightful look on the internment of her people in her valedictory address:

> Sometimes America failed and suffered. Sometimes she made mistakes, great mistakes. America hounded and harassed the Indians; then remembering that they were the first Americans, she gave them back their citizenship. She enslaved the Negroes; then remembering Americanism, she wrote the Emancipation Proclamation. She persecuted the German Americans during the First World War; then recalling America was born of those who come from every nation, seeking liberty, she repented. Her history is full of errors, but with each mistake she has learned. . . .Can we the graduating class of Amache Senior High School believe that America still means freedom, equality, security, and justice? Do I believe this? Do my classmates believe this? Yes, with all our hearts, because in that faith, in that hope, is my future, our future, and the world's future.

After World War II, Marion Konishi opened a sushi restaurant in Chicago, operating it for thirty-four years.[57]

The anti-Japanese feelings, however, were real for the Shigekuni family. Tom Shigekuni took advantage of the freedom to leave the camp when one day he traveled to Lamar, a town west of Granada. When Tom sought to board a return bus to Granada, the bus driver said to him, "Not you, you dirty Jap." He closed the door and denied Tom transportation to his home at Camp Amache.[58]

Camp Amache officially closed on October 15, 1945, although many internees had left earlier. Those with children in school remained until the summer of 1945. As late as July, there remained four thousand people in camp. Some families were able to return to the Los Angeles area, others went to Denver, while some remained in the Granada area.

The Shigekunis Return to California

The Shigekuni family returned to California, but not to Los Angeles. The War Relocation Authority sent them to Piedmont, California, where Yonetaro and Shizuyo Shigekuni worked as domestic servants for a Chinese family. Piedmont was an upper-class neighborhood in the hills east of San Francisco.[59] The Shigekunis lived very near Piedmont High School, but Chinese residents told Tom he could not attend the local school. He was informed, "Your kind go to Oakland Technical High School." He had to ride public transportation three miles each way to attend school. Isolated in Piedmont, he remembers, "I saw few Japanese Americans there, and I didn't like the area."

The general population in California remained hostile to the returning Japanese. However, Tom remembers that members of Churches of Christ were the exception. They welcomed Japanese Christians. He recalled how members of Churches of Christ remained loyal to the Japanese Christians, as at the outbreak of war, even though they were put at personal risk.[60]

Tom was the youngest member of his family. His older brother, Tsuneo (Tunny), had moved to Milwaukee, and his middle brother, Henry, was in Elmhurst, Illinois, working in a nursery growing gardenias. Feeling alone, Tom informed his parents that he was going back to Los Angeles. His parents agreed to go with him. The Shigekuni family again became involved in the nursery business, locating in a highly populated area of Jewish families. Said Tom, "The Jews were great to us. Without them, we'd have no business."

The Shigekunis returned to the nursery business with nothing to show for their success before the war. Fortunately, the man who bought their nursery truck three years previously sold it back to the Shigekunis at the same price he paid. Tom and his family established Centrose Nursery, which became a very successful business. They even opened branches of the nursery throughout Los Angeles. The Shigekuni parents continued in the business until Yonetaro's death in December 1967; Shizuyo continued working until retirement at the age of ninety-three. She lived until 1997, passing away at the age of 102. Shizuyo looked forward to again meeting her young daughter Fumiko, who had committed herself to Christ, thus inspiring her entire family to be baptized. She never forgot what Fumiko told her before she died: "I'm going to meet Jesus."

Thomas applied to and received admission as a freshman at UCLA. D'Lila, registrar at George Pepperdine College, hearing of his decision, told Tom to withdraw from UCLA and enroll at Pepperdine. He told her that his parents could not afford his attendance at Pepperdine. They had just returned from the internment camp and were penniless. George Pepperdine, the founder of the school, hearing of Tom's dilemma, paid for everything. After Pepperdine, Tom attended the University of Southern California Law School. After graduating, for forty-five years he practiced law in Southern California, retiring in 2011.[61] Tom and his wife, Ruth, attended the Redondo Beach Church of Christ. "The people there are true Christians and welcome everyone no matter their race, economic standing, or other differences. I can't speak more highly of the integrity of the members of our church."[62]

Life, as the years passed, changed greatly for the Shigekunis. "When I [Tom] bought my first home in Los Angeles, there were restricted covenants on where Japanese could buy. I had to buy in Gardena, an area populated by many Japanese Americans. For the past thirty-five years, I've lived in the coastal city of Palos Verdes Estates. . . . When I first moved here, there were few Asians. It's very different now."[63] Somehow, someway, this family had emerged triumphant from their trials, fueled by their love of Christ.

The Westside Church of Christ Meets Again

Hirosuke Ishiguro returned to Los Angeles on October 8, 1945. He was met at the train terminal by his friend Erroll Rhodes. The two men kept busy with numerous issues, including finding living quarters for the returning evacuees. The Los Angeles church, eager to reopen its doors, did not immediately regain the use of its former building, as two families had rented it for their residences. The renters, although notified in May 1945, did not vacate the meetinghouse until February 1946. The building had to be redecorated. In the meantime, Erroll and Bess Rhodes met with the returnees in a Japanese Christian's home when they began arriving in August 1945. This arrangement would continue until their building was ready in February.[64]

Even before Thomas Shigekuni enrolled in George Pepperdine College, the young man remembered George Pepperdine befriending the Westside Church of Christ. He would often attend their services before the government sent Thomas and his family to Camp Amache. It was not unusual for George Pepperdine, after members of the Westside Church of Christ returned from Amache, to invite the youth of the church for a wiener roast or barbeque on the grounds of his home on West Adams Street.[65]

The language situation had not changed much since 1942. Therefore, Ishiguro preached for the older Japanese Christians, while Rhodes preached for the younger generation. This situation was indicative of things to come. With the death of the older generation, a church for a Japanese-speaking congregation would no longer be needed. In the 1970s, the Westside Church of Christ constructed a new building at 2531 West Jefferson Boulevard in Los Angeles, serving Japanese Christians. In 2002, the church disbanded and gave the building to Pepperdine University. The proceeds from the sale of the building are dedicated to scholarships at Pepperdine University in memory of Hirosuke Ishiguro and the Westside Church of Christ.[66]

Los Angeles and California have changed dramatically since 1942 when all Japanese people were sent to internment camps. A hated people are now accepted as American citizens. And there is no longer a Japanese Church of Christ. Now veritably all Japanese Americans speak the English language and worship in integrated churches. Life is much different from the years in Camp Amache, "that horrible time period." The Shigekunis and other Japanese Christians like them had lived through a great but difficult cultural change in American history. And it was their faith in Christ, along with Christian fellowship extending beyond all notions of race and nationalism, that brought them through into peaceful and prosperous times, a transition from darkness into light.

Endnotes

[1] Editor, *Christian Chronicle*, "Letters to the Editor," accessed December 23, 2016, http://www.christianchronicle.org/article/letters-to-the-editor.

[2] "Camp Amache, the Mountain Branch of the Santa Fe Trail," accessed December 22, 2016, http://www.santafetrailscenicandhistoricbyway.org/amache.html.

[3] Jacobus TenBroek, Edward N. Barnhart, and Floyd W. Matson, *Prejudice, War and the Constitution* (Berkeley: University of California Press, 1958), 84.

[4] Ibid., 39. The authors present a comprehensive overview of Caucasians, attitudes toward Asians—both Chinese and Japanese.

[5] Ibid. 51.

[6] Morton Grodzins, *Americans Betrayed: Politics and the Japanese Evacuation* (Chicago: University of Chicago Press, 1949), 2–111.

[7] "Ozawa v. United States (1922)," accessed December 23, 2016, http://encyclopedia.densho.org/Ozawa_v._United_States/.

[8] S. H. Hall, "Consistent Missionary Work," *Gospel Advocate*, December 8, 1932, 1308.

[9] S. H. Hall, "H. Ishguro," *Gospel Advocate*, November 25, 1920, 1141.

[10] Robert S. King, "Does It Pay?," *Gospel Advocate*, October 16, 1930, 1001.

[11] Erroll Rhodes, "The Work in Tokyo," *Gospel Advocate*, February 10, 1927, 127.

[12] S. H. Hall, "Ishiguro's Work," *Gospel Advocate*, March 15, 1923, 253.

[13] F. B. Shepherd, "With Ishiguro in Los Angeles," *Gospel Advocate*, October 16, 1930, 1000.

[14] Toku Mazawa, Letter, *World Vision*, April, May, June 1940, 4.

[15] S. H. Hall, "Japanese Church in Los Angeles Reopens," *Gospel Advocate*, May 23, 1946, 492.

[16] S. H. Hall, "The Japanese Mission," *Gospel Advocate*, August 27, 1925, 820, 821; B. D. Morehead, "Our Trip to Los Angeles," *Gospel Advocate*, August 27, 1925, 821.

[17] Don Carlos Janes, "News and Notes," *Missionary Messenger*, November 1941, 1092.

[18] Michi Weglyn, *Years of Infamy: The Untold Story of America's Concentration Camps* (New York: William Morrow and Company, 1976), 46.

[19] Ibid.

[20] Jacobus TenBroek et al., *Prejudice, War and the Constitution*, 100.

[21] Ibid.

[22] Ibid.

[23] Ibid.

[24] Ibid.

[25] Suzanne Stamatov, "Japanese-American Internment Camps in New Mexico 1942–1946," accessed December 23, 2016, http://www.newmexicohistory.org/people/japanese-american-internment-camps-in-new-mexico-1942-1946. The Lordsburg camp in 1944 became the "dumping grounds" for 5,500 German uncooperative noncommissioned prisoners of war. The camp was constructed to house 3,000 men. It was a camp also for Italian prisoners of war. Millie Pressler, "Lordsburg Internment POW Camp," accessed December 23, 2016, http://newmexicohistory.org/places/lordsburg-internment-pow-camp.

[26] S. H. Hall, "Japanese Church," *Gospel Advocate*, May 23, 1946, 492.

[27] Michi Weglyn, *Years of Infamy*, 76.

[28] Ibid., 77; Daisuke Kitagawa, *Issei and Nisei: The Internment Years* (New York: Seabury Press, 1967), 53, 54.

[29] Jacobus TenBroek et al., *Prejudice, War and the Constitution*, 125.

[30] Michi Weglyn, *Years of Infamy*, 77.

[31] Ibid., 78–80.

[32] Thomas Shigekuni, whose family was interned at Camp Amache in Colorado, remembers their times in Santa Anita and Camp Amache. He shared with the author these memories on several occasions. On May 1, 2013, he responded to a series of questions sent to him. Tom was about twelve years of age when his family was transported to Camp Amache.

[33] Kitawaga, *Issei and Nisei*, 64, 65.

[34] Michi Weglyn, *Years of Infamy*, 80, 81.

[35] Tom Shigekuni in response to questions, May 1, 2013.

[36] Konrad Linke, "Santa Anita (Detention Facility)," *Densho Encyclopedia*, accessed December 20, 2016, http://encyclopedia.densho.org/Santa%20Anita%20(detention%20facility)/.

[37] Michi Weglyn, *Years of Infamy*, 84.

[38] Bonnie J. Clark, "Amache (Granada)," *Densho Encyclopedia*, accessed December 23, 2016, http://encyclopedia.densho.org/Amache_%28Granada%29/.

[39] Thomas N. Shigekuni, "'Faith Odyssey' Evokes a Cousin's Response," *Christian Chronicle*, July 2002, 31.

[40] Michi Weglyn, *Years of Infamy: The Untold Story of America's Concentration Camps*.

[41] Konrad Linke, "Santa Anita (Detention Facility)," *Densho Encyclopedia*, accessed December 20, 2016, http://encyclopedia.densho.org/Santa%20Anita%20(detention%20facility)/.

[42] Thomas N. Shigekuni, Letter, *Christian Chronicle*, July 2002, 31.

[43] S. H. Hall, "Japanese Church," *Gospel Advocate*, May 23, 1946, 492.

[44] Correspondence with Thomas Shigekuni, May 1, 2013.

[45] Email from Frances Palmer, who was three years of age when she went with her parents and grandparents to Amache internment camp. She was known then and for several years as Fumi Itow. April 8, 2013.

[46] S. H. Hall, "Japanese Church," *Gospel Advocate*, May 23, 1946, 492.

[47] Thomas N. Shigekuni, *Japan: An Odyssey of Faith*, a booklet published in 2002. Copy in possession of Robert Hooper.

[48] Ibid. All quotations and information in this paragraph are from Thomas Shigekuni's letter to the editor of the *Christian Chronicle*.

[49] Ibid.

[50] Jonathan Shikes, "Forward into the Past," *Westword News* (Denver), September 13, 2001, accessed December 20, 2016, http://www.westword.com/news/forward-into-the-past-5067922/.

[51] Thomas James, *Exile Within: The Schooling of Japanese Americans, 1942–1945* (Cambridge, MA: Harvard University Press, 1987), 43.

[52] Ibid., 63.

[53] Bonnie J. Clark, "Amache (Granada)," *Densho Encyclopedia*.

[54] Correspondence with Thomas Shigekuni, May 1, 2013.

[55] Bonnie J. Clark, "Amache (Granada)," *Densho Encyclopedia*.

[56] Bever's son, Dr. Ron Bever, is a retired professor at Oklahoma Christian University. He has a photograph of his family with members of the Japanese church taken on March 1, 1943. The Shigekuni family is in the photograph.

[57] Richard Reeves, *Infamy: The Shocking Story of the Japanese American Internment in World War II* (New York: Henry Holt and Company, 2015), 175, 291.

[58] *Westword News*, September 13, 2001.

[59] Editor, *Christian Chronicle*, "Letters to the Editor," accessed December 23, 2016, http://www.christianchronicle.org/article/letters-to-the-editor.

[60] The attitude of Americans was generally anti-Japanese during World War II, often encouraged by an anti-Japanese press and propaganda in Hollywood films. Yukikazu Obata composed a paper on attitudes of members of American Churches of Christ toward Japan and its people during World War II. He titled his 2012 paper "Knowing Your Enemy: How American Churches of Christ Viewed the Japanese People during WWII," Special Collections, Beaman Library, Lipscomb University, Nashville, Tennessee. Obata studied religious journals among Churches of Christ during the war years. He did not find any overt anti-Japanese feelings in the papers and magazines. *The Christian Leader* of Cincinnati, Ohio, came the closest to advocating an anti-Japanese attitude. He concluded that American Christians who knew missionaries who had served in Japan were more likely to see at least some of the Japanese as brothers and sisters in Christ.

[61] Ibid.

[62] Correspondence with Thomas Shigekuni, May 1, 2013.

[63] Ibid.

[64] S. H. Hall, "Japanese Church," *Gospel Advocate*, March 23, 1946, 492, 493.

[65] Thomas N. Shigekuni, "My Memories of George Pepperdine," a printed memory written on June 28, 2010, copy in the possession of Robert Hooper; Thomas N. Shigekuni, *Japan: An Odyssey*.

[66] Westside Church of Christ, accessed December 22, 2016, http://www.westsidechurchofchristla.org.

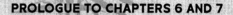

A DEVASTATED PEOPLE AND THE
COMING OF MILITARY CHRISTIANS

The final events of the war between Japan and the Allied nations took place with the dropping of atomic bombs on Hiroshima and Nagasaki on August 6 and 9, 1945. Less than a month later, on September 2, the surrender of Japan took place aboard the USS *Missouri*. Having led the victory in the Pacific, General Douglas MacArthur was appointed as the head of the Allied occupation of Japan. President Truman, with advice from MacArthur, chose to postpone the formal surrender until Sunday, September 2, because he wanted all the Allies represented: on that day there were 250 war ships in Tokyo harbor from many nations from around the world represented at the surrender of Japan, bringing a conclusion to World War II.

Even though the surrender was multinational, the United States was solely responsible for the post–World War II occupational government, with General Douglas MacArthur as Supreme Commander for the Allied Powers (SCAP).[1] The government would remain in place until 1952 when Japan regained her independence, although many close ties remained with the United States (i.e., military bases remained on Japanese soil).

The new government, imposed from the top down, was a democracy, but with certain specifications, including not allowing Japan to initiate war. The United States hoped that the establishment of a democratic government would prohibit the growth of communism in Japan. Furthermore, before the passage of the imposed constitution, MacArthur initiated equal rights for women, freed political prisoners—including communists—and implemented a new land policy that broke up large land holdings.[2] But the new government could not immediately solve the problems facing the devastated Japanese people.

It is next to impossible to convey in words the conditions prevalent in Japan at the close of World War II. When the American occupational force arrived in Japan, they were appalled at the total destruction they saw everywhere. The economic structure of the nation had been totally destroyed. The average American knew of the physical destruction of Japan only through photographs in magazines, newspapers, and Movietone News. They saw the burned out cities but could not see defeat. And of course, everyone remembered the nuclear destruction of Hiroshima and Nagasaki. As a result, the Japanese people faced a tremendous housing shortage. In the Ibaraki Prefecture, and certainly elsewhere, a host of people lived in caves two and three years after surrender in 1945. Others lived in makeshift houses in shanty towns. As of 1948, 3.7 million families continued to have inadequate housing. Seeing such devastation, it amazed Edwin Jocke, Jr., a special presidential envoy, that the Japanese had held out in war as long as they did.[3]

In Tokyo, the destruction was so complete that five million of its seven million inhabitants left the city, looking for places to live. Added to the devastation of Tokyo, sixty-five more Japanese cities had an estimated 40 percent of their urban areas destroyed. This left 30 percent of the population homeless, a percentage that adds up to nine million men, women, and children without quality living conditions. John Dower, in his classic study, quoted an observer: "In every major city, families were crowded into dugouts and flimsy shacks or, in some cases, were trying to sleep in hallways, or on subway platforms, or on sidewalks." The rural areas were not exempt; living standards fell to 65 percent of the prewar standards.[4]

The number of Japanese who died on faraway islands, or in Manchuria, China, Indo-China, or the Philippines, is staggering. The often cited number is 1.74 million military personnel at the time of surrender. Add civilian deaths and the number rises to 2.7 million. These numbers add up to 3 or 4 percent of the total population of Japan in 1941. Compare these numbers to the military deaths of the United States: 418,000 of a total population of 132,000,000. Few US civilians died as a result of war. Even more amazing, at the end of the conflict, as many as 6.5 million Japanese, including 3.5 million soldiers and sailors, stranded in faraway places, faced difficulties returning home to Japan.[5]

Among the homeless were thousands of children left orphaned, with parents dying in battle or as a result of terror from the skies. In many cases, they may have simply become separated from mothers and fathers. As of February 1948, there remained 123,510 orphaned or homeless children. They lived wherever they could find shelter: "railroad stations, under trestles and railroad overpasses, in abandoned ruins." They survived in every sort of way, by stealing, recycling cigarette butts, selling newspapers, even picking pockets. Some teenage girls turned to prostitution. Often officials rounded up these young women like cattle and housed them in detention centers. It took years for these children to become a part of society or even be allowed to enter the educational system.[6]

Hunger was rampant. In fact, hunger was a concern in Japan even at the beginning of World War II. And many Japanese soldiers, by war's end, were dying of malnutrition. Factory workers, needed for the war effort, suffered from beriberi, caused by a lack of nourishment. As a result, a large percentage of work hours were lost every week. Rice, the staple of the Japanese diet, was often not available. Instead, the people ate barley and sweet potatoes. When these were in short supply, they substituted anything available—acorns, grain husks, peanut shells, and even sawdust. To make matters worse, the 1945 rice crop was a disaster—only 40 percent of a normal year. Early in October 1945, the minister of agriculture learned that Tokyo had only a three months' supply of rice. As a result of these reports, it was thought that as many as 8,000,000 Japanese would die of starvation. These deaths might have occurred, had the United States not shipped boatloads of food to Japan, a program that continued until the end of occupation in 1952.

Instead of the normal diet of steamed rice, many people lived on a thin gruel, made with a limited amount of rice. To make matters worse, most of the food supplies ended up on the black market. The rich dined well in specialty restaurants, while the poor people were taught how to prepare bamboo shoots as food. Resulting from a lack of wholesome food, in both 1946 and 1947, the caloric intake of the Japanese people dropped as low as one quarter to one-third of the needed 2,200 calories. Because of a lack of food, elementary children were, on average, smaller in 1945 than in 1937.[7]

It was into this depressed nation that missionaries from America brought hope to a tired and defeated people. The Japanese had been involved in war since 1931, when through conquest they gained control of Manchuria. After fourteen long years of war, left broken down and in shambles, Japan desperately needed a new beginning.

First Arrivals from Churches of Christ: Soldiers and Airmen Look for a Church Home

When the occupational forces of the United States entered Japan, the military members of Churches of Christ looked for and quickly discovered the Zoshigaya church in Tokyo. Two men, including Harold Savely, reported their meetings with the Japanese church. Savely had arrived in Tokyo on September 17, 1945, only 15 days after the official surrender of Japan. Soon after his arrival, he penned two letters to S. H. Hall, the minister for the Russell Street Church of Christ in Nashville, telling of his visit to the Zoshigaya church.

Hall published both letters in the *Gospel Advocate*. Savely had spent Sunday, September 23, locating Christians in Tokyo, especially noting his visit with Yunosuke Hiratsuka, who was a longtime preacher for the Kamitomizaka church in Tokyo. Since firebombing destroyed their building during the war, the burned-out members joined the Zoshigaya church. The church elected Hiratsuka an elder, and he also served as a minister until 1943. Hiratsuka was anxious to contact J. M. McCaleb, Harry Fox, and O. D. Bixler.[8] He looked forward to his Christian friends returning to Japan as quickly as possible.

In a second letter, Savely wrote that the Japanese Christians "asked me to *please* tell the brethren in America, everywhere, that they still remember them and have not ceased to pray for them. Their great wish is to see *many* fellow workers come to Japan as soon as possible and help them. They need them so much!"[9]

A second soldier, Major Clyde H. Bynum, of the Fifth Air Force and a member of the Auburn, Alabama, Church of Christ prior to World War II, arrived in Japan on October 13, 1945. Stationed thirty-five miles north of Tokyo, he and a few men met each Sunday on base for worship. Bynum's girlfriend sent him the articles from the *Gospel Advocate* written by Harold Savely (the articles written by S. H. Hall containing letters from Savely) that included information about the Zoshigaya church in Tokyo. Bynum and his friends located the church, and "each Sunday some of the members rode in a jeep or train to worship with the church there." Transferred to Tokyo, Bynum advertised in *Stars and Stripes*, giving the address of the Maiji Building where he and others began an American military church. On February 17, 1946, twenty-seven men met for worship. Because the men were in transition, the numbers fluctuated, the largest being thirty attendees. The leaders arranged the church's meetings so the men could also attend the Zoshigaya church.[10]

The vast majority of the military personnel stationed in Japan at the end of the war were soon relocated to the United States. These men told the churches in America about the needs of the Japanese people. Beginning in 1948, the Auburn, Alabama, Church of Christ supported Charles and Norma Doyle as missionaries to Japan. Very likely, Major Bynum influenced the decision. Over the next several years, military personnel connected with Churches of Christ contributed substantially to the work of churches on military bases and even to the establishment of the Yoyogi-Hachiman church in Tokyo. They were the foundation for Churches of Christ in the Tokyo area of Japan after World War II.

Endnotes

[1] John W. Dower, *Embracing Defeat: Japan in the Wake of World War II* (New York: W. W. Norton, 1999), 33–43. Dower's massive study of Japan after World War II until 1952, when the occupation ended and Japan returned to self-rule, is very thorough.

[2] Ibid., 60–84.

[3] Ibid., 44.

[4] Ibid., 44–46, 115.

[5] Ibid., 45, 48.

[6] Ibid., 62, 63.

[7] Ibid., 93–97.

[8] S. H. Hall, "News from Japan," *Gospel Advocate*, November 1, 1945, 608.

[9] S. H. Hall, "Japan Heard from Again," November 29, 1945, 671.

[10] Homer P. Reeves, "The Church in Tokyo," March 7, 233; Pryde E. Hinton, "The Opportunity of the Centuries in Japan," April 25, 1946, 403.

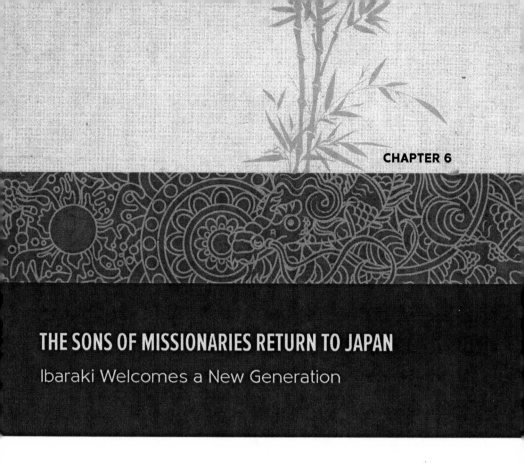

CHAPTER 6

THE SONS OF MISSIONARIES RETURN TO JAPAN

Ibaraki Welcomes a New Generation

On October 10, 1947, Harry Robert Fox, Jr., and his wife, Gerri, sailed for Japan on board the SS *Marine Swallow*, the first of the young missionaries to enter the war-torn country. On the same ship was O. D. Bixler, returning to Japan after his 1946 appointment in Japan as "representative missionary." They arrived at Yokohama on October 23 after thirteen days on the Pacific Ocean.[1] The war had been over two years when a new, younger group of missionaries eagerly, but with trepidation, entered Japan.

The young missionaries who chose to go to Japan had no idea how they would be accepted. They could possibly be seen as "outsiders" coming to Japan as victors looking to dominate a defeated people. They certainly had heard the reports of the success of Fox, Sr., and Bixler in Japan. But

171

how would this new generation of American missionaries be accepted by a former "enemy"? They had no idea what to expect.

But before these young missionaries could enter Japan, it was necessary to qualify for the task. This was the responsibility given to Orville D. Bixler, who turned to George Benson, a former missionary to China and then president of Harding College, for help in getting Churches of Christ interested in Japanese missions. Benson, in turn, conveyed Bixler's hopes and dreams for Japan through the religious papers read by members of Churches of Christ.

Bixler's travels throughout the length and breadth of Japan revealed that the Japanese people were eager to have Churches of Christ to organize and operate schools for their young people. According to Bixler, the American occupation forces shared this enthusiasm for schools. Applauding the revelations from Bixler, Benson wrote, "I hope that we will not be disappointed in the response in both personnel and in financial support to enter these open doors in Japan and to render a great service to our Master in heaven."[2] Harding College would answer the call with at least four of its graduates and their wives among the first to enter the open doors of Japan.

It had been twelve years since Harry Robert, Jr., and Logan Fox had been in Japan. Their father and mother, Harry Sr. and Pauline, and their seven children left Japan in 1935 because of Harry's health problems. From 1934 forward, the Christian community in Nashville became central to the Fox family, with Harry Robert, Jr., emphasizing the great impact that Nashville had on him: "My years at Lipscomb were among the most enjoyable in all my life."[3] In the meantime, Harry Fox, Sr., became an employee of Lipscomb when the college appointed him business manager. In addition, the board of directors elected him to the board. He also became the preacher for the campus church.

The Fox parents enrolled their children in the campus school and college. Both Harry Robert and Logan were exceptional students while at David Lipscomb College. Harry Robert, the oldest child, garnered most every honor except Bachelor of Ugliness, the premier honor for a Lipscomb male student. His good friend, C. W. Bradley, received that honor. Harry

Robert graduated Lipscomb in 1942. Logan, like his brother, was totally involved in campus activities, especially in dramatics and public speaking. Logan graduated in 1943. Both young men returned to Los Angeles to finish their undergraduate degrees at George Pepperdine College. Between Lipscomb and Pepperdine, Harry Robert spent one year at Harding College where he came under the influence of J. N. Armstrong.[4]

Not all of Harry Robert's education occurred in the classroom. He committed himself to Jesus in 1933 when J. D. Fenn baptized both Harry and Logan. However, as Harry Robert reviewed his life, 1932 may have been the turning point of his Christian walk. At age eleven, Harry Robert listened to George A. Klingman at the Highland Church of Christ in Louisville. Most preaching he had previously heard was routine, matter-of-fact sermons. But Klingman was different; he filled his sermon with joy. As years passed, he listened to and received his life's direction from such men as J. N. Armstrong, R. C. Bell, G. C. Brewer, and E. H. Ijams. These preachers and teachers gave direction to Fox's total Christian life; and along with Klingman, they emphasized the grace and love of God.[5]

Logan had known for some time that he would return after World War II to Japan as a missionary. Harry Robert, however, faced a major spiritual crisis because he was not convinced that missionary work was his calling. Pressured on every side to return to Japan, he said of himself what Paul felt: "O wretched man that I am. Who shall deliver me from the body of this death?" Responding to his crisis, Harry Robert told of his dilemma: "What death? The death of agreeing that I was indeed obligated to perform a duty I felt unable to perform."[6]

In May 1942, a trip resolved his inner conflict when, with his father and Logan, he heard E. Stanley Jones at McKendree Methodist Church in downtown Nashville. Listening intently to every word the former missionary to India spoke, Harry Robert recalled later: "By the time the sermon was over I had received the answer to my ten-year quest. I had been shown what 'Christianity' was all about, namely a 'religion' centered in the person of Christ." Continuing, he said, "I had now been given a central, *personal* focus for my faith and my life. Christ had come alive and *real* for me!" The next morning, when Harry Robert attended his classes at Lipscomb, even his fellow students noticed a difference in their friend. From that day forward, he knew he would return with renewed dedication to Japan as a missionary.

Following Lipscomb, the brothers enrolled in George Pepperdine College, where they earned their college degrees. While a student at Pepperdine, Harry Robert met Geraldine Paden, the sister of the Paden brothers who led mission efforts in Italy after World War II. They married on September 8, 1944. Almost a year earlier, on September 23, 1943, Logan married Madeline Clark. Following graduation, Harry Robert enrolled in Union Theological Seminary in New York City. While a student there, O. D. Bixler called to encourage him to go to Japan. He perfectly fit the requirements for admission into Japan as a missionary. Knowing this to be his call, he dropped out of the degree program and, with the approval of the faculty, attended the classes without credit. Needing financial support, he approached Long Beach, California's Ninth and Lime Church of Christ. They agreed to sponsor him.

In the meantime, Logan Fox entered the University of Chicago, where he earned a master's degree in psychology. He was teaching at George Pepperdine College when he received his call to return to Japan. The church near the campus, the Vermont Avenue Church of Christ, agreed to support Logan and Madeline in Japan, the country of his birth.

"Be Still and Know God": Harry and Gerri Arrive in Japan

Getting their first glimpse of the devastation in Yokohama, Harry Robert described what they saw as they traveled across Japan. He noted the housing shortage and the shanty towns in the cities: "If the housing shortage seems severe in America it is ten-fold worse here, and what houses we have to live in are cold from lack of heat and dark for lack of light." Destitution was rampant among the majority of the people: "Anyone who has anything at all is never safe from robbery." On one occasion, they returned home to find they had been robbed of food and clothing, things needed most by a destitute people. Roads were almost impassable. The trains were so overcrowded that catching a ride between the cars was oftentimes the only travel mode available. Harry Robert believed it would take years for the situation to improve.[7] The larger cities, bearing the brunt of the bombing, had not yet recovered. They had been totally destroyed by firebombings, with thousands of people dying in the raids.

With the exception of Rhodes, Bixler, and Hettie Lee Ewing, Harry Robert and Gerri Fox were the only Church of Christ missionaries in Japan. Bixler, having lived in Japan since 1918, except for the war years, became acquainted with important men in government and business. His friendship with government officials led to an offer of land in Ibaraki for a school. This became the focus of the young missionaries arriving in Japan in 1947 and 1948.

Harry Robert was at home in Japan, but what an adventure for Gerri Paden Fox. Writing to the Japanese people in 1970 after returning from a visit to Japan, she recalled bewilderment when leaving the ship in Yokohama, gazing upon the horrors of war and its aftermath:

> Why did God choose for me to live in Japan? I can only—from my own prayerful quest—find God and myself first of all, and then give to you the benefits of what you have drawn out of me and all you have revealed to me. I am forever different because of living among you, intimately for 10 years, and distantly for another 20 years.
>
> I came to you first at age 23, expecting our first child, fearful—and overwhelmed to see what my country had just done to your country. That was my pain in relation to you in my youth in 1947.
>
> Out of the conflict of wanting to run away, but knowing deep down that I had seen too much of your suffering in those early post-war years, to ever forget. There was no place to run— for the memories would go with me, plus the awareness that I had not stayed and helped.

Later in the essay she revealed her innermost feelings: "Again, why did God choose Japan for me? My conclusion is—that you [the Japanese people] are so much like the real me—that when I got lost myself, from birth or early childhood—he sent me to you to restore myself . . . you also helped restore me to that yearning within to 'BE STILL AND KNOW GOD.'"[8] Being a missionary's wife—and especially the wife of Harry Robert Fox, Jr., a man who was, according to Gerri, 90 percent Japanese—made for a heavy burden during those early years of living among the Japanese people and so far away from America.

Back in Yokohama, Harry Robert was contacted by a judge in the Tokyo courts by the name of Brother Inomata, requesting him to teach a weekly Bible class for himself and nine other judges. What a challenge this must have been for Harry Robert—a class of ten judges! This was quite an opportunity for the young American missionary. On January 12, 1948, he held the first session. "Ten men were present and most of them showed a keen interest in the Christian religion."[9] From these studies, Harry baptized one of the judges, a Judge Oga.

This and other opportunities would cause Harry Robert to be in a dilemma a few months later—should he remain in the Yokohama-Tokyo vicinity or should he move northward to Ibaraki? While dealing with his dilemma, in November, he welcomed his father, Harry Fox, Sr., to Japan. He had overseen the transportation of almost two hundred goats from the United States for the benefit of the poorer Japanese people. They would provide milk every day and also serve long-term for breeding purposes. It was a project of "Heifers for Relief," a nonprofit organization that helped the needy in impoverished countries.[10] Harry Robert, recognizing the importance of the goats to the Japanese, wrote, "It is hard to describe in words the great deprivation which millions of the people in Japan who are still suffering as a result of wartime destruction which America escaped entirely."[11] Other goats would arrive in the summer of 1948.[12]

As important as these events were, they were nothing compared to the birth of Harry Robert and Gerri's first son, Kenneth. He arrived five weeks early on January 5, 1948. All planning had been predicated on an expected delivery date of February 9. Harry Robert referred to January as the "great interruption." He now fully understood "why the Occupational Government has consistently refused the entrance into Japan of babies under a year old. There simply are not the facilities in war-ravaged Japan for parents to give such infants the care they need." He added, "For a while we almost reached the brink of despair, but the Lord delivered us and gave us strength in our time of need."[13]

Young Harding Graduates Arrive

The Fox family received a morale boost on January 16, 1948, when three young couples—Virgil and Lou Lawyer (sponsored by Southside Church of Christ, Fort Worth, Texas); Charles and Norma Doyle (sponsored by the Auburn, Alabama, Church of Christ); and Joe and Rosa Belle Cannon (sponsored by the Fern Avenue Church of Christ, Toronto, Canada)—arrived in Yokohama. All the men were recent graduates of Harding College. O. D. Bixler met them, shedding tears of happiness at their arrival. They immediately went to Erroll Rhodes's home, where an excellent American meal awaited them.[14]

Arriving on the SS *Flying Scud* on April 5, 1948, Logan and Madeline Fox joined the four young couples destined to settle in the Ibaraki Prefecture. On arrival, Logan reflected, "We realize that the beginning of the fulfillment of years of dreaming was at hand. At last we are in Japan!" The Logan Foxes lived a month with his brother's family in Totsuka, near Yokohama. It was time well spent. After thirteen years' absence, he needed time to become reacquainted with Japan. Logan was impressed by the guidance and support Bixler gave to the young missionaries: "It is because of [Bixler's] efforts and his contacts that we are as well prepared as we are to enter into the door of opportunity God has opened for us."[15]

Another missionary couple arrived in Japan on May 2, 1948, when R. C. and Nona Pauline Cannon (sponsored by Central Church of Christ, Pasadena, California) arrived in Yokohama. R. C. (Carroll), a Harding College graduate of 1939 and also a graduate of Pepperdine College, was thirty years of age and considered the "old man" among the new missionaries. Edwin Washington McMillan encouraged Cannon to replace Bixler as the clearing person for missionaries from Churches of Christ.[16] Cannon reluctantly accepted the responsibility. As a result, the Cannons remained in the Tokyo region until 1949 when they joined the faculty of the soon-to-be established Ibaraki Christian College. The early team for the influential Ibaraki institution (discussed in Chapters 8 and 9) was now in place.

Edwin Washington McMillan Leads the Way

The young men and women who made their way to Japan in 1947 and 1948 carried the heavy workload in Ibaraki for ten solid years. However, the work of a very mature preacher from an established church in Memphis, Tennessee, must be recognized for his contributions to mission work in Japan. During the fall of 1947, the Union Avenue Church of Christ sent Edwin Washington McMillan on a fact-finding tour to survey the possibility of supporting mission work in Japan. The elders of Union Avenue were especially interested in establishing a Bible school.

E. W. McMillan had preached for the Central church in Nashville; the College church in Abilene, Texas; and then the Union Avenue church from 1941 to 1950. Born in 1889 in New Baden, Texas, he brought a mature perspective to Japan and became an important advisor for the young missionaries.

The day McMillan flew out of the Memphis airport, five hundred members of the Union Avenue church gathered to see him off on his historic exploratory trip to Japan. The 1,200-member church provided $3,327 to cover his expenses. This was only a small monetary contribution that Union Avenue would make to mission work in Japan. Their greatest gift, yet to come, along with what other churches contributed, supported the founding and building of Ibaraki Christian College.[17]

In preparation for McMillan's visit to Japan, Harry Robert accompanied O. D. Bixler on the first of November to Ibaraki, where they met with Japanese Christians at Omika, the proposed site for the Bible school. The next morning, a Sunday, the two missionaries drove to the school site where they met 250 people gathered for worship on the lawn. Harry Robert, in his earlier years in Japan, had never seen such a large number of Japanese people gathered for worship. The largest crowd he remembered was no more than fifty persons. "The day was perfect for such an outdoor meeting, and the radiant sunshine all about us was paralleled by an equally warm and radiant spirit of Christian good-will." Bixler urged his Japanese brethren to match the zeal of their American brethren toward evangelizing Japan. He invited everyone to be present on November 16 when E. W. McMillan would be in Omika to survey the proposed location for the school.[18]

Shortly after McMillan's arrival in the middle of November, he joined O. D. Bixler and Harry Robert in Bixler's jeep for a ninety-mile adventurous journey to Omika. On arrival, they witnessed eleven persons baptized in the Pacific Ocean. On Sunday morning, they met with Japanese Christians for worship. Ryohachi Shigekuni, from the Ota church, preached.

The Americans and Japanese Christians, as one body, partook of the Lord's Supper. Later in the day, McMillan spoke to the expectant audience. Bixler interpreted for him. Said Fox, "It was one of the greatest speeches I have ever heard because of the magnificent spirit in which it was delivered. Needless to say, the whole Japanese audience was deeply impressed. This would have been so had not even a single word of his speech been translated, such a spirit transcends all linguistic and cultural differences, and men intuitively understand."[19] A number of men, both Japanese and American, arms entwined, gathered in prayer on the site for the proposed school.

McMillan returned to Memphis where he reported in January 1948 to the Union Avenue church and other invited churches and individuals. All preachers for Memphis Churches of Christ were present. The large assembly listened with rapt attention to McMillan's report of what he had experienced in Japan and the visit to the location of the proposed Ibaraki Christian College. He told of speaking through an interpreter seventeen times with good attention. However, he understood that Bixler's alleged premillennial views concerned many in his audience. This concern had to be solved before American Churches of Christ, he believed, would support missions in Japan.

An Issue That Would Not Go Away

Despite many difficulties, McMillan's enthusiasm for mission work in Japan did not diminish: "From the state of Ibaraki, one hundred miles northeast [of Tokyo], to the state of Shizuoka, one hundred miles southwest [of Tokyo], the Japanese people are calling for spiritual leadership." Interestingly, O. D. Bixler, early in Japan, had been emphasizing the call of the Japanese people for intentional instruction in Christianity.[20]

The issue of premillennialism, however, would not go away. Bixler announced, "I am stepping aside from any position of prominence in such a way that will please and enable you to work out your own program in Japan. But please do that." He further stated that he would cooperate fully with those who opposed him so that missionaries would come to Japan. However, such statements did not satisfy everyone. E. R. Harper, a strong opponent of premillennialism since the 1930s, suggested Bixler might change his views on the biblical texts in Revelation. The missionary answered Harper that he could not conscientiously change his long-held positions on Revelation 20—the chapter where John discusses the thousand-year reign of Christ. Christians debated whether it should be interpreted literally or symbolically—and what does "literal" mean?[21] In September 1949, a spokesman for the Union Avenue church emphatically stated, "The Union Avenue church is not now supporting, and will not support, a premillennialist."[22]

The editor of the *Gospel Advocate*, B. C. Goodpasture, interviewed Bixler when he visited Nashville. He told Goodpasture, "I am proposing to step down and out and turn it over to you brethren if you will go and get the job done." Goodpasture agreed with Bixler's decision. Then the editor urged churches to support mission efforts in Japan. "There seems to be no doubt that Japan is a promising field for the gospel. The church must not fail to send faithful men who will preach Christ to the disillusioned millions of Japan. These people with empty hands and hungry hearts look to America for help. This is a Macedonian call we must answer."[23]

The Bixler situation was bittersweet. The young missionaries in Japan spoke with very positive feelings about the help Bixler had given them on their arrival. He, along with the Rhodes, an avowed premillennialist, on January 16, 1948, met the young couples from Harding College at shipside when they arrived in Yokohama. For them, it was good to see American faces greeting them as they came ashore. Bixler cared for them in Tokyo until March 11, when they moved northward to Ibaraki. Joe Cannon noted, "Brother Bixler has been a great blessing to us. Through him we have made many wonderful contacts with Christian brethren in Japan—young and old." He added, "Brother Bixler is very fine to work with. The Japanese respect him highly."[24] In April, Bixler returned to the States. Later he would return to Japan to renew his mission work in Tokyo.

The Dream Becomes Reality: The Beginnings of Ibaraki Christian Schools

Before leaving Japan, Bixler, along with Harry Robert and Carroll Cannon, attended the board meeting for the new Christian high school scheduled to begin classes on April 19. The board of directors, with oversight of the proposed schools, decided to purchase for $6,000 the thirty acres that had been under option for a year. The long-term desire was to build a Christian college. But first they would begin with a high school. The board chose Virgil Lawyer as principal of the school. Joe Cannon was put in charge of the kindergarten and would also serve as business manager. Charles Doyle would conduct the night school. Japanese friends, both Christian and non-Christian, had raised 800,000 yen ($16,000) toward the opening of the school. They urged the opening for April 1948.

The missionaries received a warm welcome in Hitachi-Taga. There were children literally dancing in the street. The Hitachi Company offered tours of their facility. The city officials informed the missionaries that they would give 80,000 yen worth of lumber for the school. One man in Mito gave 200,000 yen for the educational effort, while a group of Japanese men gave another 200,000 yen for the school. Much of this Japanese support was the result of the favorable impression made by O. D. Bixler on his return to Japan in 1946.[25]

The three young Harding graduates were busy in Omika, preparing for the opening of the Christian school on April 19, not many days away. There was also an urgent call for evangelism.

Renewing Evangelism in Ibaraki

Ibaraki was the ideal section of Japan to renew mission work. Although pre–World War II missionaries had not converted large numbers, six churches had met regularly at the outbreak of the war. Before the war, the concentration of missionaries and native preachers in Japan was in Ibaraki.

The young men and women in Japan recognized the impact of the prewar missionaries. Immediately on arrival in Ibaraki, the young missionaries stated, "The work of former missionaries here has laid a commendable foundation. The Japanese Christians are very zealous and sincere in wanting to build a new Japan after the will of Christ."[26] O. D. Bixler underscored the strong possibility for evangelism when in 1947 he had a tremendous response to his preaching. He baptized seventy-nine persons of the two hundred believers baptized in concert with other American and Japanese teachers and preachers.[27] Here, both Japanese and Americans were baptized side by side, as brothers and sisters, in the wake of wartime animosity and destruction. Among the Christians in Ibaraki, Christ was more important than Americanism and Japanese nationalism.

It was of utmost importance that the young missionaries—Virgil and Lou Lawyer, Joe and Rosa Belle Cannon, and Charles and Norma Doyle—move quickly to Ibaraki. Language study in Tokyo had to wait. They could hire teachers in Omika to instruct them in the Japanese language—a process that continued for a year. It was Ryohachi Shigekuni who suggested Shion Gakuen as the name for the school, representing the four graces mentioned in Luke 2:52.

But first, they had to find places to live. Fortunately, Japanese Christians had been preparing for them. On arrival, they had a month to prepare for the opening of the high school. Also, there was a pent-up demand for missionaries to build on the foundations laid by pre–World War II missionaries. The six churches established by the earlier missionaries needed to be resurrected. The three young couples from Harding College and the sons of prewar missionaries had a major task before them. But with youthful vigor and a deep faith in God, they were equal to the task.

The housing needed by the missionaries was ready on arrival. The Doyles and the Cannons settled in Hitachi-Taga where Christians had prepared a duplex for them. Six miles away, Virgil and Lou Lawyer began housekeeping in a regular Japanese-style house. It was also furnished by Japanese Christians.[28] Lou Lawyer, having never experienced rural Japanese houses, remembered that her kitchen had a dirt floor.[29]

April 19 was soon upon them—the promised school had to open. By their hard work and dedication, it opened on time in a temporary building, surprisingly offered by a non-Christian, until the board of directors could construct a permanent building.[30] But it must not be forgotten that the school could not have opened had not the Union Avenue church in Memphis and its preacher, E. W. McMillan, provided the $6,000 to purchase thirty acres of a golf course in Omika owned by the Hitachi Company. With the cooperation of Japanese Christians, community friends, and American missionaries, the school opened as planned. It was a story of successful cooperation among former "enemies"—a true testament to the unifying power of Christian fellowship.

On opening day, 60 students—chosen from 110 who applied—enrolled on the tenth-grade level. The faculty included eight Japanese and two American teachers. McMillan announced, "That day the church made history in Japan." This was true in more ways than one. The school would be co-educational, unheard of in pre–World War II Japan. To employ the Japanese teachers, it was necessary to raise $400 every month for salaries. Again the Union Avenue church came to the rescue, providing salaries for the first three months.[31]

In order to work full time for the establishment of a top-quality high school and college in Japan, McMillan resigned as pulpit minister of the Union Avenue Church of Christ. However, the church continued to support McMillan's financial needs, including his travel expenses. They also remained committed to the financial needs of the schools. This was very important to the future of Ibaraki Christian College and high school.

The board of directors needed $100,000 to cover the cost of beginning the high school and college.[32] To facilitate his work in raising the necessary funds, McMillan moved to Abilene, Texas, to be nearer to those who were supporting the mission efforts in Ibaraki.[33] He would return to Japan in 1949 to oversee the opening of the college.[34]

While the opening of the school was important, equally so was the evangelization of the towns and cities of the Kuji River Valley. Harry Robert Fox, Jr., however, was torn between remaining in the Yokohama-Tokyo region and going with Logan to Ota. His work among the judges in the Tokyo court system must have had some impact on his dilemma—eight judges were attending the class in January 1948. He also had two other Bible classes and was preaching for the military church in Tokyo. With the arrival of Logan, Harry Robert was soon convinced that he, Gerri, and Kenny should join the missionaries and school staff in Ibaraki. Evidently Logan used as a good reason for moving to Ota the fact that their parents had lived and worked there. Said Harry Robert, "So we are quite happy over the prospects of moving up there around the first of June."[35]

Logan and Harry Robert made sure they were in Omika when the school opened on April 19. They enjoyed a reception given by Japanese Christians for the missionaries who had arrived in 1948. "Many beautiful expressions of Christian love and appreciation were extended to them by the Japanese brethren, and all present felt greatly strengthened and encouraged."[36] Harry Robert assured Christians in America that the school would never replace evangelism; instead, it "will rather serve to stimulate an increase in Evangelism."[37]

On April 30, the missionaries and Japanese Christians were in Yokohama to wish O. D. Bixler Godspeed as he boarded the *General Gordon* for the United States. He had spent two six-month very appreciated tours in Japan. Harry Robert spoke of him: "He had the thankless task of re-establishing the work over here amidst the difficulties of postwar conditions. We thank God for his faith and unflagging zeal which enabled him to carry on alone in the face of many discouragements."[38]

Although they could not yet speak Japanese, Doyle, Cannon, and Lawyer ventured into their communities, sharing the gospel of Christ through an interpreter. The three preachers held services at Hitachi-Taga and Ishiuchi. Virgil Lawyer baptized nine persons, eight from Hitachi. But there were other concerns facing the communities. Even though the people did not have an abundance of food, the greatest need was clothing—which was especially true for the many orphans, as many as five thousand, in rural Ibaraki. They were thankful for churches in America for sending clothing, but they needed much more.[39] There would continue to be a call for clothing over the next two or three years.

May was a good month for the Fox brothers. The Vermont Avenue and Ninth and Lime churches purchased a Ford automobile for Logan and Harry Robert. It had come to Japan on the ship with Logan and his family. Thus the brothers had transportation for traveling to more distant places for preaching engagements. They surmised that the automobile would allow them to do four times more work than traveling by public transportation. In May 1948, they received an invitation from Japanese Christians to come to Daigo, the location where their uncle, Herman Fox, had spent twenty years prior to World War II. They wished to welcome the Foxes back to Japan.

The Fox Brothers Return to Their Roots

The welcome involved much more than the remaining members of the Daigo church. A large meeting gathered in the Agricultural High School's auditorium, where nearly a thousand students and townspeople listened to a Christian message from the brothers. As they reminisced, memories flooded their minds. They remembered as youngsters trampling over the green rolling hills. They had walked the grounds of the agricultural school, but few people cared for the Christianity their father and uncle preached. The administration of the school would never have invited them to speak to the students. In 1948, everything had changed. The students and faculty listened intently to all the brothers had to say. At the end of their presentations, three persons confessed their belief in Christ. Immediately, they went down to the Kuji River for baptism. Said Harry Robert, "Thus, once more we had the pleasure of reaping fruit in a place where the ground had been patiently worked for many seemingly fruitless years."[40]

The following week Logan and Harry Robert accepted an invitation tendered by the Ota High School PTA to speak on their faith in Jesus Christ. This was a tremendous opportunity. Parents, teachers, and even city leaders, including the mayor and vice-mayor, gathered to hear the story of Jesus. Again, Harry Robert recalled the past: "During our former stay in Ota we were never favored with such wide-spread receptivity." Toward the end of the month, they returned to worship with the Ota church. "[I]t was an inspiration to worship with that fine group of Christians. . . . That afternoon three young ladies of high school age were baptized upon their confession of their faith in Christ."[41]

On June 7, both Fox families traveled to Ota when they moved into the house they had left in 1935. It was always referred to as the Morehead house, built by Barney and Nellie Morehead when they were in Japan between 1925 and 1930. Shortly after moving to Ota, the two families, according to custom, called on all their immediate neighbors, presenting each household with a gift. They also asked for their friendship. Within a few days, the neighbors returned the visits, bringing gifts to their new neighbors. They were accepted members of the community.

By the middle of the month, the brothers and wives opened boxes of food and clothing sent by Long Beach—Harry Robert's sponsoring church. After supplying the needs of Ota, they carried most of the clothing to the orphans' home at Nukada, a home begun by Brother Michio Suzuki soon after becoming a Christian. He had established the home in 1945 when he recognized the great numbers of homeless youngsters in Ibaraki. The remainder of the clothing was taken to Fukui. The community had sustained a major earthquake on June 28, which may have been as strong as the 1923 earthquake that destroyed Yokohama and Tokyo. Preliminary reports indicated that between five thousand and eight thousand lost their lives. Fortunately, the earthquake happened in a less-densely populated area of Japan.[42]

Even though Lawyer, Doyle, and Cannon had rushed to Ibaraki to open the school, Joe Cannon enthusiastically reported in August 1948 that thirty-eight persons had responded for baptism since their arrival on April 1. The Japanese people openly responded to Christianity. Since the end of World War II, three hundred baptisms happened throughout Japan. The cumulative number included the work of O. D. Bixler, Erroll Rhodes, and Japanese preachers.

The three Harding graduates also began publishing a monthly paper in Japanese called *Light and Life*. Using the energy only available to young adults, near the end of 1948, they also began a weekly paper called *Taga E No Fukuin* (The Gospel for Taga), distributed by a newspaper agency in Taga.[43] Additionally, Charles Doyle conducted an English night school three days each week. By the fall, he had enrolled 250 students studying the Bible while learning the English language.[44]

O. D. Bixler, although in the United States, reported the organization of twelve new Churches of Christ during the previous twenty-two months. He added, "None of us realized that such a great awakening, such open doors, would come in our lifetime." He remembered how difficult it had been to reach the Japanese people prior to World War II. Even though up to eighteen missionaries had served in Japan from 1918 to 1941 (from all accounts the numbers were forty or more), he was pleased that sixteen missionaries had already come to Japan since 1945.[45] The future looked very promising.

In Ota, the Fox families lived in the same house they had shared with their parents from 1930 to 1935. Prior to the move to Ota, the senior Foxes had lived in Tanakura in Fukushima Prefecture from 1924 to 1930 when Barney Morehead invited them to oversee the work in Ota. In July 1948 the brothers, full of memories, made a trip to Tanakura to hopefully renew friendships from twenty-eight years prior. Their father baptized few people during those years. "The people as a whole simply were not receptive to the gospel." Even though there were only a few baptisms, the Fox brothers' father and mother had taught a large Sunday school with 150 or so students.

However, on their return to Tanakura, they had a welcome surprise. An older gentleman, whom their father had baptized in 1930, welcomed the brothers. Now eighty years of age, he was pleased to see the two men who were only youngsters, ages nine and seven, when they moved from Tanakura. Harry Robert observed, "He still showed the same interest in the church and expressed a deep longing to meet with brethren once more." The Foxes assured their aged Christian brother that they would return to Tanakura to take him to Ota where he could share in worship with fellow Christians.[46]

Neither of the Fox brothers participated in teaching during the first year of the school. They kept busy filling the calls from churches, schools, and non-Christian groups. In August 1948, Harry Robert and Logan were invited to speak to a teachers' convention in Ota on the theme of "Education in Democracy." Because America had been victorious over Japan, the people wished to hear how democracy and Christianity had helped the United States defeat their country—there had to be a relationship. Logan spoke on the "History of American Democracy," while on the second day, Harry Robert discussed "Freedom and Responsibility." After each day's lectures, the speakers conducted question-and-answer sessions. Possibly because the Japanese had worshiped the emperor and Japan had lost the war, most questions concerned Christianity. The brothers emphasized how Christian principles had given rise to democracy in the founding years of the United States.[47]

In 1947, even before the arrival of Americans, Japanese Christians in Ibaraki began a gathering for Churches of Christ from throughout Japan. From August 25 through 28, 1948, a second meeting gathered at the summit of Nishi-yama (West Mountain) near Ota. The American missionaries compared it to the annual Yosemite Bible Encampment in California. Thus in 1948 all five missionaries, along with a number of Japanese evangelists, eagerly participated in the event. Christians came from almost every church in Japan. Each attendee was asked to bring enough rice for their daily meals. This meant that not only would all worship together; they also had their meals together, making the entire event a spiritual exercise.

The day began at 5:30 a.m. with a devotional, then breakfast at 7:00 a.m. From 7:30 to 8:30, each person shared in one type of work or another (e.g., washing dishes). For the next two hours, they had three presentations followed by a half an hour learning new songs. From 11:30 a.m. to 2:00 p.m., the attendees had time to visit and eat lunch, followed by three more speeches until 4:00 p.m., followed by thirty minutes of hymn singing. Until 7:00 p.m., they enjoyed another period of visiting and dinner. The day continued with introductions, since so many Japanese Christians had been denied fellowship during the war years, and hearing reports from the churches, followed by a question-and-answer session. Bedtime was 9:00 p.m.

The average daily attendance was seventy-five, with some of the sessions reaching one hundred attendees. The speeches covered a wide range of topics emphasizing basic Christian needs, remembering the lack of understanding among the many new converts. The presentations, shared by Japanese and American preachers and teachers alike, included R. Shigekuni, "Prayer"; Logan Fox, "The History of the Church"; Harry Robert Fox, "The Grounds for Belief in God"; Virgil Lawyer, "Organization of the Church"; Joseph Cannon, "Worship"; S. Mio, "Christian Character"; S. Oka, "The Obedience of Faith"; and M. Kikuchi, "The Revelation of God's Grace in Christ's Sacrifice" and "Christianity and Communism," a topic very important in Japan in the 1940s. With enthusiasm, each person in attendance agreed the gathering should be an annual event.[48]

Free to Evangelize

The first semester of Shion Gakuen—the Christian school—ended in July. This gave the three men who had been involved with the school since April 19 time to spend in week-long preaching opportunities. And it was a very successful summer. Joseph Cannon reported the results in both total attendance and conversions: Taga, 235 attendees; Hitachi, 580 present; Ishiuchi, 165 attendees; and Omika, 360 persons present. The total number of conversions was 118; since March the total was 156. After each preaching session, the custom was to have a question-and-answer period, often lasting an hour or two after the preaching service. Cannon marveled at the complexity of the questions presented to him during these meetings.[49]

The most important September event for the Fox brothers was an American-style gospel meeting in Ota, scheduled for September 26 through October 2. However, neither brother was prepared for the sickness of not one but both men, all within the short span of one week. They had decided that Harry Robert would do the preaching; then Logan, after the preaching session, would respond to the questions from the attendees. Everything had been planned—even the style of sermon Harry Robert would preach, with topics such as "What about God?"; "What about Christ?"; "What about Salvation?"; "What about the Christian Life?"; "What about Your Soul?"; and "What about the Future?" To accommodate the expected crowds, they rented the junior high school auditorium. They placed advertisements in the local paper, even providing the sermon titles. Three nights before the meeting, the Ota church met in fervent prayer. Everything was ready . . . except the preacher.

Before the meeting began, Harry Robert developed a severe cold; Logan had to preach and handle the question-and-answer sessions the first two nights. For the next two nights, Harry Robert, having recovered somewhat, carried out the sessions as planned. Then on the fifth day of the meeting, Logan fell prey to an even worse sickness than had attacked his brother. Out of necessity, while Logan was in bed, Harry Robert finished the meeting. Amazingly, even with the interruptions of their well-laid plans, fourteen persons responded for baptism.[50]

Experiencing for several months the ready acceptance of the gospel of Jesus Christ by the Japanese people from Yokohama to Ibaraki, Logan Fox praised Churches of Christ in America for their support of the missionaries in Japan: "Never before have so many individuals and so many congregations been interested in unselfishly sharing with the Japanese people the good news about Jesus Christ." He then recalled his experiences in Japan as a youngster. "Those of us who were in Japan in pre-war years and saw the stolid resistance that Christian missionaries met then can still hardly believe what we see now. Prior to World War II a force of half-a-dozen missionary couples baptized less than fifty a year. Now an equal number of workers baptized over 300 [in less than a year]."[51]

E. W. McMillan, although in the United States, kept the interest in the Japan mission work alive, especially the efforts expended in Ibaraki. Early in

1949, he wrote glowingly of the six couples in the Kuji River Valley. Where direct preaching had not been successful among the Japanese before World War II, the young missionaries were having great success in gathering large assemblies for preaching and question-and-answer sessions. As a result, he mentions that in only six meetings some two hundred persons responded for baptism.

Yet despite all their success in winning souls for Christ, a great concern among the missionaries was the large number of homeless children in Ibaraki. In 1949, Churches of Christ had only one small home for orphans, operated by Michio Suzuki. For lack of facilities and funding, he was only able to care for fewer than a dozen children. To meet the demanding needs of the large numbers of homeless Japanese children, their young lives completely shattered by war, McMillan, ever concerned for the needs of Japan, issued a call for Christians in America to donate just $10—money sufficient to care for one child for an entire month. It was a sum every Christian could give to meet the needs of thousands of homeless in Japan.

Always interested in every facet of Christianity, education remained at the top of E. W. McMillan's dreams. He believed a Christian college to be the future of Christianity in Japan. He foresaw an accredited high school and then a college where a standard curriculum would be offered, plus a nursing program and special Bible programs to educate preachers and church leaders. With a good college-trained leadership for churches, there would in the future be no need to send missionaries to Japan. To underscore his optimism, in less than a year, there were five hundred church members in Ibaraki—a good foundation for the future, especially underscored with a good educational foundation that would eventually manifest as Ibaraki Christian College.[52] There was still so much work to be done.

Christianity or Communism?

With the end of World War II, Japan was completely prostrate. The emperor had confessed that he was not a god. The Japanese people had grown to maturity with a commitment to their emperor—now where would they turn? Communism called for a completely secular society. To many, this seemed to be the best alternative because their god was only a man. Thus, in Japan, communism gained a strong following after World War II.

Deliberately, the Soviet Union did not return Japanese prisoners of war immediately to Japan. These ex-soldiers were taught communist doctrine before they were sent home. They would provide a means of gaining a strong communist presence in the politics of Japan.

In addition to these former soldiers, intellectuals who had been imprisoned before the war by the Japanese government were now free to teach communism. Historian John Dower states, "When Tokuda Kyūichi and several hundred other communists were released from prison, they became celebrities and instant heroes in a society whose old heroes had suddenly been toppled." General MacArthur, concerned, watched the growth of communism in Tokyo and beyond. To respond to the rise of communism, on June 6, 1949, he instituted a "Red Purge," then taking a bold step, "he ordered 34 members of the Party's central committee [to be purged]; the next day he extended this purge to 17 top editors of the party newspaper," who were removed from their positions.[53]

This surge of communism and MacArthur's strong opposition to it gave the six young men in Ibaraki many opportunities to present a contrast between communism and Christianity. Harry Robert Fox, Jr., knew the Japanese young people were seeking a "way." Communism presented a real challenge—it was an attractive alternative for a people who had lost their god, the emperor.

On October 21, 1948, Harry Fox Jr. traveled to Urizura to speak to a select group of young men. They requested that he speak on "Christianity and Communism." Writing in his monthly newsletter concerning communism, Harry Robert stated, "The communists are working early and late to sell the young people on communism as the Way, and more Japanese are hearing of communism than they are of Christ." But Fox believed, "yet in most cases where the Christian side of the story is told it is more successful in winning assent than is communism." Fearful that communism would continue to be a choice for young people, Fox urgently called for more missionaries to come to Japan to confront communism's secular appeal.[54] He emphasized Christian love and a focus on Christ as the true king rather than a political philosophy based on domination and control.

Thus Fox emphasized another way to combat communism—with Christian compassion. Sufficient food was difficult to come by among the

Japanese, but getting clothing, especially winter clothing, was much more difficult. Therefore, the six couples in Ibaraki constantly called for churches to send clothing to Japan. In the Hitachi-Taga area, the Harding couples distributed clothing as soon as they received shipments from the States. Joseph Cannon told Americans of the horrible situations endured by thousands of Japanese people: "Hundreds in the bombed areas are living in tin can shacks and hovels. Their clothing is ragged and dirty." The Christians responded generously, with a fellowship that extended beyond the false boundaries of nationalism or war, and had no trouble distributing all the clothing the churches could send to Japan.[55]

The Japanese people, financially unable to purchase clothing, appreciated the clothing sent by American Christians. Some even wrote letters to Joe Cannon, Charles Doyle, and Virgil Lawyer expressing their gratitude. One letter, from a widow without means to support her children, stated:

> Dear Mr. Cannon and Mr. Doyle: I want to inform you that I am a poor woman that received many good clothes some days ago. I wanted to express my gratitude, but couldn't because of my child's illness. My husband died one year ago, and now I am bringing up three children. I am facing a hard living with many troubles, but I live on only to see the growth of my children. I thank you indeed for your good clothes. Be careful of your health.
>
> Masa Yashimari

Inflation and scarcity of all consumer goods multiplied the difficulties of the average Japanese family.[56] But these hardships were seemingly no match for the power of Christian fellowship.

In early November 1948, the Ota church "began a full scale relief distribution." At the end of November, they continued to provide clothing for the community. "It has been done just in time because winter weather struck us on the 28th with sub-freezing temperatures." Harry Fox believed "the distribution of clothing helps to back up and confirm what we say in preaching the gospel of love; that the love of Christ is REAL, and is of higher quality than any other, extending even to enemies! Most of the people over here need clothing even worse than they do food, and when Christians show concern to meet their most urgent physical need the people are deeply appreciative." He concluded, "The winter has only begun and there are many months of freezing weather ahead."[57] Christian love far surpassed the political ideology of communism.

Progress Continues: A New Year, A New Dawn

December 1948 was a very busy month. On December 11, the board of directors of the Shion Gakuen assembled on the campus to begin construction of a classroom building. Logan Fox, in a ceremonial groundbreaking, turned the first spade of dirt, followed by each board member taking his turn. Immediately contractors began laying the concrete foundation. Carpenters, busy preparing lumber for the building, were rushing in January to erect the building in time for the opening of the school in April. If the building could be finished in April, the proposed college would open. The structure would be two stories, with classrooms for 120 high school students and 100 college students. Already on campus was the Quonset hut that would be used for home economics, and the first faculty house neared completion. The dream of E. W. McMillan, the recently arrived five American families, and Japanese Christians who urged the beginning of the schools was becoming a reality.[58]

In late March 1949, the Hitachi-Taga trio of missionaries had been in their field of work for almost a year. They amazed themselves at the results. The first year of school was behind them, and plans were in place for an even greater beginning in April. As they looked at evangelism throughout Japan, they reported 425 baptisms. Joe Cannon and Virgil Lawyer had organized a preacher's study class for Japanese men, meeting once each week for two hours. Lawyer drilled the students on Scriptures and sermon delivery, while Cannon taught preparation and organization of sermons. Twenty-five men enrolled, with an average of sixteen men attending each class. Such classes were viewed as important because "it is necessary for the church to have leadership now." Incidentally, the oldest attendee was a seventy-year-old man who had been baptized only a year before.[59] This older brother quickly engaged zealously in sharing the gospel. Cannon told how the elderly brother had found a woman on the verge of suicide. Having been caught selling goods on the black market, she had everything she possessed confiscated by authorities. The Christian man, showing compassion, provided her with food. In May 1949, he was seeking work for her.[60] He changed the woman's outlook on life.

The Fox brothers, working inland up the Kuji River Valley, had spent their first year in evangelism and answering calls from schools and cities to discuss Christianity. Within a year, some twenty churches were meeting, triple the number meeting before the war, putting strain on the missionaries' efforts to teach and encourage new Christians. To make matters worse, they could not get gasoline for their automobile. In December, they did not get their ration card for the month until the 28th! The 1948 Ford automobile often sat idle for lack of gasoline.

During the month, Harry Robert and Logan traveled to each church in their sphere to conduct Christmas programs. Harry Robert explained, "In war torn and poverty stricken Japan there are so few pleasures to be enjoyed that the people welcome every opportunity of having a little fun. When this pleasure can be of the wholesome kind afforded by Christmas it is only right that we do what we can to help them have such an experience." These parties began on December 19 and continued until December 30. Most often the Christmas programs coincided with Sunday preaching services. Usually there were those who asked for baptism, and in December it was not unusual to break ice in the Kuji River for this purpose. At Karasuyama, Harry Robert and those involved in the baptismal service walked an hour and a half to the river and back. The next day they repeated the trip when a young man asked for baptism.[61]

On March 21, 1949, the most important event of the month, and maybe the most important since the missionaries arrived in Japan after World War II, was the gathering in Mito of all Ibaraki churches. And what a pleasant surprise it was! The church in Mito was relatively new. Over five hundred persons, mostly Christians, assembled—what a joyous occasion! Never had such a large crowd gathered for worship. "The congregational singing compared favorably with that to which we Americans had been accustomed in the States, and that was another 'first' for the Japanese churches." Harry Robert Fox, on the occasion, allowed his mind to return to a past year. "I remember the first time I ever visited America and heard the marvelous singing in the churches over there [and] how impressed I was, and longed for the day when I could hear the same in Japan. At Mito this longing was fulfilled."[62] O. D. Bixler, who had just returned to Japan along with a friend from America, Robert Gill, enjoyed the gathering of Christians unlike any Bixler had seen in his many years in Japan.[63] The meeting gave new energy to everyone, including the missionaries and especially the Japanese Christians.

On March 19, Logan and his family moved into their home on the school campus. It was the house Harry Fox, Sr., and his family built in 1923 when they moved to Tanakura. When Harry Robert and Logan visited Tanakura in July 1948, they investigated the possibility of moving the house to the school campus. After finding the house in good condition, they made plans for the move. It pleased both Fox families to locate the house on campus. Neither family had had separate living quarters since they had married four and five years ago, respectively—and now they had their own homes.[64]

The Impact of Japanese Christians

It is impossible to convey how busy all five men were in the first year and several months they had been in Japan. Of course, the three Harding men had responsibilities with Shion Gakuen for the first school year. Thus they had limited time to spread far afield for evangelistic work. On the other hand, the Fox brothers traveled widely up the Kuji River Valley, visiting old churches and establishing new ones. Harry Robert and Logan also had two Japanese preachers who on many occasions traveled with them. The person who had held the churches together in the Ota area was Ryohachi Shigekuni. He was a very stabilizing force for Christians in Ibaraki during the war—and a very important person who helped the Fox brothers reach out in a wide area during their first year in Japan. He was also a major force in establishing the high school and the college in 1948 and 1949.

The other Japanese Christian, Masaichi Kikuchi, who had worked with Erroll Rhodes in Omiya prior to World War II, became a valuable worker alongside the Fox brothers. Rhodes and Kikuchi had established a church at Urizura, the home of Kikuchi, a few miles south of Omiya. When Harry Robert and Logan located in Ota, Kikuchi quickly made himself available to the brothers in evangelizing the interior of Ibaraki. According to Harry Robert, "He paved the way for us into almost every town and village in north-western Ibaraki. He arranged appointments for us in so many places that we had a hard time keeping up with him!"[65] Not only was he an effective evangelist; he was very helpful in the follow-up nurturing of Christians and churches. (Kikuchi is discussed more fully in Chapter 8.)

Preaching and teaching opportunities came from surprising places. In March 1949, Harry Robert, Logan, and Ryohachi Shigekuni accepted an invitation from a priest to speak at a Shinto shrine. The priest asked them to discuss "Democracy and Christianity." Harry Robert mentioned that he and Logan had passed the shrine many times as young boys. He never imagined the possibility of an invitation from a Shinto priest to teach in his shrine. There were more invitations to speak than they could fill.[66] One invitation Harry Robert and family accepted was to travel to Shizuoka, two hundred miles south of Ota, the city where Sarah Andrews and Hettie Lee Ewing lived and worked prior to the war. Ewing, having returned to Japan, invited the family down for Harry Robert to preach for two days, once on Saturday and twice on Sunday. Returning on April 7, Harry Robert had "to enter immediately into a full schedule of activities," including teaching in the inaugural year of Ibaraki Christian College.[67]

At the moment, the most important activity facing the six young families—with Nona and Carroll Cannon now located in Ibaraki—was the opening of Shion Gakuen Bible College on April 18. The classroom building, begun in December, was finished in time for the opening of school. While the Fox brothers had not been involved in teaching during the first year, they had been involved in a very intensive language study so they could teach their college classes in Japanese.[68] R. C. and Nona Cannon moved to Omika for the opening of both the high school and Bible college. Dr. Frances Campbell, from Pepperdine, joined the faculty to teach the sciences.

The faculty welcomed sixty students to initiate the Christian college. It was a historic day! Virgil Lawyer expressed joy when four hundred people gathered for the opening of the second session of the high school and the inaugural year of the college. He shared through the *Christian Chronicle* how thrilling it was to be present when a new Christian college opened. Paying tribute to the pre–World War II missionaries, Lawyer wrote, "Much has been said about what has been done in Japan since the war, but let us remember that unless brethren had been here to sow the seed we would not be reaping the harvest today."[69]

Logan Fox, the newly appointed academic dean of the college, reported a total of 180 students, with 120 in high school. They came from seven prefectures. All students studied the Bible an hour each day. Fox also wrote of the opening of the schools, "The story behind the building of this Christian school in Japan is a thrilling story of the victory of faith over doubts, fears, prejudices, and the discouragements of long lonely years." He paid tribute to E. W. McMillan, now president of the high school and college, for his commitment to building a school in Japan. And he gave tribute to the Union Avenue Church of Christ in Memphis, Tennessee, for their financial support.

But Logan Fox did not limit his accolades to Christians in America. He gave much credit to Ryohachi Shigekuni, who came back to Japan in 1927 from the United States to teach the gospel to his people. A mainstay of Churches of Christ for twenty years, he was an enthusiastic supporter of the concept of a Christian college in Japan. His twenty years had been spent mostly in Ibaraki Prefecture, living in the Morehead house in Ota after 1935. When missionaries found it necessary to leave Japan in 1940, it was Shigekuni who "faithfully served the Ota church and sister congregations in Ibaraki Prefecture" during the years of war. Fox said of him, he "patiently taught . . . wisely counseled . . . [and] quietly ran a dairy which provided milk for undernourished children."

A second Japanese Christian, Shiochi Oka, who converted with an entire church in Taga to Churches of Christ from the Presbyterian faith only two years before, brought his expertise to the college as business manager. He had twenty-five years of experience in Japanese colleges.[70]

To gain the maximum benefit from their time, all families, with the exception of the Harry Robert Foxes, now lived on or near the campus. Harry Robert and his family remained in Ota, eight miles from Omika. Five days each week, he commuted to teach his classes, teaching only in the mornings. Logan and Madeline Fox provided Campbell a small apartment, while the Carroll Cannons provided in their home an apartment for E. W. McMillan when he arrived in July. He would continue living with them for the remainder of his time in Japan.[71]

The last of May and into June, Harry Robert and Gerri Fox had to rush their son Kenny to an American hospital in Tokyo so he could be treated by American doctors. He had an infection, and after two or three days, he was much better, but he had to spend sixteen days in the hospital before being dismissed on June 15. Harry Robert, using his time well, searched for used books for the school's library. While Kenny was in the hospital, he and Gerri on June 5 went with Logan to Otsuki, fifty miles west of Tokyo, where Logan preached for the two-year-old church. Ed Brown and his wife, graduates of Abilene Christian, would work with the church after their arrival on June 7, 1949. Harry Robert also had the opportunity to meet with the church in Tokyo for the first time. Returning to Ibaraki, Kenny was completely recovered and at home "running around as friskily as before."[72]

The opening of the Bible college did not decrease the evangelistic responsibilities of the missionaries. Only Logan Fox and Frances Campbell gave full time to the school. The calls for evangelism increased; thus evenings and weekends were busy times for everyone, and it was difficult to fulfill all the calls for spiritual help. There was definitely more work than the six young missionaries could handle. They continued calling for more men and women to come to Japan. A few would come over the next several years, but never enough to meet the needs of the school or the requirements for evangelism.

It had been a very busy first year that far exceeded the expectations of the six young, idealistic missionary families. They looked enthusiastically and optimistically to the future.

Endnotes

[1] Harry Robert Fox, Jr., "My Life as a Missionary to Japan," unpublished essay. A copy is in Special Collection, Beaman Library, Lipscomb University, Nashville, Tennessee.

[2] George S. Benson, "Open Doors in Japan," *Gospel Advocate*, February 27, 1947, 195.

[3] Personal letter from Harry Robert Fox, Jr., January 5, 2012.

[4] Personal conversation with Harry Robert Fox, Jr., October 23–25, 2013.

[5] "Personal Conversion Testimony of Harry Robert Fox," unpublished paper shared with the author, October 23, 2013. A copy is in Special Collection, Beaman Library, Lipscomb University, Nashville, Tennessee.

[6] Personal Conversion Testimony of Harry Robert Fox.

[7] Harry Robert Fox, Jr. (ed.), *Japan Christian*, November 1947. Fox gave monthly reports to his sponsoring church and his friends for the entire time he was in Japan. It is a first-person account of the first ten years of post–World War II mission work in Ibaraki Prefecture and Fox's travels to other areas of Japan. These newsletters are in Special Collection, Beaman Library, Lipscomb University, Nashville, Tennessee.

[8] Gerri Paden Fox, "To My Dear Brothers and Sisters." This is an essay to Japanese Christians written after a trip to Japan in 1970. A copy of the essay is in Special Collection, Beaman Library, Lipscomb University, Nashville, Tennessee.

[9] Harry Robert Fox, Jr. (ed.), *Japan Christian*, December 1947.

[10] This organization continues today as Heifers International, headquartered in Little Rock, Arkansas.

[11] Harry Robert Fox, Jr. (ed.), *Japan Christian*, December 1947.

[12] Ibid., November 1947; Charles R. Brewer (ed.), "Foxes and Goats for Japan," *World Vision*, February 1948, 10.

[13] Harry Robert Fox, Jr. (ed.), *Japan Christian*, January 1948.

[14] Charles Doyle, "Doyle Says Japanese Opportunity Greater than Reported; Growth Seen in Numbers Converted in '47," *Christian Chronicle*, March 24, 1948, 1, 4.

[15] Logan Fox, "Logan Fox Writes from Japan," *World Vision*, July 1948, 16.

[16] E. W. McMillan, "Present Conditions: Future Plans for Japan," *Firm Foundation*, April 24, 1948, 3.

[17] E. W. McMillan, "The Voice of Opportunity—China and Japan," *Gospel Advocate*, March 11, 1948, 259.

[18] Harry Robert Fox, Jr. (ed.), *Japan Christian*, November 1947.

[19] Ibid.

[20] E. W. McMillan, "The Voice of Opportunity," *Gospel Advocate*, March 11, 1948, 259.

[21] B. C. Goodpasture, "Bixler's Statement Concerning the Work in Japan," *Gospel Advocate*, August 21, 1947, 628; E. W. McMillan, "Indications among Brethren," *Firm Foundation*, March 23, 1948, 3. For a brief introduction to O. D. Bixler and his role in the premillennial controversies, see Yukikazu Obata, "The Apocalyptic Origins of a Church of Christ Missionary: O. D. Bixler's Early Years in the United States (1896–1918)," *Discipliana* 58 (1998), 22–32.

[22] B. C. Goodpasture, "The Union Avenue Congregation and Premillennialists," *Gospel Advocate*, September 29, 1949, 610.

[23] B. C. Goodpasture, "Bixler's Statement Concerning the Work in Japan," *Gospel Advocate*, August 21, 1947, 637.

[24] Joseph Cannon, "Cannons Tell Plight of Japanese in War's Aftermath; Have Room in Home of Kagawa, a Religious Leader," *Christian Chronicle*, March 3, 1948, 6.

[25] Charles Doyle, "Report of Japanese Mission Work," *Gospel Advocate*, March 3, 1949, 139, 140.

[26] Joseph Cannon, "Japan's Challenge Outlined by Worker Sent into Field under Toronto Congregation," *Christian Chronicle*, March 3, 1948, 1.

[27] No author, "Opportunities in Japan Told by McMillan in Discussing Attitude of Leading Men in State Positions," *Christian Chronicle*, March 3, 5.

[28] C. W. Doyle, "Status of Christian Work in Japan," *World Vision*, June 1948, 9.

[29] Personal conversation with Lou Lawyer.

[30] E. W. McMillan, "Present Conditions: Future Plans for Japan," *Gospel Advocate*, July 29, 1948, 727.

[31] Ibid.

[32] Ibid.

[33] Frank L. Cox, "McMillan Returns to Texas," *Firm Foundation*, October 19, 1948, 3.

[34] E. W. McMillan, "Conditions and Plans for Japan Work," *Christian Chronicle*, June 30, 1948, 1.

[35] Harry Robert Fox, Jr. (ed.), *Japan Christian*, April 1948.

[36] Ibid.

[37] Ibid.

[38] Ibid.

[39] Charles Doyle, "Status of the Work in Japan," *Firm Foundation*, June 29, 1948, 8.

[40] Harry Robert Fox, Jr. (ed.), *Japan Christian*, May 1948.

[41] Ibid.

[42] Ibid., June 1948.

[43] E. J. A. Kennedy, "Toronto Church Gives Report on Japan," *World Vision*, August 1948, 10.

[44] Joseph Cannon, "Now Is the Time in Japan," *World Vision*, November 1948, 7.

[45] O. D. Bixler, "Ripe Harvest in Japan," *World Vision*, November 1948, 8.

[46] Harry Robert Fox (ed.), *Japan Christian*, July 1948.

[47] Ibid., August 1948.

[48] Ibid.

[49] Joseph L. Cannon, "The Summer Meetings in Ibaraki and Their Results," *Firm Foundation*, November 2, 1948, 10.

[50] Harry Robert Fox, Jr. (ed.), *Japan Christian*, September 1948.

[51] Logan Fox, "Aboard the Japan Band Wagon," *Firm Foundation*, October 5, 1948, 8, 9.

[52] E. W. McMillan, "Developments in the Japanese Work," *Firm Foundation*, January 18, 1949, 2, 3.

[53] John Dower, *Embracing Defeat: Japan in the Wake of World War II* (New York: W. W. Norton, 1999), 52, 230, 272.

[54] Harry Robert Fox, Jr. (ed.), *Japan Christian*, November 1948.

[55] Joseph L. Cannon, "Your Clothing at Work," *Firm Foundation*, May 10, 1949, 6.

[56] John Dower, *Embracing Defeat*, 114–20.

[57] Harry Robert Fox, Jr. (ed.), *Japan Christian*, November 1948.

[58] Ibid., December 1948.

[59] Likely author Joseph Cannon, "The Gratitude of the Japanese," *Firm Foundation*, March 29, 1949, 4. In the same issue, there are articles titled "More Conversions in Japan—Year's Total 425," 4, 5; and "Our Preacher's Study Class in Japan," 5.

[60] Joseph L. Cannon, "Clothing at Work," *Firm Foundation*, May 10, 1949, 6.

[61] Harry Robert Fox, Jr. (ed.), *Japan Christian*, December 1948.

[62] Ibid., March 1949.

[63] R. C. Cannon, "Interest of Japanese Youth in Religion Leads Workers to Put Emphasis on School," *Christian Chronicle*, March 23, 1949, 2, 3.

[64] O. D. Bixler, "Crisis in Japan Demands Church Act Promptly to Retain Advantage Held over Catholics, Commies, All Others," *Christian Chronicle*, July 7, 1948, 5; Joseph L.

Cannon, "Visits to Hospitals and Homes Reveal Eagerness of Japanese for Christianity, Cannon Says," *Christian Chronicle*, February 8, 1949, 7; Charles W. Doyle, "Doyle Outlines Challenge of Japan [*sic*] Pleads for Additional Workers to Rise to Great Opportunity There," *Christian Chronicle*, March 9, 1949, 1.

[65] An unpublished essay on Masaichi Kikuchi written by Harry Robert Fox, Jr., for the writer, November 2013. A copy is in Special Collections, Lipscomb University, Nashville, Tennessee.

[66] Likely Harry Robert Fox, Jr., "Bible School in Japan Opens This Month, Workers Needed," *Christian Chronicle*, April 13, 1949, 8.

[67] Harry Robert Fox, Jr. (ed.), *Japan Christian*, April 1949.

[68] Ibid., June 1948.

[69] Virgil L. Lawyer, "New College in Japan Opened; 180 Students to Attend School," *Christian Chronicle*, May 4, 1949, 1.

[70] Logan Fox, "150 Students Attend School in Japan Stressing New Freedoms," *Christian Chronicle*, July 13, 1949, 7.

[71] Harry Robert Fox, Jr. (ed.), *Japan Christian*, April and May 1949.

[72] Ibid., May and June 1949.

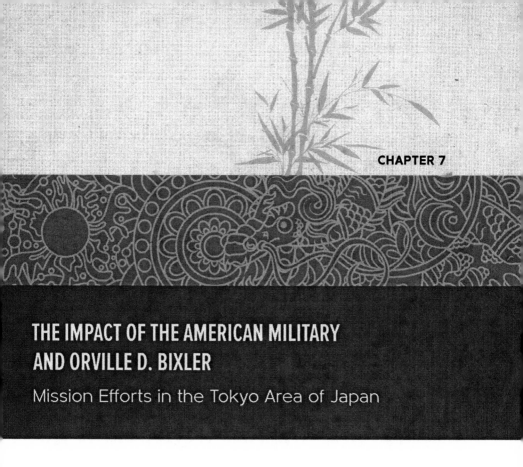

CHAPTER 7

THE IMPACT OF THE AMERICAN MILITARY AND ORVILLE D. BIXLER

Mission Efforts in the Tokyo Area of Japan

A fter the bombing of Hiroshima and Nagasaki to end World War II, Americans quickly changed their attitude toward the Japanese. This was especially true of American Christians, who were left to consider several questions: Would they continue to consider the Japanese as an enemy, or would they instead reach out to a defeated people? Would they heed the advice of Harry Fox, Sr., who saw the carnage of Nagasaki and reminded his brothers and sisters in Churches of Christ of Romans 12:20, "If your enemy hungers, feed him"? Would they follow in the footsteps of members of Churches of Christ who worked directly with Japanese Americans interned in camps? It seems that a majority of Churches of Christ saw Japanese Christians as Christians first, a fellowship that extended beyond any false notions of wartime propaganda and nationalism.

The compassionate attitudes of American Christians could be seen in the military's almost immediate response to the needs of Japanese Christians as they entered Japan within months after the end of World War II. For the next several years, military personnel would be engaged in attending to the physical needs of the Japanese. Even more, they were involved in evangelism, mostly by providing financial help to missionaries who came to Japan. They truly represented to Christians back home in America how to forgive the enemy and then to reach out to them in Christian love and fellowship.

Returning to a Nation Torn by War

When the first military personnel arrived in Japan in 1945 on a relief and recovery mission to help rebuild the infrastructure of their once enemy, one of their first goals was to seek out the legendary Zoshigaya church. Originally founded by J. M. McCaleb early on in his ministry, Zoshigaya had been a historic first stop for all new US missionaries coming to Japan prior to World War II. It was a safe haven and a place of transition—some certainty and assurance in an extremely uncertain and intimidating situation. They eventually found the fabled church. But upon their arrival, the deflated troops discovered that the Zoshigaya church was no longer affiliated with the US Churches of Christ; under the leadership of Japanese nationals, Zoshigaya had joined the government-sponsored Japanese national Christian church at the outbreak of the war. With tensions still high, it could no longer provide US missionaries with the centralized meeting location and safe haven they needed upon arrival in Japan. The would-be peace ambassadors were left out in the cold, with no room at the proverbial inn. Already their task was marked by hardship, and it was only the beginning of a long and treacherous journey to establishing a new era of peace in Japan.

It was for this reason that longtime Japanese missionary Orville D. Bixler dreamed of establishing a Church of Christ in the center of Tokyo. He had first come to postwar Japan in 1946. Returning to the United States in 1947, he re-entered Japan in 1948. Accompanied by Robert Gill from Kentucky, the two men escorted some 250 goats to Japan for the needy people. Bixler, as noted in the previous chapter, was responsible for encouraging missionaries to go to Japan; once there, he aided them in getting acclimated to a different world. His impact on mission work in Japan at such a trying time when Christ's love was needed most cannot be overlooked.

Because of his long history as a missionary in Japan (since 1918), Bixler had made close friendships with influential Japanese men in both business and government. These relationships were invaluable to US missions to Japan after World War II and allowed the highly influential Ibaraki Christian schools (discussed more in Chapters 8 and 9) to purchase property in Omika at a reasonable price.

Bixler selflessly gave to the postwar efforts in Japan, even when it meant giving up the leadership post he loved most to ensure the mission would carry on without incident. While encouraging the American church to reach out to and love their enemies, Bixler became a lightning rod for controversy—he was believed to hold a premillennial view of Revelation. To squelch this concern, he willingly gave up his leadership position so Churches of Christ would support mission efforts in Japan, and he even resigned from the Ibaraki Christian school board of directors in April 1948. The mission to spread the love of Christ in such dark times was just that important to Bixler—even if it meant stepping aside so that progress could continue.

In the place of Bixler, E. W. McMillan, the most important nonmissionary person advocating mission work in Japan, persuaded R. C. (Carroll) Cannon to accept the position to oversee missionaries coming to Japan from Churches of Christ. Graduates of Harding and Pepperdine Colleges, Carroll and his wife, Nona, were sponsored by the Pasadena, California, Central Church of Christ; they were the first missionaries from Churches of Christ to settle in Tokyo after World War II. Alone in a great city, the Cannons began reaching out to the Japanese people, inviting them to Bible studies in their home. After a home Bible study, one young Japanese man said to Cannon, "I have never heard such teaching; it beats heavily upon my heart."[1]

Soon after Carroll and Nona Cannon arrived in Japan, they met Dr. King Goto, a man beyond sixty years, who had been confronted with Christianity thirty years prior to the war. Goto had "maintained that one could not be scientific and believe the New Testament record of Christ.

Hence, through the years he had remained skeptical." Dr. Goto received his medical degree from Harvard University and had been successful in the practice of medicine in Japan for many years. When Cannon heard his story, he became determined "to confront him again with the reality of Jesus Christ."[2] The two men spent many active hours in discussing the Christian religion. Cannon shared with Goto *Therefore Stand: A Plea for a Vigorous Apologetic in This Critical Hour of the Christian Faith*, by Wilbur Smith. He told his Japanese friend that the book provided the most convincing arguments for Christianity.

On June 4, 1948, as Carroll and Nona were leaving the mission house where they lived, Dr. Goto waved briskly for them to stop their car—he needed to talk with them. His face was animated—"an unusual sight," according to Cannon, "in this land of defeated people." Even before the automobile came to a stop, Goto urgently proclaimed to the Cannons, "I must speak to you just a minute. I have been convinced of the reality of Christ; I want to be a Christian." That night Cannon baptized him. A few days after his baptism, Goto told Cannon with deep feeling, "Now I have a peace of mind I never had before, and could never have without Christ."[3] This was exactly the peace that Cannon and other missionaries like him sought to bring the Japanese people in such a dark time. One small victory at a time, Cannon pressed on in unfamiliar and at times hostile circumstances, reclaiming for Christ what was once nearly destroyed by war and blind hatred.

Besides teaching the Bible in Tokyo homes, the Cannons drove some fifty miles into the Yamanashi Prefecture to share the message of Christ in two mountain towns. Carroll taught a Bible class and Nona instructed the Japanese in the English language. In one of the villages, they attracted some 150 young people every Sunday for Bible study. There were multiple calls from other villages for Bible classes, but the Cannons could not accept the invitations because of their commitments in Tokyo. The Japanese people were ready to welcome the peace of Christ into their lives as they rebuilt not only their nation but their spirit. Urgently, Carroll Cannon made a call for at least two young couples to come to Japan, especially to minister in Yamanashi Prefecture. Seeing special needs in the rural state, he added that a Christian woman could be of service to the Japanese by not only teaching the Bible but also instructing on sanitation and child care. "The people," said Cannon, "have little knowledge of health, hygiene, and cleanliness." He told readers across the ocean in America that the prefecture was the location of majestic Mount Fuji and one of the most beautiful areas of Japan. He quickly added that any missionary coming to Yamanashi must be interested in country folk.[4] But even more so, prospective missionaries back home needed to be open to the true spirit of "love your neighbor," casting aside all bias and wartime propaganda to work alongside former alleged "enemies" to partake in a healing process in Christ.

Missionaries for Yamanashi Prefecture

Cannon's call for missionaries to minister in Yamanashi resulted in two interested young couples who had just graduated college. The first couple consisted of Edward Brown, a spring 1949 graduate of Abilene Christian College, and his wife Edna. Sponsored by churches in Anson and Hamlin, Texas, the Browns arrived in Yokohama on July 8, 1949. So the Browns could begin teaching immediately on arrival, Carroll Cannon had made arrangements for Brother Yamaguchi, the second person he had baptized in Japan, to assist the young couple in Otsuki.[5]

The other missionaries answering the call of Yamanashi were William and Norma Carrell from Martinsville, Indiana. Like the Browns, they were graduates of Abilene Christian College. Sponsored by the Sears and Summit Church of Christ in Dallas, Texas, the church provided $200 of their support and channeled other churches' funds to the Carrells. After the war, Carrell had been stationed with the army of occupation in Japan; thus William knew something of Japan and its people. Certainly, this knowledge inspired him to return to Japan as a missionary to share the Christian religion. Arriving on August 15, 1950, aboard the freighter *War Hawk*, the Carrells joined Ed and Edna Brown in Otsuki. The Browns and the Harry Robert Fox family offered them a warm welcome in Yokohama.[6]

With housing not yet available for the Carrells, the two families shared a small four-room house. Not long after the Carrells' arrival, a fire destroyed the kitchen, leaving only three rooms for two families. Even though the two families did not have adequate living quarters, they were able to raise sufficient money by late 1950 to construct the finest church building among

Churches of Christ in Japan. Providing seating for 250 persons, the cost of construction was only $3,000.

The work in Otsuki, using a Japanese brother to translate for the Americans, flourished. At times, however, the two missionaries, not yet speaking Japanese, invited Logan and Harry Robert Fox, Jr., to hold special gatherings for them. Having Americans preach to the Japanese in their language always seemed to bring about positive effects. Early in 1951, Logan Fox spoke at Otsuki, resulting in eight baptisms. Altogether, three preaching sessions that year resulted in twenty-four baptisms.

The year, however, brought word that Edna Brown's mother, suffering from leukemia, was near death. In July, lacking immediate funds, the Browns had to sell their automobile and also take out a loan to finance their emergency trip home. They arrived in Texas just in time for Edna's mother to see her daughter and grandson before her death. Instead of remaining in the States for a long furlough, they immediately raised the funds to return to Japan in November, selflessly returning to work among a downtrodden and defeated people in need of God's love.[7] In the meantime, the Carrells had moved to Uenohara, where they established a viable church, "[a] lovely white church house, situated in a beautiful rice field on the main highway."[8] The building, constructed in 1951, had seating for 120 people. It also had four rooms as a residence for the Carrells.[9]

During his family's furlough in 1951, Harry Robert Fox, Jr., spoke at the Abilene Christian College Lectureship. Although the speech focused on Ibaraki, he early mentioned the two families in Yamanashi. He noted first that the Browns and the Carrells were graduates of Abilene Christian College, a mention not lost on his audience. Then Fox complimented the two missionaries: "I personally feel that they are doing the most outstanding piece of 'located work' of any in Japan." Compared with the overloads carried by the men in Omika, "the brethren in Yamanashi are concentrating on a limited number of places and building up some fine local congregations."[10]

In 1954, after five years of incredible service among the Japanese people, Ed and Edna Brown returned to the United States so Ed could pursue a master's degree at Abilene Christian College.[11] The Browns would not return to Japan. It should be noted that Brown was the first ACC graduate to go to Japan as a missionary. At the 1955 ACC Lectures, Brown shared with the lecture attendees what had been accomplished in Yamanashi Prefecture during the five years he was in Japan. There were now two congregations, where there had been none prior to World War II, both with fine buildings. The churches, with four doctors and five teachers, had good leadership. One of the churches had a preschool with seventy students taught daily by Christian teachers. The goal for the missionaries was to establish mature churches with good local leadership.[12]

William and Norma Carrell took a furlough in 1954 but remained in the United States only six months.[13] In 1957, having trained native leadership for Uenohara, the Carrells relocated in Koganei, fifteen miles west of downtown Tokyo, where they established a church in William's home office. By late 1957, Carrell had baptized twenty-seven people in the new location.[14] However, he began working in concert with other missionaries at the new Yoyogi-Hachiman church, involving himself in a number of activities sponsored by both the English-speaking and Japanese churches.

Carroll and Nona Cannon, responsible for the Browns and the Carrells locating in Yamanashi, chose to move to Omika in the spring of 1949 to teach Bible at the new Ibaraki Christian College. This meant that O. D. Bixler remained the resident missionary in Tokyo. Even before World War II, Bixler had a special vision for mission work in Tokyo. Always in his plans was a hospital serviced by Christian doctors. Returning to Japan after the war, his dream had enlarged. He was determined to see that central Tokyo had a viable church with sufficient space for multiple ministries.

Bixler's Vision for Tokyo

Before returning to Japan in 1948, Bixler urgently told the Churches of Christ that Japan faced a crisis. He recognized that the Japanese people were now free from a dominating military-led government. "Their minds have been unshackled thru the severest chastisements." From his experiences prior to World War II and his time in Japan immediately after the war, Bixler believed the Japanese people "already love the Christ because of what they have seen of His love in the lives and action of Christians before and since the war."[15] However, two major decisions faced Japan in 1948, involving communism and Catholicism. How would the people respond?

Communism, Bixler believed, was rushing to enter the open hearts of the Japanese people. Even though he surmised that the people were opposed to communism, still "their needs cause them to listen to the offer made [to] them first. What will our answer be in the Judgment; if we do not 'Rise out of sleep' and get there before Satan has closed the door?" According to Bixler, Catholicism was just as active in postwar Japan as communism. The Catholics sent a thousand missionaries to Japan after World War II. Referring to his missionary efforts prior to World War II, Bixler asked, "Will we sit idly by while others buy up the opportunities *given* [to] us thru sacrifices already made?"[16]

Japanese people of all walks of life welcomed Bixler, from the poor in Ibaraki to political and business leaders in Tokyo. There were numerous situations where people awaited baptism until Bixler came to their communities. He quickly made friends with men of importance when he first came as the representative of Churches of Christ to oversee the coming of new missionaries to Japan. And from those first months in Japan, Bixler had his eye on a building in central Tokyo to carry on the work he envisioned. The royal family, according to Bixler, favored the success of the central Tokyo project. He had friends among the emperor's kin.

At least one businessman offered a million yen ($2,000) toward the building. The Taga Works and the community of Ibaraki had already donated a million yen. He told his readers back home in the States that members of Parliament were backing the project. Of major importance to Bixler was the support of doctors and teachers "of first rank." In the midst of his plans, evangelism remained an important part of his mission to Japan. "Our work in the last year has resulted in six or eight new churches."[17]

Having enlisted Japanese political and medical leaders in support of the central Tokyo church, Bixler shared six urgent reasons why Churches of Christ should help in providing a central location for Christian activity in Tokyo. First, he reminded his readers that Christians in central Tokyo did not have a place for worship. The old Zoshigaya church of J. M. McCaleb was on the outskirts of the city, not easily reached, and since the war, it had been overtaken by the government-sponsored Japanese national Christian church. Second, "We have no place for teaching and training workers." Third, there was no place to meet those seekers who were searching for the truths of Christianity. Fourth, there was a need for child-care facilities. Fifth, central Tokyo lacked a place for medical facilities where four Christian doctors could practice medicine to the glory of God. And sixth, the facility would provide a place "for the training of the future homemakers of Japan." He believed a school would provide a thousand places for teaching sewing to young women.[18]

As can be seen, Bixler had great plans for the Central Tokyo Church of Christ. He called on churches and individuals to invest in a building that would house everything he wanted to do. The building under consideration was a three-story structure within a block of the million-dollar Rockefeller Institute. Therefore it had a good location at a reasonable price. The total cost of the building would be $125,000. Japanese friends had already given or promised to give some $40,000. He gave several formulas for Churches of Christ to answer the call for paying the remaining cost of the building. If 500,000 members of Churches of Christ gave just 25 cents each, the building would be paid for. Or if 1,000 Churches of Christ gave $125 each, then the facility would be a reality. He concluded, "Do you know that on the future of Japan hangs the future welfare of the Orient?"[19]

The final plans were not exactly as Bixler proposed prior to his return to Japan. Instead of acquiring the existing building, he purchased land in the Ochanomizu district near the center of Tokyo. Here Bixler proposed the construction of a larger facility that would meet the needs he had listed in the religious papers. Led by Woodrow Whitten, Christians in Los Angeles purchased the land. A house on the property served as a meeting place until a larger facility could be constructed. After he sold a portion of the land, Bixler had funds to begin construction of a six-story reinforced concrete building. Both the Japanese-speaking and the English-speaking GI churches would use the new structure.[20]

Bixler's vision for a church in central Tokyo caught the attention of George Gurganus. A 1939 graduate of Harding College, he and his wife Irene and their two children, Janet Kay and Lynette Gay, arrived in Japan late in 1949, joining Bixler in Tokyo.[21]

Bixler believed that Gurganus would be only the first of many missionaries who would locate in Japan's largest city. However, as was true of J. M. McCaleb in the early twentieth century, Bixler became disappointed when large numbers of Americans failed to join him in Tokyo. Besides Gurganus, the only Americans to join him were Dr. and Mrs. Shermann, a dentist who would become an associate of the medical team to be located in the new building. Determined to prove the young missionaries in Ibaraki wrong (they had warned Gurganus that it was nigh on to impossible to work with Bixler), Gurganus believed he could share in Bixler's vision for Japan. However, within a year he discovered, just as others before him, that he could not accept doing everything dictated by Bixler.

Another church on the west side of Tokyo was the result. With the aid of the military church that had once met in the Bixler building and then in the Kaijo Air Force Chapel, Gurganus established the Yoyogi-Hachiman Church of Christ. The church began in September 1950 at a downtown men's club. The church quickly moved to construct, with financial help from the Cornell Avenue church in Chicago, a building in one of the finest residential areas of Tokyo. After only seven months, on March 28, 1951, when worship services convened, two hundred persons, mostly non-Christians, attended the opening of the new building.[22]

The Military and Churches of Christ

To more fully grasp the importance of the American military to the Yoyogi-Hachiman church, it is necessary to note their involvement and leadership in church activities. Just as Corporal Harold Savely and Major Clyde Bynum were much interested in having worship opportunities in Tokyo, men such as Captain E. S. Lowrie demonstrated similar interests. Lowrie arrived in Japan in February 1949. At the time, it was difficult to locate a Church of Christ. He specifically noted the work underway in Ibaraki and plans forming in the United States and Japan for purchasing property for a central church in Tokyo. After searching, he located the church Carroll Cannon had assembled, where some fifty Japanese and three or four Americans were meeting in a public auditorium. But the meeting place was not satisfactory for the military.

George Gurganus, while working with Bixler, developed a close working relationship with military personnel. The military church began meeting in a building on the property purchased by Bixler. Gurganus and Bixler, following Bixler's dream, had established the Tokyo Bible Center.

The military church met there until October 1950 when it moved to the New Kaijo Air Force Chapel. Beginning with a total attendance of twenty, the numbers increased to as many as fifty people from the army, navy, and air force and their families, along with civilians. This church, through its weekly contributions, supported the Bible Center mission work in Japan. As of March 1951, Lowrie reported the church had contributed $1,400 to Japanese mission programs during the previous eleven months.[23]

Soon thereafter, Gurganus, unable to work with Bixler, left the Bible Center. The teaching program deteriorated and finally ceased. According to Lowrie, Gurganus was so discouraged with the conflicts at the Bible Center that he thought about returning to the United States. At this juncture, the military personnel and missionaries encouraged Gurganus to organize another church in Tokyo. To aid him in this new venture, the military church pledged Gurganus 60 percent of its weekly contribution to support the purchase of land and the construction of the building. In the meantime, Gurganus began meeting with Japanese Christians in a public hall in the neighborhood while the building was under construction.

The new building had only an auditorium. Almost immediately, it proved to be inadequate for their needs. On the first Sunday the church met in the new building, one hundred children who desired to study the Bible had to be turned away. As a result, the military church meeting at the Kaijo Chapel committed to raising the funds necessary to construct an educational wing.[24]

Bixler's Relationship with Other Missionaries

Bixler made a second call for missionaries to join him in the development of a Christian high school in Tokyo. The very wealthy Mitsui family asked Bixler to operate their private high school in Keimei. The Mitsui family wanted it operated as the Keimei Christian High School. Needing a Christian faculty, Bixler asked members of Ibaraki Christian College and High School faculty to move to Tokyo to help administer the school. No one from Ibaraki, with the exception of Ryohachi Shigekuni, accepted his invitation. Harry Robert Fox, Jr., stated that Bixler "lacked the gift of functioning in any kind of group project. He was, on the other hand, richly gifted to serve as an individual—which had been true of him in pre-WW II in Ibaraki." After a short while, Shigekuni resigned from the administrative position of the high school and moved to Yokohama, where he preached for the Nogeyama church.[25]

The failure of Bixler to work with other missionaries in Japan had become well-known both in Japan and the United States. In 1952, while Logan Fox was visiting among Churches of Christ in America, he raised questions about O. D. Bixler and his relationship with the Ibaraki missionaries. In an *Advocate* article, he emphasized that Bixler was in Tokyo, 95 miles from Ibaraki, and had no involvement with the school. The concern of most Americans was Bixler's views on millennial issues. Fox stated emphatically that neither he nor any missionary in Ibaraki held to the premillennial views attributed to Bixler.

The inability to work with Bixler was much larger than a difference in theology. First, stated Fox, "[M]ost of us in Japan have learned through bitter experience that cooperation with Brother Bixler is impossible. To work with Brother Bixler one must be willing to do everything his way, or not at all." Secondly, "In order to reach the 'high and mighty,' Brother Bixler goes much further than would seem best for a preacher of the gospel in trying to win friends and converts by giving gifts and doing favors." Concluding, Fox stated, "I hold no animosity toward Brother Bixler. . . . [I]t is my sincere opinion that Brother Bixler can best serve the cause of Christ in Japan by returning to the United States."[26]

Members of the military stationed in Japan also recognized Bixler's inability to work with his fellow missionaries. An unidentified soldier called the return of O. D. Bixler to Japan a dark cloud on the Japanese horizon. He concluded, "All of the missionaries with whom I talked openly stated that Bro. Bixler's return to Japan was the one thing that could wreck or at least considerably cripple the Lord's work in Japan."[27]

Concern for the divisive nature of Bixler's inability to work with other missionaries influenced the two sponsoring churches of Gurganus and Bixler to send representatives to investigate the situation. A member of the Cornell Avenue church in Chicago and a representative of the Acadia, California, Church of Christ first came to Japan in 1950. For two years the churches attempted to solve the problem. Unable to do so, their recommendation to the missionaries included (1) develop your programs independent of Bixler and seek harmony among yourselves, and (2) in correspondence with sponsoring churches or with the press, "clarify your relations, or lack of relations, with Bixler." A letter, signed by Edward M. Brown, George Gurganus, and William L. Carrell, was a response to the findings of the two churches. It stated emphatically, "We cannot recommend [Bixler's] program as worthy of the support of faithful Christians."[28]

Not all missionaries in Japan held negative attitudes toward Bixler. At Bixler's death in 1968, Erroll Rhodes, who followed Bixler to Japan in 1919, said of him, "O. D. Bixler was one of my closest friends. Our association in the work of the gospel in Japan was nearly fifty years." He added, "Brother Bixler was a man of vision. He wanted to spread the gospel of Christ in as many ways as possible." Rhodes gave Bixler credit for starting Ibaraki Christian College. He stated it was Bixler who asked George Benson to go to Memphis to persuade E. W. McMillan to go to Japan to help start Ibaraki Christian College. Even the critics of Bixler praised him for his vision.[29]

Bixler continued his work without the support of the majority of American missionaries. The Bixler family's involvement with the Keimei Christian Academy continued after his death. Bixler had returned to the United States in 1948, and on this trip he married D'Lila Symcox, registrar at Pepperdine College. For the next nineteen years, both worked together at the high school where they had their home.[30] There were young men who came to Japan to work with the Bixlers. In 1953, Edwin Thomas Marsh of Sellersburg, Indiana, joined in the work of the Christian high school and other work under the direction of O. D. Bixler.[31] Bixler's son, Dean, also joined his father in Japan. But for the most part, the success of the Yoyogi-Hachiman church can be seen as a result of the inability of both American and Japanese Christians to work with Bixler.

Yoyogi-Hachiman Church: Military Contributions and Japanese Leadership

As stated previously, military members of Churches of Christ were important to mission work in Japan. The military church in Yokohama decided the churches in Japan needed a printing press to publish Bible-related materials, including books, for Japanese Christians. The GI congregation, averaging twenty-five to thirty members, began meeting in August 1951 and by June

1952 had saved $900 for the press. Needing to raise $3,000, they appealed to American Christians for help. The press became a reality. It was located at the Yoyogi-Hachiman church building.[32] In addition to purchasing a printing press, the military churches also provided dormitories, a Japanese preacher's home, and a special room for printing work at the church.[33]

In addition, the establishment of a radio program was the idea of the military churches. Colis Campbell, first supported by premillennial churches in Louisville, began working with the Yoyogi-Hachiman church after a furlough in America. He announced that a radio program, beginning on January 2, 1955, would provide a fifteen-minute broadcast every Sunday morning. The military churches paid the full cost of $100 each week for the program. Young people of the Yoyogi-Hachiman church formed a thirty-member chorus to provide music.[34]

In 1952, the Yoyogi-Hachiman church began an encampment for Japanese young people, under the direction of Colis Campbell. Youth camps were important to George Gurganus. He had begun Camp Hunt while at Hubbardsville, New York. Located on Lake Motosu, near Mount Fuji, the numbers attending continued to increase until 1955, when 175 youngsters attended from 5 prefectures and 23 participating churches. In 1953, 38 young people responded for baptism. In 1955, there were 31 baptisms.[35] Instructors for the camp were missionaries from throughout Japan, including teachers from Ibaraki Christian College.[36]

Some years are more important than others in the history of a church. This was certainly true of the Yoyogi-Hachiman church. Moving to the Yoyogi-Hachiman church on October 31, 1954, according to Norman Clothier, the military church "was largely responsible for the establishment of the Japanese congregation less than four years ago and has cooperated in every possible way with the Japanese brethren in their efforts to build up the work." Americans worshiped in English on Sunday afternoons.[37]

Despite financial difficulties and the wonderful contributions of the military churches, the goal of the Yoyogi-Hachiman church, like every church in Japan, was to become self-supporting. Yoyogi-Hachiman church was the first church in Japan to achieve independent status. On September 26, 1954, the announcement made to an overflow crowd thrilled those gathered for worship. The budget for the church of 140 members was $90 a month. Gurganus explained that the church, made up of single persons of college age and a few young married couples, represented mission efforts throughout Japan. To meet their goal of self-sufficiency, the church doubled its contribution.

Possibly the answer to why the church was able to respond to the challenge was its excellent, mature leadership. Among the leaders was Judge Koichi Inomata of the Tokyo High Court. A former Methodist, he converted to Churches of Christ under the instruction of Erroll Rhodes soon after World War II. His wife and two children were also Christians. In the fall of 1956, he spoke on the Harding College lectureship.[38] Dr. Masami Takata, a leader and preacher, was a medical doctor and also held a PhD, but he gave up a career in medicine to preach the gospel, thus healing people's spirits and hearts, not just their bodies. To prepare himself for teaching the Bible, he attended Harding College for a semester. A third respected leader of the church was J. Matsumoto. He had a degree in engineering from one of the finest universities in Japan and a master's of science in engineering from Johns Hopkins University in Baltimore. The full-time minister for the church was Yukio Mori.[39]

The life experience of Yukio Mori is a fascinating story. Reared in the state of Ibaraki, near Hitachi, Mori was in grade school when World War II began in December 1941. Each morning the government required all students to bow to the emperor. He even won a contest for the student who wore the least clothing to support Japan's war effort. After a while, the schools closed to allow the youngsters to work in the factories; Mori sometimes worked twelve hours a day. The Hitachi factory was often the target of American bombers and shelling from ships offshore. One day when he and some fellow workers had a day off from their work, the American Navy shelled the city and destroyed the factory. After the war, Mori met Joe Cannon and Charles Doyle. Attending Ibaraki Christian College, he heard the good news of Jesus Christ and responded to baptism. He desired to preach. His father, however, demanded that he attend law school. Confronted with communism while in law school, he often shared with Colis Campbell the issues he faced every day. When attending the Motosu Christian Camp in 1953, he was determined to preach, even over the objections of his father. To prepare himself to preach, he, like Dr.

Takata, attended Harding College for one semester. Returning to Japan, he became the preacher for the Yoyogi-Hachiman church, replacing Dr. Takata, who reentered the practice of medicine while serving as associate minister of the church.[40]

When the church became self-supporting, George Gurganus chose to drop his support from the United States and accepted a teaching position with the air force. In 1954, after a furlough in the United States, he became educational advisor for the US Air Force at the Tokyo International Airport. In 1956 he accepted the appointment to be education director.[41] However, he and Colis Campbell would continue a cooperative relationship with Yoyogi-Hachiman. Specifically, they continued a preacher training program, the printing of gospel literature, a summer encampment at Lake Motosu, and in a shared desire to establish another congregation in Tokyo.[42]

The Military and the Far Eastern Fellowship

Even though the total number of men who made up the military churches in Japan was never more than 125, the group that met at Yoyogi-Hachiman involved itself in a wide variety of Christian activities. George Gurganus stated in 1956 that "no post-war report on the church in Tokyo would be complete without telling of the work of the American congregations. . . . These groups have contributed more to the work than it is possible to mention at this time."[43] This was certainly true. The Far East Fellowship was the most ambitious work of the military churches. The first of these meetings took place November 21–26, 1955. The invited speaker was Dr. James D. Bales of Harding College. All sessions were held at the Yoyogi-Hachiman building.

Six American military congregations in the Tokyo area cooperated in the five-day program. These churches met at the Yokosuka Naval Base Chapel, the Yokohama Chapel Center, Grant Heights Housing Area, Johnson Air Base, Tachikawa Air Base, and the church at Yoyogi-Hachiman. The men who prepared the program in 1955 were Captain Edwin Tester and Captain William Mabry of the Tachikawa church. The first fellowship was so successful that the military churches decided to make it an annual event.[44]

The next several years of the Far East Fellowship was like a who's who in Churches of Christ. In 1956 it was H. A. Dixon, president, Freed-Hardeman

College, Henderson, Tennessee. The following year, Dr. Batsell Barrett Baxter, member of the speech and Bible departments, David Lipscomb College, and minister for the Hillsboro church, Nashville, Tennessee, was the featured speaker. In 1958, Dr. J. D. Thomas, Abilene Christian College, came to present lessons to the Christians, both Americans and Japanese. In 1959, the newly appointed president of Pepperdine College, Dr. M. Norvel Young, was the speaker for the occasion. The desire, according to W. H. Betts (an airman at the Tachikawa Air Base), was to choose men associated with colleges connected with Churches of Christ "so they might become aware of the need for evangelists to come over into Macedonia and preach the word."[45] The importance of the Christian colleges for foreign missions did not go unrecognized by the young military personnel.

Reaching Out with Radio and Print Literature

The numbers of full-time missionaries in Japan began declining in the mid-1950s, with only William and Norma Carrell continuing to minister in Tokyo. Besides personal evangelism, Carrell became involved in a number of areas to more widely spread the message of Christ. Involved from the beginning, Carrell helped produce the Sunday broadcast over JOKR—"Radio Tokyo." From the time the program was first aired on January 2, 1955, until 1958, the audience grew from 350,000 to 1,000,000 listeners. The speakers on the program were both Japanese and Japanese-speaking American preachers. Harry Robert Fox, Jr., traveled from Ibaraki on several occasions to record five-minute lessons for the program.[46] Every week the program received between thirty and fifty requests for a correspondence course.

The missionaries in Japan needed Bible study material in the Japanese language. Until William Carrell developed a correspondence course in 1956, there was no way to reach the majority of the people with the message of Jesus. Carrell created the lessons in English; then a Christian woman, Yasuko Homma, a specialist in writing Japanese textbooks, rewrote the manuscript in fluent and beautiful Japanese.[47] By January 1958, a total of 3,200 Japanese had enrolled in the correspondence course. A number of Japanese Christians worked with those enrolled in the twenty-lesson series.[48]

New Outreach Opportunities by Japanese Christians

Quietly, without any fanfare, another church began meeting in Tokyo. Young men, graduates of Ibaraki Christian College, had come to Tokyo to find employment. Living in the Oji district of Tokyo, they formed a church with hardly anyone knowing about it. These young men, baptized in Ibaraki, began meeting in a large upstairs room of a Sister Akamatsu's home. She was an eye doctor who had moved from Karasuyama. Harry Robert Fox, Jr., had baptized her son and daughter a few years before. The young church, desiring to reach out to their community, invited Harry Fox to preach in a meeting beginning on February 23, 1952. It must have made the families at Ibaraki Christian College proud of these young Japanese Christians—to form a church without calling on American missionaries and then to become personally involved in evangelism.[49] This was always the goal of foreign missionaries.

Equally as important, within three years the Yoyogi-Hachiman church began to reach out to Uenohara and Okinawa, an island with a population of 600,000 and a major American military installation. The Uenohara church, established by William Carrell, was in 1957 no longer directed by an American missionary. To support a native preacher, Yoyogi-Hachiman church sent 5,000 yen to help the church. The Japanese churches were making progress toward becoming independent congregations.

Okinawa: Work among the Military and Japanese Nationals

Okinawa came to the attention of American churches in 1952 and, closer by, the Yoyogi-Hachiman church in Tokyo. Calvin C. Daniel, Jr., a former student at Abilene Christian College, arrived that year with the army to serve on the island's military base. Military Christians gathered in the Rycom army chapel had never considered preaching to the Okinawans until Daniel arrived. He contacted George Gurganus, inquiring as to the possibility of sending a Japanese preacher to work among the Japanese people on the island. In the meantime, Daniel encouraged the Rycom church to support a native preacher. On December 28, 1952, with George Gurganus accompanying them, Mr. and Mrs. Shigeo Saito, both graduates of Ibaraki Christian College, arrived in Okinawa to begin evangelizing the island. In August 1953, they invited Brother Nagano from Ibaraki to conduct evangelistic services in Naha, with twenty-one persons responding for baptism. In December 1953, the Saitos returned to Ibaraki.

The background of Saito is a story that must be told. Harry Robert Fox, Jr., while in 1947 instructing Tokyo judges in the Bible, met Shigeo Saito, Judge Inomata's secretary. The young man had an interesting history. He served in the Japanese military during World War II. Trained for the Kamikaze Corps as a suicide pilot—men who crashed their planes into American ships, dying for the emperor—Saito was within two weeks of flying a suicide plane when the war came to an end. Baptized by Erroll Rhodes in Yokohama, young Saito lived for a while with R. C. and Nona Cannon in Tokyo. When the Cannons moved to Omika in 1949, Saito followed them and enrolled in Ibaraki Christian College to prepare himself for ministry. Two weeks made a difference in the life of Shigeo Saito and Japanese Churches of Christ. Pleased with the commitment of ICC graduates, the missionary-teachers gladly announced that Saito was being replaced with another graduate, a Brother Hatakeyama. Saito then went on to Okinawa, where his presence is still felt today among the faithful.[50]

Over the next few years, the Yoyogi-Hachiman church continued providing preachers for the Okinawa mission, leading to the establishment of three churches.[51] The military church, now focused on the island, continued support for preaching in six villages.[52] Naha continued to be a fertile field for the gospel. Sixty-two had been baptized by August 1955. There were four baptized at Koza and twenty-two at Itomen, a total of eighty-eight.[53]

In the meantime, the Rycom church sought an American preacher to come to Okinawa. In May 1955, Charles Butler and his wife arrived in Okinawa to work, for the most part, with the American church. Supported by the Rycom church and the Central church in Amarillo, Texas, Butler's goal was to work with the one hundred ever-changing members of the military church and "to help train and indoctrinate native teachers and evangelists."[54] In August 1955, Butler, in cooperation with a native Okinawan, Brother Uza, held a six-day session of sermons at Ishikawa. At the end of the six days, seventy-six persons had been baptized, followed by five others during the following month.[55]

In August 1957, Charles Butler and his wife returned to the United States. On leaving, he gave a summary of the results during their stay on Okinawa.

During the 25 months on the island, 285 persons had responded to the preaching of the gospel. Of this number, 217 were baptized, including 32 Americans and 185 Okinawans. During his stay on the island, three native churches began meeting. Butler believed the military church was stronger, having constructed their own meetinghouse. The GI church also helped an Okinawan church construct a meeting place. He mentioned specifically that Yoshiaki Shigekuni, the son of legendary Ryohachi Shigekuni, was serving a year working among the Japanese people. It had been a productive 25 months on Okinawa.[56] The efforts of the Rycom and the Yoyogi-Hachiman churches were quite productive on Okinawa.

In March 1957, Freed-Hardeman College announced that George Gurganus would join its faculty in the fall semester as chairman of the college's English department.[57] Announcing his return to America, Gurganus wrote, "I have never regretted leaving a place more in my life than now. The Lord has been good to us and has blessed our work. Our dream of a self-supporting, self-governing Japanese church has been realized, and it gives us a feeling of deep satisfaction." Gurganus mentioned that Robert Nichols had arrived in April to join William Carrell in Tokyo.[58] However, most missionaries in the Tokyo area had returned to the United States.

"Love Your Enemies": A Salute to American Military Churches

It is impossible to overemphasize the importance of the American military to the Churches of Christ in the years of World War II and immediately after the worldwide conflict. American chaplains, including Frank Traylor and John C. Stevens. Traylor was a 1936 graduate of Abilene Christian College, who served in the South Pacific. John C. Stevens, a 1938 graduate of ACC served in Europe participating in the invasion of Normandy and the Battle of the Bulge. After serving in the chaplaincy, Stevens taught history at Abilene before he became president of Abilene Christian College. The chaplains, not to mention all members of Churches of Christ who served in the military, prepared the way for American missionaries around the world. American military personnel, because of the war, experienced a world and cultures they had never dreamed existed. The development of Churches of Christ would not have been possible in Tokyo, not to mention Europe and the remainder of the Far East, without men and women who served in the US Army, Navy, Marines, and Air Force as a result of World War II. A number of veterans returned to the areas where they had served to share the message of Jesus Christ with a defeated people.

It is important to note that members of the military, on returning home, emphasized the need to share the message of love with the former enemy. This helped the soldiers' home congregations become involved in supporting missionaries among the Japanese. They took to heart Harry Fox, Sr.'s call to American Christians: "If your enemy hungers, feed him."

Endnotes

[1] R. C. Cannon, "Cannon Tells of Opportunities for Teaching Christianity to Japanese," *Christian Chronicle*, June 9, 1948, 3.

[2] Burton Coffman, "Mission—Far East," *Christian Leader*, September 29, 1953, 3.

[3] R. C. Cannon, "Japan Worker Baptizes Leading Physician, Formerly Skeptical but Now Happy in Christianity," *Christian Chronicle*, August 25, 1948, 5.

[4] R. C. Cannon, "Workers Urged for Yamanashi Area in Japan; To Reach All Calls for Teaching among Villages," *Christian Chronicle*, September 1, 1948, 5.

[5] No author, "Edward Brown to Sail for Oysuki, Japan Next June," March 9, 1949, 1; September 7, 1949, 4.

[6] Harry Robert Fox, Jr. (ed.), *Ota Christian News*, August 1950.

[7] No author, "Death Brings Browns to States; Will Stay Here Three Months," *Christian Chronicle*, August 8, 1951, 1; Edward Brown, "Brown Goes to Japan after Visit in States," *Christian Chronicle*, November 7, 1951, 1.

[8] Burton Coffman, "Mission—Far East," 3.

[9] No author, "New Building in Japanese City Give Workers Opportunity for Expansion of Work, Growth," *Christian Chronicle*, March 26, 1952, 7.

[10] Harry Robert Fox, Jr., "The Work of the Church in Japan," *Abilene Christian College Lectures* (Austin: Firm Foundation Publishing Company, 1951), 83.

[11] No author, "Edward Brown Returns after 5 Years in Japan," *Christian Chronicle*, October 6, 1954, 7.

[12] Edward Brown, "The Work in Japan," *Abilene Christian College Lectures* (Austin: Firm Foundation Publishing Company, 1955), 189.

[13] No author, "Carrell Tours States Narrating Japan Work," *Christian Chronicle*, November 17, 1954, 1.

[14] Batsell Barrett Baxter, "Tokyo—World's Largest City," *Gospel Advocate*, January 2, 1958, 2.

[15] O. D. Bixler, "Crisis in Japan Demands Church Act Promptly to Retain Advantage Held over Catholics, Commies, All Others," *Christian Chronicle*, July 7, 1948, 5.

[16] Ibid.

[17] Ibid.

[18] Ibid

[19] Ibid.

[20] A letter dated August 12, 2013, from Harry Robert Fox, Jr., to Robert Hooper. This letter is in Special Collections, Beaman Library, Lipscomb University, Nashville, Tennessee.

[21] No author, "Chicago Church Sends Two More Workers to Japan," *Christian Chronicle*, November 2, 1949, 6; Personal information for George Gurganus was taken from Batsell Barrett Baxter and Norvel Young (eds.), *Preachers of Today: A Book of Brief Biographical Sketches and Pictures of Living Gospel Preachers*, vol. 2 (Nashville, TN: Gospel Advocate Company, 1959), 172.

[22] George Gurganus, "The Work in Tokyo," *Firm Foundation*, November 27, 1956, 766.

[23] R. C. Cannon, "Information for Men Coming to Japan," *Gospel Advocate*, March 15, 1951, 171.

[24] The information for the foregoing narrative was recorded in the *Gospel Advocate* by Captain E. S. Lowrie, a member of the military. This is the most complete story this writer has discovered detailing the inability of O. D. Bixler and George Gurganus to work together, which resulted in the beginning of the Yoyogi-Hachiman Church of Christ. E. S. Lowrie, "The Church in Tokyo, Japan," *Gospel Advocate*, March 27, 1952, 205.

[25] Ibid.

[26] Logan J. Fox, "The Work of O. D. Bixler," *Gospel Advocate*, October 9, 1952, 650.

[27] A serviceman, "G. I. Gives On-the-Ground Sketch of Work in Japan and South Korea Area," *Christian Chronicle*, March 26, 1952, 1.

[28] Edward M. Brown, George Gurganus, and William L. Carrell, "Investigator Sent to Study Worker Relationships in Japan; Advises to Develop Own Program Independently," *Christian Chronicle*, December 17, 1952, 7.

[29] Oneida Jaquess Cook, *[Biography of O. D. Bixler]* (Tokyo: Shiro Obata, 1985), 170. The book, with the exception of supplementary material by Americans, is written in Japanese. The title given may not be totally accurate, as it was added by librarians at Harding University.

[30] Ibid., 170, 184.

[31] Howard T. Marsh, "To Assist Brother Bixler in Japan," *Word and Work*, August 1953, 183; No author, "Missionary Notes," *Word and Work*, December 1953, 281.

[32] Captain James B. Jolley, "A Printing Press for Japan," *Gospel Advocate*, June 19, 1952, 404.

[33] Batsell Barrett Baxter, "Tokyo," *Gospel Advocate*, January 2, 1958, 2.

[34] No author, "First Program for Tokyo Area Slated January 2," *Christian Chronicle*, December 8, 1954, 6.

[35] Colis Campbell, "Motosu Christian Camp," *Gospel Advocate*, October 15, 1953, 684.

[36] No author, "31 Young People Baptized at Motsu Christian Camp," *Christian Chronicle*, September 28, 1955, 5.

[37] Norman I. Clothier, "Tokyo G. I. Church Moves," *Firm Foundation*, November 9, 1954, 9.

[38] George Gurganus, "The Work in Tokyo," *Firm Foundation*, November 27, 1956, 766.

[39] Norman I. Clothier, "Tokyo," *Christian Leader*, December 7, 1954, 593.

[40] No author, "Yokio Mori Will Leave for Japan Early in July," *Christian Chronicle*, June 15, 1955, 3.

[41] No author, "George Gurganus Added to Freed Hardeman Faculty for Fall Term," *Christian Chronicle*, March 19, 1957, 6.

[42] Norman I. Clothier, "Tokyo," *Christian Leader*, December 7, 1954, 593.

[43] George Gurganus, "The Work in Tokyo," *Firm Foundation*, November 27 1956, 766.

[44] No author, "Far East Fellowship in Tokyo Termed History Making Event," *Christian Chronicle*, December 21, 1955, 1.

[45] M/Sgt. W. H. Betts, "Servicemen in Japan Raise Workers' Fund," *Christian Chronicle*, February 2, 1960, 4.

[46] Harry Robert Fox, Jr. (ed.), *Kuji-Valley News*, July 1955.

[47] No author, "Bible Correspondence Course Is Started in Japan by Carrell," *Christian Chronicle*, August 8, 1956, 1.

[48] Batsell Barrett Baxter, "Tokyo," *Gospel Advocate*, January 2, 1958, 2.

[49] Harry Robert Fox, Jr. (ed.), *Ota Newsletter*, February 1952.

[50] Harry Robert Fox, Jr. (ed.), *Kuji-Valley News*, November 1953.

[51] G. H. P. Showalter, "The Okinawan Mission Work," *Firm Foundation*, April 27, 1954, 8.

[52] On January 31, 2016, the author met Edwin Bell, age ninety-three, at the Jones Chapel Church of Christ in Franklin, Tennessee. Bell served on Okinawa with the air force and was a member of the Rycom church during the 1950s. He has interesting stories about Charles Butler, an American missionary who came to Okinawa to serve the military church. Butler chose to eat native food, becoming quite ill on several occasions. This may have been a reason he did not remain on Okinawa more than twenty-five months.

[53] No author, "Charles Butler Reports on Work with Okinawan Churches," *Christian Chronicles*, August 3, 1955, 3.

[54] Ibid.

[55] No author, "An Average Week in the Life of an Okinawa Preacher," *Christian Chronicle*, October 12, 1955, 3.

[56] Charles Butler, "Coming Home," *Firm Foundation*, August 20, 1957, 543.

[57] No author, "Gurganus Added to Freed Hardeman Faculty," *Christian Chronicle*, March 19, 1957, 6.

[58] George Gurganus, "Gurganus Family Returning after Eight Years in Japan," *Christian Chronicle*, May 28, 1957, 7.

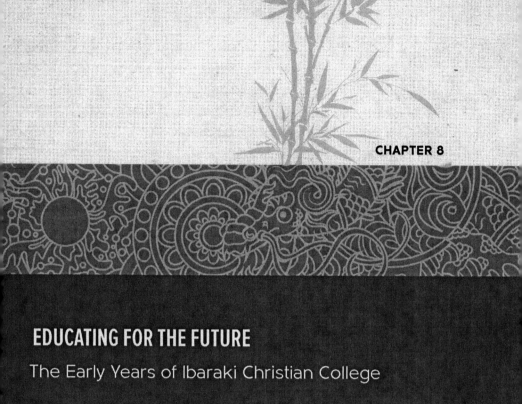

CHAPTER 8

EDUCATING FOR THE FUTURE
The Early Years of Ibaraki Christian College

I n some small way, the idea of a Christian college in Japan began with a discussion between James A. Harding and David Lipscomb about the need for a Bible school in Nashville, Tennessee. That conversation led to the founding in 1891 of the Nashville Bible School. In 1924 Barney and Nellie Morehead graduated from David Lipscomb College, the former Nashville Bible School, and in 1925 went as missionaries to Japan. The Moreheads determined that if a Christian school were good for Nashville and Tennessee, one could also be good for Japan.

The Vision Becomes a Reality

The Moreheads, because of family concerns, returned to the United States in 1926, where Barney used the opportunity to raise funds to start a school. Robert S. King, an elder of the Lipscomb College church, accepted the challenge of raising funds for the school. Emerging from that idea was the King Bible School organized in Ota, Japan, in the 1920s, where the Moreheads settled as missionaries and organized a church. The post–World War II missionaries, especially the Fox brothers, both born in Japan, made the connection between Morehead's King Bible School in pre–World War II Japan and Ibaraki Christian College. Their father had operated the school when the Moreheads returned to the United States. E. W. McMillan, a graduate of Gunter Bible College in Texas, also caught early the vision of a Christian college in Japan.

Two years after first visiting Japan and Ibaraki, McMillan returned as president of Ibaraki Christian College and High School during the summer and fall of 1949. Seeing what had taken place since April 1948, McMillan emphasized the importance of Christian colleges to foreign missions: "An important influence in this rise of Christian work is the emphasis colleges have given missions on their [Christian college] lectureships."[1] In addition, each campus had missions clubs that met weekly or monthly. Abilene Christian College was the first school to offer formal mission classes for its students before the end of World War II.

As early as 1892, David Lipscomb and M. C. Kurfees urged J. M. McCaleb to establish a college in Japan. His response was that a constituency of Japanese Christians was not available to support a school. Commenting on this discussion, over fifty years later, Logan Fox stated, "Brother McCaleb was undoubtedly right in what he said, though I am not convinced that a school could not have been built and operated for the good of the Christian effort in Japan."[2]

McCaleb's conclusion was not the attitude of an idealistic group of young men and women who went to Japan in 1947 and 1948. Nor was it the attitude of E. W. McMillan. Following World War II, there was a pent-up desire among Churches of Christ for the support of foreign missions and Christian schools. And in Japan, there were also a number of Japanese Christians who called for a Christian school in their country. Ryohachi Shigekuni, probably the leading Japanese evangelist who survived the war, was involved in the initial discussions about Ibaraki Christian College. Shiochi Oka, a new convert following World War II who would become business manager of the Christian schools, became inspired by the vision of the Americans.

Oka's vision of a Japanese Christian college would ensure, in his mind, the future of Christianity in Japan. He foresaw an accredited high school and then a college where a regular curriculum would be offered, including a nursing program and special Bible offerings to educate preachers and church leaders. With a college-trained leadership program for churches, in the future, there would be no need to send missionaries to Japan. To underscore his optimism, there were already five hundred church members in Ibaraki who were newly converted or reclaimed from those converted prior to the war—a good foundation for the future.[3]

Evangelism in the Land of the Rising Sun: McMillan's Return and the Legacy of the Foxes

Most of McMillan's presidency was in absentia; he lived in the United States, giving his time and effort to raising funds to support the college. When McMillan returned to Japan on July 18, 1949, he would be involved for a short time in the inaugural year of the college. Although the schools were between sessions, all students, high school and college, and many Japanese Christians gathered on July 19 to hear the first president of their school. Afterward, the students and faculty played a baseball game, with McMillan, age sixty, playing two innings with each team—the high school won. Said Harry Robert Fox, Jr., "Brother McMillan coming into our midst has been an inspiration and a source of great encouragement to all of us. He has our full confidence and we are thankful for his leadership."[4]

On the following Sunday, McMillan spoke twice to a welcoming area-wide meeting of churches. In the afternoon, he related his experiences while traveling around America in support of the mission efforts in Japan. He enthusiastically told his Japanese audience about the work of Churches of Christ in other regions of the world—Germany, Italy, France, and Africa. Harry Robert Fox wrote after listening to McMillan, "The Japanese were delighted to hear all these facts and were thankful for the generosity of their American brethren who were making such a great contribution toward the salvation of Japan."[5]

The first year of the college and the second year of the high school had begun in April before the arrival of McMillan. The name given to the college was Shion College. However, on December 27, 1949, the board changed the name to Ibaraki Christian Education Community. American Christians, called on to support the college, would be more comfortable with the new name.

With the schools on vacation, the seven men, including McMillan, spread throughout the Kuji River Valley in evangelistic efforts. At the end of August, Harry Robert Fox reported "the most eventful and fruitful month since we came to Japan a year and ten months ago." In the Ota area there were eighty-three baptisms and a similar number in the Hitachi-Taga and Mito areas. On August 1, Harry Robert went to Tanakura, where he baptized seventeen persons in five days, doubling the size of the church.

From August 8 through 13, a special week's meeting convened at Omika in the college auditorium. The year before, the missionaries described this gathering as a Yosemite-type encampment. Christians came from all over Japan to participate in the meetings. The difference from the 1948 meeting was the nightly evangelistic effort, with McMillan preaching. At the end of the week, five persons responded for baptism. McMillan also gave three lectures on the qualifications of elders and deacons.[6] The six young evangelists and school staff recognized the future needs of new churches forming every month. They needed more instruction than they could provide.

Charles Doyle, reporting in the *Christian Chronicle*, noted that 150 persons had been baptized in fifteen meetings throughout the state of Ibaraki. At Ota, Logan preached in a meeting where thirty-five persons responded for baptism. In a later report, he noted the baptism of fifty-six persons. The meeting attracted large crowds, with a hundred or more people crowding into the building. As many as three hundred more stood outside where the church had erected speakers. The preaching and the question-and-answer periods lasted 2.5 hours, with only a few persons leaving. During the month of August, Harry Robert Jr. baptized seventeen in Urizura, and Carroll Cannon baptized sixteen in Omiya. At the same time, eighteen responded to McMillan's preaching at Hitachi. Joe Cannon, Virgil Lawyer, and Charles Doyle baptized fifteen persons at Takahagi.[7]

During August of 1949, Harry Robert Fox, Jr., traveled to the locations where his father, Harry Sr., and his uncle, Herman, labored with little success in the years before World War II. Postwar evangelism brought much greater results. In Tanakura, the only mission point outside of Ibaraki, the location of Harry Sr.'s ministry, his son baptized seventeen persons, doubling the size of the church. The last meeting of the month was at Daigo, where Herman had settled in 1923. Although he remained there throughout his stay in Japan, he had little success.

The meeting, scheduled for only three days, met on the first two nights at the Daigo Home Economics School. On the final day, they had to meet elsewhere. The evangelistic effort was a tremendous success. Five persons responded for baptism during the first two days. They immediately went to the Kuji River. On the morning of the third day, the owner of the Home Economics School asked for baptism, followed by twenty-seven of her students. Following preaching on the third night, five persons from Daigo requested baptism the next morning prior to the preacher leaving for home. All totaled, Fox baptized thirty-eight people. This was the largest number he had ever baptized in such a short time.[8]

However, Fox would not take credit for the success of the evangelistic effort. From the time he and Logan arrived in Ota, they were helped by Shoji Tachi, a second-generation Christian. He had spent two days each week for several months in Daigo, preparing for the preaching by Harry Sr. His parents, merchants in Ota, had been baptized by Barney Morehead. Afterward, many of the residents of Ota refused to trade with them because they had converted to Christianity. Through it all, the Tachi family remained faithfully connected with the church in Ota. Shoji and his two sisters followed their parents in accepting the truths of Christianity. Shoji, conscripted into the Japanese army, served in Manchuria for the duration of the war. He was not well when he returned home following Japan's surrender. Finally recovered, he gave credit to American soldiers for his renewed health. They had provided him with penicillin—the wonder drug unavailable to the Japanese. According to Fox, he was a tireless worker among the churches in Ibaraki. He also worked in the business office of Ibaraki Christian College. Truly he was another of Harry Fox's Timothys.[9]

McMillan's Impact on Japan

E. W. McMillan left Japan for the United States on November 1, but on October 16, 1949, the churches in Ibaraki gave him a heartfelt sendoff. Then on the night of October 25, all the Americans met to bid him farewell. On the 26th, along with Carroll and Nona Cannon, McMillan met in Tokyo with General Douglas MacArthur. McMillan had asked by telegram for a meeting to discuss Ibaraki Christian College and its place in Japan. Arriving for the meeting, MacArthur rose and crossed the room to welcome his visitors. Sitting in a semicircle, the general asked McMillan to tell him about Ibaraki Christian College. They talked for twenty minutes. As the three guests rose to leave his presence, MacArthur said to them, "If you get into any trouble out there, just let me know."[10]

Harry Robert, speaking for every missionary, wrote glowingly to the Christians in America about McMillan's visit:

> His presence with us was an inspiration and a source of great encouragement. We were impressed by his utter sincerity and by the fact of his service here on foreign soil. To see a man of his stature giving up the comforts of life in America to serve in a place like this was a new experience for me. I shall never forget, nor cease to be thankful for it. May God raise up more men like him who will heed the call for laborers in the desperately needy but chronically neglected areas of this world.[11]

It had been a great several months for all involved—McMillan, the American missionaries, and the Japanese Christians.

At the end of his experience, McMillan shared his impressions of his time in Japan. He reported that since the end of World War II, there had been 1,525 baptisms, most of which were in Ibaraki. During the past summer, the total number of baptisms in Japan was 394, with 354 in Ibaraki. There had been 29 revival meetings in the prefecture during the summer. Now he reported a total of 20 native preachers along with 15 student preachers sharing in the success of the gospel. At the end of World War II, 6 churches survived in Ibaraki. In 1949 there were 23 thriving churches. Reflecting on Japan, he wrote, "Two years ago the people were frenzied, nervous, full of fear, ready to try anything. That made it dangerous from the viewpoint of baptizing them [the respondents] too soon."

Two years made a great difference: the "Japanese . . . still have a serious feeling of insecurity, but they are not so ready to jump at just anything. They ask questions, they argue the comparative values of alternatives—communism, Christianity, etc. They ask freely about Protestantism, Catholicism, Humanism, etc." He recalled his last Sunday in Japan. He had preached for an hour, followed by a question period lasting another hour—what a great experience! McMillan closed his report by praising the six families in Ibaraki: "I am certain that no finer or loyal groups of missionaries have been sent to foreign mission fields than we have in Ibaraki Ken."[12]

E. W. McMillan was an inspiration for all the missionaries, and his presence at the college revealed the enthusiasm the young men had for preaching and teaching throughout Ibaraki. That enthusiasm is evident in Harry Robert Fox's newsletter at the beginning of the second half of the school year: "Those of you who have attended any of the Christian schools in the States know just how rich can be the experience. . . . I wondered for a long time if it would be possible to produce anything comparable. . . in Japan. No longer do I wonder, for right here before us such a school has become a reality." The first thing visitors noticed when on campus was "How bright and filled with light is this school!"

Japan was only four years removed from a devastating, emotionally draining war. Harry Robert, noting the emotional conditions of the young men entering the college, wrote: "Most of the boys had impassive faces when they entered last April—some so burdened they couldn't look any of us in the eye. At first we couldn't get them to talk. Then little by little they began to talk. . . . [and] often revealed themselves to be in despair—no hope, no meaning, nothing to look forward to nor live for." He mentioned one young man, emotionally distraught, who told him that because there was no way out, his best friend had committed suicide. "What a changed person now! During the summer he obeyed Christ in baptism and is today filled with joy and hope in the Holy Spirit."[13]

Meet Masaichi Kikuchi

A close Japanese Christian friend of the Fox brothers was Masaichi Kikuchi. Following the return of missionaries after the war, Kikuchi was among the most zealous in reaching his people with the gospel of Christ. In May 1948, when the Foxes moved to Ota, Kikuchi "made himself available to us in evangelizing extensively in Ibaraki Prefecture. It didn't take us long to become aware of how gifted he was as an evangelist!"

One unusual place where Kikuchi made an appointment for both Fox brothers was the tuberculosis sanitarium near Urizura. (Because TB was so prevalent in Japan, in December 1949, Harry Robert, Gerri, and Kenny, while visiting the sanitarium, were x-rayed and found free of the disease.)[14] Many of the elderly patients accepted Christ while in the hospital but had no home after their release. Kikuchi shared with the Fox brothers his dream of establishing a home for the aged. He also told a newly formed tiny mountain church at Odano his dream. The members of the church gave him enough trees for lumber to build the first unit of the home "for the needy aged" in Urizura. He named the facility Nazare-en (Garden of Nazareth).

The demand for admission to the home was so great that Kikuchi had to expand almost immediately. Harry Robert said, "So, by the Grace of God and contributions from caring individuals the home was expanded to care for more than 400 persons over time in four divisions—1) Non-disabled, 2) Disabled (physically), 3) Blind, and 4) Mentally disabled." The home continues its service in the twenty-first century. The administration of the home has, from the very beginning, remained in the Kikuchi family. The church in Urizura has continued to provide religious services in the home, resulting in a number of conversions.[15]

All American missionaries at this time, especially the Fox brothers, recognized the importance of Japanese preachers to the success of their work in Japan. Many of these Japanese workers had been converted to Christianity by the early missionaries. They remained faithful to Christianity during one of the most difficult times to do so. Everywhere they went during the war, they found opposition. The story of Masaichi Kikuchi and his close relationship with the Fox brothers shows the impact a the pre–World War II missionaries had on the continuity of Churches of Christ in Ibaraki

Prefecture. He certainly caught the spirit of Jesus in reaching out to his own people, in both preaching and caring for the elderly.

Postwar Progress Continues, but Needs Still Remain

The Christmas season had arrived for Ibaraki Christian College, and on December 17, 1949, Gerri Fox and Dr. Frances Campbell, science professor at the college, held a party at the Fox home for the youngsters from a local Christian orphanage founded and operated by a Brother Suzuki. The children were transported by automobile, and they were so excited about attending a party and riding in car for the first time that they hadn't slept the night before. Gerri and Frances gave each child a generous supply of clothing sent by churches in America. Especially appreciated were girls' dresses sent by the Long Beach church. The church sent enough dresses to share with other children not at the party. The gifts made all of them "wonderfully happy."[16]

On Christmas Eve, a hundred young people of the Ota church, led by Gerri and Logan Fox, spent the evening walking the streets of Ota singing Christmas carols. Harry Robert, who was away in Tanakura for a preaching appointment, commented on the caroling: "This has really impressed a lot of people favorably because it is such a contrast to the drunken conduct of the pagan religions at holiday time."

Harry Fox Jr., in the midst of visiting churches throughout the region, found time to be home on December 26 to share a Christmas dinner with other missionaries at the Carroll Cannon home. Yet the time together with other American missionaries was very sobering. Noting the millions of Japanese people yet unreached, the past accomplishments were minuscule. Fox remarked, "Surely looked at from the human standpoint the situation looks hopeless. But we know that nothing is impossible with God, so we are inspired to keep pressing on believing that He will bless these efforts in His own way and that He will achieve the realization of all His purposes without fail." The missionaries continued to send out "a Macedonian call" for others to join them "on behalf of these lost men and women" in Japan.[17] For the most part, the calls remained unheard.

Soon the new year brought more progress. A landmark date for Churches of Christ in Japan was the opening on January 14, 1950, of a meetinghouse in Hitachi, a church formed by Christian brothers Lawyer, Joe Cannon, and Doyle. The cost of the building was $2,000, donated by individual Christians and churches in America. The missionaries believed a similar building in the United States would have cost $10,000. The building seated 250, and on special occasions it could be reconfigured to seat 350 people. The building had two major features—a baptistery and preacher's study—unknown in other buildings in Japan.[18]

The work of the American missionaries and their Japanese compatriots continued. And while progress was made over the next few years, the average Japanese citizen had still not recovered from the war. Housing remained substandard, the food supplies were less than needed to sustain full caloric intake, and there was insufficient clothing for the wintery season. Inflation continued to be a problem. Housing remained a concern, and some families still lived in Hitachi's caves. These were major discussion topics among the six missionary families in the Kuji River Valley. Ibaraki Prefecture remained dominated by a rural population. These rural people tended to be poorer than those in urban regions of Japan. One concern of the American missionaries was their own living standards, much higher than members of the local churches and their nonbelieving neighbors. Evidently the missionaries had discussed the topic in their monthly meetings and the time spent together at the Ibaraki Christian schools. Harry Fox Jr. noted, "From the very day that each of us arrived over here each has been deeply disturbed. [Even] though the nation as a whole has in some respects improved considerably during the past few years our sense of disturbance refuses to go away." Reflecting the attitudes of his fellow missionaries, he continued, "The pressure of this reality has borne so heavily upon us this month that we have hardly been able to think or talk of anything else."[19]

Harry Robert Fox, Jr., used words reflecting his fellow missionaries: "It is we Christians I am so troubled about. Our professions of loyalty to a crucified Saviour sound so hollow when we ourselves make so few *real* sacrifices. Worse still, all of our talk about the superiority of spiritual blessings over things material sounds absurdly unbelievable when coming from automobile-driving, refrigerator-owning, well-fed Americans. . . .[W]e stand practically no chance of convincing the average Asiatic have-not that the Kingdom of God *actually* means more to Christians than the abundance of things we possess."[20]

A few days before he wrote his newsletter, Harry Robert had an experience involving teachers meeting at a nearby junior high school. They had asked to see inside the Fox home in Ota. "After concluding their inspection, one of them expressed the sentiment of the whole group when he spoke up and said, 'You owe it to the Japanese people to teach all of us how to live like that.'" Fox concluded, "[W]e are too well off to touch them spiritually."[21] As a response, the Fox brothers sold their automobile. The missionaries in Ibaraki felt the divide more than missionaries in the urban areas of Japan. They were living among rural, less affluent citizens of Japan.

In the midst of voicing what seemed to be a major concern of the American missionaries, their work had to continue. On March 31, 1950, the school year came to an end. The progress of the school year pleased everyone. In January the high school received accreditation, followed by the college in March. Accreditation meant greater opportunities for Christian service to the young people of Japan. Looking forward to the next school year beginning on April 17, the high school would enroll 180 students, and the projected enrollment for Ibaraki Christian Junior College was 100 students.

On the evening of March 31, the Americans met for a potluck dinner. It was a time to reflect on the past year and look forward to a new year. It was also a time to say good-bye to Dr. Frances Campbell, who had been so important for establishing science programs for the high school and college. She had been in Ibaraki for two years at her own expense. Not only did she teach sciences; she also taught Bible classes in Mito and Tokyo. Through these classes, a number of persons accepted Christ, including Professor Yamaguchi. Very important for Ibaraki Christian College, the professor moved from Tokyo to chair the biology department. Harry Fox said of Frances Campbell, "She has been a true friend to all and will be greatly missed when she returns to her duties at Pepperdine College early in May."[22]

"The Unity of the Spirit": Collaboration among the Ibaraki Staff

Since 1948, the young men from Harding College had focused their preaching on the lower Kuji River towns. In the meantime, the Fox brothers evangelized the regions of northwest Ibaraki and southern Fukushima. In some ways, this separate focus was intentional. The graduates of Harding College saw the graduates of Pepperdine College as "liberal." And those who graduated from Pepperdine—Harry Robert Fox, Jr., Logan Fox, and Carroll Cannon—viewed the Harding boys as too conservative. This attitude remained until every person became involved in the founding of and then teaching every day in Ibaraki Christian College.

Years later, Harry Robert recalled those early years. In an essay entitled "My Life as a Missionary to Japan," he recognized that the establishment of Ibaraki Christian College was the factor that meshed the two attitudes: "[W]e found ourselves having a hard time working with each other [in evangelism]. But having to be together on the ICC campus five days a week, month after month and year after year we became well enough acquainted with each other that we learned to love, trust and respect each other and to feel comfortable working together." He continued, "We discovered that in spite of our differences what we had in common, namely, our relationship to Jesus Christ and His gospel of reconciliation, enabled us to become aware of 'the unity of the Spirit.'"[23]

Ten years after the Harding men and their wives came to Japan, Charles Doyle arrived at the same conclusions. He recalled: "The making or breaking of a missionary depends on how much he learns from his experiences on the field. I do not claim to be exemplary, but I feel that my ten years here have wrought certain changes in me. These can be presented under two heads: first, my attitude toward fellow workers has changed from a negative, critical one to one of positive appreciation, and secondly, my method of working has changed from an extremely individualistic, non-cooperative one to that of a group effort."[24]

He further stated that he had a tendency to be critical of the preaching, speech, and mission methodology of his fellow missionaries. "I had been trained to fight certain sectarian errors and evils, and when these traditional enemies failed to cross my path in Japan, I turned my guns on my fellow workers."[25] He continued, "My conclusion now is that this type of thinking is absolutely suicidal on a mission field. If we don't learn to be less irresponsibly independent and mutually helpful we may as well fold up the tent of world missions and silently steal away."[26]

Doyle continued his confession: "Ten years ago when we were so mutually exclusive and suspicious the only work that kept us associating with each other was the school work at I.C.C." He concluded that he had learned that two or more persons can work together yet be free and independent, "This seems to me to be the real meaning of Christian freedom."[27] Ibaraki College continued to progress, with a mission to remain unified by the spirit of Christ and focused on their work, particularly in the face of new world conflicts that threatened to disrupt the spirit of fellowship fostered by the college's vision and divide the world once again.

Communism and Its Impact on Evangelism and the Ibaraki Christian Schools

By 1950, communism had become a major concern for Western democracies. The Soviet Union erected the Iron Curtain separating Eastern from Western Europe. To protect Western Europe from communist expansion, the United States funded the Marshall Plan to rebuild the continent as a bulwark against the spread of communism. In 1949, the communists defeated the Nationalist government in China. The United States lost its major ally in the Far East. There was the likelihood of communism moving into the Balkans and the Middle East—leading to the Truman Doctrine to aid Greece and Turkey. It seemed the Soviet Union was behind an international conspiracy to rule the world. The rising tide of communism in Japan concerned General MacArthur. With the coming of the Cold War in the 1950s, the issue of communism was widespread in the United States.[28]

The concern was not lost on Christianity, specifically Churches of Christ in the United States and Japan. E. W. McMillan, speaking at Harding College on their annual Bible lectures in 1950, told his audience, "The entire Far Eastern World today—India, China, Korea, Japan, and the smaller islands nearby—educationally, politically, economically and religiously is confronted with two great alternatives, and only two . . . communism and Christianity." He noted how General MacArthur desired to come home, but "he spoke of the unrest, the fear and the burden in every heart. . . . He told graphically of communism and its many ways of doing its work. . . . [He] stressed the fact that the job in the Far East will be well done only when Christian faith is the guide in each life."[29]

The issue became more urgent when in June 1950 North Koreans stormed across the 38th parallel to overrun South Korea. As a result, Korea became a battlefield between communist-inspired North Korea and United Nations–defended South Korea. Korea had been divided along the 38th parallel since the conclusion of World War II, the northern portion under the sway of the Soviet Union. South of the 38th parallel, the region was controlled by the West, dominated by the United States.

Never officially called a war, the police action continued until 1953 when the two sides reached an agreement that the 38th parallel would remain the divide between North and South Korea while negotiators continued seeking a peaceful solution. The Korean action had a substantial impact on Japan. With the loss of China, Japan became the major ally of the United States in the Far East.[30] The American occupation ended in 1952, even though US military bases continued in Japan.

However, the war had little impact on the Ibaraki region of Japan. It remained basically a rural area. Only later would Hitachi become a major player in the economic revolution of Japan. In the Tokyo and Yokohama areas of Japan, there were numerous American military bases where military personnel aided in establishing military churches. This was also true of the Shizuoka region, where Sarah Andrews and Hettie Lee Ewing ministered. There was little military presence in Ibaraki.

Rumors, however, were rampant in the United States about Japanese mission work and the Korean conflict. And, of course, the missionaries in Japan quickly heard from their American friends. Virgil Lawyer responded to the rumors. "No, Ibaraki Christian College is not closing. Yes, Harry Robert Fox and his family are returning to the United States for a furlough." (He and Gerri were the first missionaries to Japan. Therefore they would be the first to return to the States, and they were the only ones on furlough.) "No, the American army has not told all Americans to get out of Japan. Neither is it true that new missionaries are not allowed in Japan." Three new families were in the process of moving across the Pacific Ocean to Japan.[31]

The most insightful reaction to the Korean conflict from a member of the mission team in Ibaraki was an article written late in 1950 by Carroll Cannon for the *Firm Foundation*, titled "If War Comes. . . ?"

Cannon emphasized President Harry Truman's "state of emergency" on December 16, 1950, when the Chinese rejected a United Nations "cease-fire" proposal. Furthermore, the Soviet Union warned Great Britain and France that the USSR was considering breaking treaty agreements made with the two countries because the USSR was in the planning stages of an agreement to rearm West Germany. The question Cannon raised was not political but one having to do with mission efforts even in places like Japan: "If war comes on a universal scale, what will happen to the mission programs in foreign lands?" The funds overseen by Union Avenue in Memphis had already declined by more than 50 percent. This, of course, was a major concern. Cannon saw the conflict as one between "Western Democracies and Russian Nationalistic Communism." If the West was victorious, then the mission efforts could be saved. Regardless, he trusted in the "unshakable" kingdom of God: "It is our faith that 'his word will not return unto him void.'"[32]

The most immediate impact was the reaction of the Ninth and Lime church in Long Beach. Harry Fox had not planned to take a furlough so soon. The missionaries had agreed to stay in Japan five years, yet after only three years in late 1950, the concerned church called the Fox family home. While away, they would leave a void in the lives of several churches founded and nurtured by their efforts. Gerri arrived in America pregnant with their second child; John was born in December. Making their headquarters in Lubbock, Texas, where Gerri's parents lived, Harry continued working on behalf of Ibaraki Christian College, traveling widely as far east as Tennessee.[33]

Despite the loss of the Fox family and concerns about budget cuts amid the threat of communism, the Ibaraki missions continued to grow. Richard Baggett and his family soon arrived in Ibaraki—the first family to come to Ibaraki since Carroll and Nona Cannon arrived in the spring of 1949—with support from the Jackson Avenue and Union Avenue Churches of Christ. Harold and Geraldine Holland also arrived in Japan in the latter part of 1950, with the support of the Harding College church in Searcy, Arkansas. Ibaraki Christian College continued to flourish amid adversity, even though the faculty had to deal with certain issues posed by the Churches of Christ in the United States.

Critics of Foreign Missions

In August 1949, Charles Doyle penned a lengthy article for the *Firm Foundation* titled "You Are Mistaken about Japan." In the article he assured the readers that the "six couples in Ibaraki are not premillennialists"; nor were they unsound in the faith. "I did not travel all the way to Japan just to present the traditions and philosophies of foolish men. . . . Most assuredly, our work is sound, and should have the confidence and backing of all loyal brethren."[34]

Going beyond the millennial issue and lack of soundness because of age, Doyle introduced an issue pervading American Churches of Christ in the years following World War II. For lack of better terms, the words "institutional" and "noninstitutional" were widely used to separate brethren in the fellowship. A minority of Churches of Christ believed that having a sponsoring church was unscriptural if other churches and individuals funneled support for missionaries through that church.

Generally speaking, the noninstitutional churches opposed cooperative efforts of churches supporting all "institutions" such as schools, children's homes, homes for the aged, and radio and television programs. Doyle concluded his article by attempting to dissuade critics of the Ibaraki mission from making false conclusions. They were in Japan, he explained, to preach the gospel of Christ and to share Christ in the Bible classes in both the high school and college—nothing else.

Although the feelings were not widespread, there were a few in America who questioned foreign mission work soon after World War II because of the great need for ministry to citizens and noncitizens in the United States. Among the first to raise questions about foreign missions was F. L. Rowe, publisher of the *Christian Leader*. Sharing his views through his paper, he urged those who supported foreign missions to respond to questions. Alternatively, he suggested preaching among the Japanese in California where there were 100,000 Japanese before World War II. "Against all of this untouched population we are already reading of certain enthusiasts planning to take the gospel to the warring nations after the war. How true it is that 'distance lends enchantment to the view.' And these starving nations will not welcome American foreigners for the next ten years."[35]

C. G. Vincent, an early missionary to Japan, was among those who responded to Rowe. He questioned how Rowe knew that "100 or 1,000" could be converted in America for the same outlay of money it would take to send a missionary to Japan. Vincent reminded Rowe that the last command given by Jesus was to begin in Jerusalem and then to Samaria and to all parts of the world. If the early Christians had remained in Jerusalem, "then neither Brother Rowe nor I would be enjoying the blessings of the gospel of Jesus Christ today." He asked Rowe to recall Paul's missionary efforts and the Holy Spirit's denial of Paul's desire to preach in Asia. The call was for Paul and his friends to cross over into Macedonia, an outlying area of Europe, to teach people far removed from Jerusalem. The same call remained true in the years following the war. Leave Cincinnati or other places in the United States, said Vincent, and "go into all the world."[36]

Moving Forward Despite Adversity

The issues raised in the United States did not deter the mission emphasis of the men who had come to Japan to share the message of Jesus Christ. During 1951, Joe Cannon, Virgil Lawyer, and Charles Doyle conducted outdoor revivals. On one occasion, Lawyer preached an entire sermon standing under an umbrella in a rainstorm, while about one hundred attentive listeners also stood under their umbrellas. E. J. Bonner of the Union Avenue church related that Virgil Lawyer stated that "they were experiencing things that he would not trade for a year's formal education." The following week, the three Harding men and Logan Fox would all be holding meetings in four separate towns—this was the culmination of a successful summer for evangelism. They reported ninety-three baptisms even before the four-meeting week.[37]

As the years passed, the Japanese missionaries realized the need for more in-depth instruction for native preachers and church leaders. Even though Bible study at the college and high school added up to 1,700 hours of study, the native men who desired to preach had little opportunity for study in formal classes.[38] Carroll Cannon reported in September 1951 that the missionaries were organizing classes for adult students beyond the junior college level. The aim of the program was (1) to provide instruction and training for church leaders, church Bible school teachers, and ministers; (2) to build strong Christ-like character; and (3) to give thorough Bible instruction and related studies—world religions, church doctrine, and church work.

The curriculum required two years and seventy-two hours to complete. All the missionaries would serve on the faculty. This ambitious curriculum compared favorably to a senior college Bible major in the United States.[39]

In April 1951, Ibaraki Christian College opened its doors to one hundred new students. Logan Fox, the dean of the college, noted that ten years previous the Japanese had bombed Pearl Harbor and plunged the United States into a bloodletting war with Japan. He continued, "To us Americans one name symbolized all that was diabolical in war-crazy Japan—Premier Tojo." Yet Kimiye Tojo, the eighteen-year-old daughter of Hideki Tojo, was among the new enrollees. Fox had been asked if the college could help the Tojo family. Tojo, found guilty of war crimes by the International Tribunal for the Far East, was hanged on December 23, 1948. The ostracized family was in financial difficulties. Fox said of the opportunity to teach the youngest daughter of Premier Tojo, echoing his father, "We feel this is a wonderful chance for us to serve our Master who taught us to love our enemies. Miss Tojo is hungry for the love of Christ, forgiveness, strength and hope."[40]

In the meantime, Carroll and Nona Cannon returned to the United States. They also took three Japanese students with them with prospects of continuing their education in American schools. Carroll began work on a PhD in religious education at New York University, and Nona received a doctorate from Columbia University in home economics. At the beginning of the fall 1953 school year, both Cannons joined the faculty of Harding College.[41]

In September 1951, Harry Robert and Gerri Fox, along with their children Kenny and John, returned to Japan from eleven months in the United States. They were anxious to resume their work in both the college and evangelism. They moved to a Japanese-style house near the campus where the Lawyers had first lived. They could not immediately take possession because the house, located in Omika, was not ready for occupancy. The straw mats on the floor needed replacing and the paper doors were in tatters. They lived with other missionaries while they made the repairs.[42]

The following Sunday, September 9, they drove up the valley to meet with the Tanakura church where Harry Robert Fox, Sr., preached from 1923 to 1930. The church was worshiping in a new building constructed in 1950 before the Foxes returned to the States. In the afternoon they visited the Daigo church. The church had never had a meeting place during all the time Herman Fox worked in the town. But when Harry Robert and his family visited on September 9, the church welcomed them in a new building. It had seating for three hundred persons and featured a four-room apartment for the preacher. It was made possible when Harry Jr., on a visit to the Grandview church in Nashville, showed slides of the members of the Daigo church. After the presentation, one of the elders, Brother Hester, contributed $1,000 for the construction of a building.[43] On a number of occasions, Fox complemented the Grandview church for their support of the work in Japan. Two individuals from the church sent $600 for the construction of other church buildings in Ibaraki. He then added, "[I] wish also to express our thanks to the entire Grandview church for their long and continuous support of the work over here."[44]

Since they arrived in Japan during the break between sessions of the schools, Harry Robert involved himself in numerous preaching engagements plus preaching at multiple places each Sunday. On October 22, 1951, the college and high school reopened. Fox taught three classes three times each week. He taught "The Life and Teachings of Jesus" to first-year college students and instructed second-year students in the New Testament epistles. By teaching these classes, he was able to reach 150 students three times each week.[45] Multiply these numbers many times over, with each missionary teaching three or four classes of Bible and Bible-related courses, and it becomes evident how much of a contribution the college made to the Ibaraki Prefecture. For the Japanese men enrolled in the special curriculum, Robert taught sermon preparation and delivery.

Each year brought new experiences for the churches in Ibaraki. When the five missionary families arrived in 1948, there were only six scattered churches. In early 1952, twenty-five congregations were meeting regularly. Throughout Japan, three thousand persons had been baptized and thirty churches organized since World War II. (Harry Robert Fox, Jr., in December 1952, stated that thirty-five churches were meeting in Ibaraki.

Either there was a miscount earlier in the year or 1952 was a banner year for establishing churches.) The vast majority of churches and conversions in Japan had taken place in Ibaraki. At the Ota church, two hundred persons had been baptized since the end of the war. The resident evangelist for the Ota church was Brother Tachi, converted during the 1930s by the old-guard missionaries.[46] He had support from the Grandview church in Nashville.[47] As was true of all rural areas where there were few work opportunities, many of those baptized moved to Tokyo to find employment.[48] Thus the attendance in churches did not reflect the large number of baptisms.

The numbers of baptisms had been down for a time, but during May through October 1951, some 270 baptisms happened in Ibaraki. Joe Cannon, writing in the *Christian Chronicle* in January 1951, introduced a sobering conclusion. First, he believed it was important to read the Japanese language, in addition to simply speaking it. He continued, "It is our desire to spend our lives in the work here, if God is willing. The work in Japan although having initial success must be approached on a long-range basis. If not, the work will die when the missionaries [leave]." As an observation, he believed the newness of the foreigners was wearing off and the native Japanese were more effectively reaching the people.[49]

With the arrival of new missionary families, including Joe Bryant and his family in April 1952, William Harris and his family on May 26, 1952, Max Mowrer and his family later in 1952, and the return of Harry Robert Fox and his family, the number of missionaries remained about the same. Two of the original families to locate in Japan chose to return to the United States on furlough, where they would encourage support for evangelism in Japan and Ibaraki Christian College. Charles Doyle and his family, arriving in the United States the first week of April, would be gone for eighteen months.[50] Logan Fox and his family, supported by the Union Avenue church for this trip, would spend much of their time raising a goal of $25,000 for Ibaraki Christian College. The Fox family left for America on April 18 with plans to establish their base in Nashville so the children could attend the Lipscomb campus schools. Their plan, like that of the Doyles, was to remain in the States for eighteen months.[51]

A Move toward Permanency

Despite the fact that the missionaries felt that churches needed permanent places to meet, in 1952 many Japanese churches continued to meet in temporary locations (i.e., homes, town meeting halls, rooms in an old factory, even in a cave). On the other hand, a growing number of churches had meeting places, including Hitachi, Tanakura, Ota (an old residence), and Daigo.

With Logan Fox and Charles Doyle in the United States in 1952, it was an excellent time to let the churches in America know the physical needs of the Japanese churches. This was the responsibility of Virgil Lawyer through the Union Avenue church in Memphis. His task was to tell of the needs of several churches but, more importantly, the upcoming construction that would take place in 1952 on a number of church buildings. He emphasized, "Our congregations far outnumber our buildings at the present time. . . . [But now there are] bright prospects for the coming year, due to the response of many churches throughout the States."[52]

The Katsuta church, with fifty members, was three years old and had been meeting in a factory dormitory room. Early in 1951, the church purchased a nice plot of land for $210 with "forty stately pine trees."[53] The Central Church of Christ in Chattanooga, Tennessee, agreed to raise $1,000 to construct the building. The church in Isabel, Kansas, sent funds as well. The building would have seating for one hundred, but it did not have classrooms or a baptistery. They believed the building would be completed in March 1952.

The second church mentioned by Lawyer was a three-year-old church in Takahagi. For Japan, it was a rather large church with fifty members. The Seventh Street and G Church of Christ, Temple, Texas, sent $1,000 for the construction of an auditorium. Charles Doyle promised to raise an additional $500 for classrooms and a baptistery. A third building was scheduled to be constructed in Kujihama for a church with thirty-five members. An individual in Santa Ana, California, promised $1,000 for the building, but they needed $300 more to purchase property.

Ota was the largest and oldest church in Ibaraki Prefecture. In 1952, the church, with a membership of about two hundred, had been meeting in a remodeled dwelling while waiting for a time to build a structure that would seat three hundred people. A member of the Pioneer Park church in

Lubbock, Texas, contributed $2,000 toward the construction of the build-
ing. There would be four classrooms but no baptistery. The Kuji River was
their River Jordan.

Several other churches needed buildings: Motoyama (sixty members),
Minami Nakago (eight members), Isohama (fifteen members), Kasama
(thirty-five members), and Mito (sixty members). Jesse Fox of the Union
Avenue church underlined that $1,000—plus $300—would construct a
building in each location. The construction of new buildings for Japanese
Christians, without funds of their own, was made possible by a fellowship
that crossed the Pacific Ocean, with Christ's love overpowering the war
that had divided the world.

The Need for New Buildings at Ibaraki Christian College

In the midst of construction efforts, Logan Fox, the dean of Ibaraki Christian
College, took leave of his work at the college in April 1952 to make a trip
to the United States on behalf of the school. The college and high school
were in need of at least two new buildings requiring the expenditure of
$20,000. The men who came to Japan were missionaries first, with their
emphasis on evangelism. They constantly reminded their sponsors and all
Churches of Christ in America that the school was not the church. Yet as
Christians, teaching young people was an important part of their mission.
The vast majority of the converts to Christianity in Japan were between
the ages of seventeen and twenty-five. The missionaries believed these
young adults were best served by having a school where they could study
the Bible each day.

The largest single amount of all funds from American Churches of
Christ after World War II went toward developing Ibaraki Christian College.
As of 1952, $60,000 had been invested in land and eight buildings for the
school—a high school building to accommodate two hundred students, a
lab building, a dining hall, a small recreational building, a junior college
building to accommodate one hundred students, a home economics building, and two dormitories, housing twenty-five students each. Where else
could an investment of $60,000 return such a reward? And to underline the
low cost of the campus, Harry Fox reminded his readers that average-sized

churches in America were spending $100,000 on new buildings, used only one-fifth the time of the buildings of Ibaraki Christian College.

The investment of $1,500 per month to maintain the teaching program was small when compared to the cost of providing full-time preachers in the United States. Harry Robert added:

> Surely all of the "seed of the Kingdom" we are privileged to sow in the hearts and lives of these hundreds of Japanese young people cannot but produce a great spiritual harvest. In the place of Buddhism, Shintoism and Emperor worship these students are being taught faith in the only God who is, and are being taught obedience to his will. Whereas previously the only cause these people knew to lay down their lives for was that of the Nation, now they are being introduced to the highest cause for which it is possible to live or die: the Cause of Christ and all that he represents.[54]

April 1952 saw the beginning of the fourth year for Ibaraki Christian College and the fifth year for the Christian high school. Reaching the youth of Japan with the gospel of Christ was a major priority for the faculty of Ibaraki Christian College—the outgrowth of the King Bible School begun in Ota in 1928. The dream of American missionaries for Christian schools in Japan was not unlike the dream of David Lipscomb and James A. Harding when they had a vision for the Nashville Bible School and Christian colleges across America. Despite the many miles and cultural differences between them, the spiritual needs of both nations remained entwined.

Endnotes

[1] E. W. McMillan, "Developments in the Japanese Work," *Firm Foundation*, January 18 1949, 2.

[2] Logan Fox, "Christian Education in a Heathen Nation," *Christian Leader*, February 2, 1954, 34.

[3] E. W. McMillan, "Developments in the Japanese Work," *Firm Foundation*, January 18, 1949, 2, 3.

[4] Harry Robert Fox, Jr. (ed.), *Japan Christian*, July 1949.

[5] Ibid., August 1949.

[6] Ibid.

[7] Ibid.

[8] Ibid.

[9] Conversation by telephone with Harry Robert Fox, Jr., December 7, 2013.

[10] E. W. McMillan, "Memorable Moments," *Gospel Advocate*, November 24, 1949, 745.

[11] Harry Robert Fox, Jr. (ed.), *Japan Christian*, October 1949.

[12] E. W. McMillan, "Churches, 1525 Baptisms Show Results of Post-War Work Done among Japanese," *Christian Chronicle*, November 2, 1949, 5.

[13] Harry Robert Fox, Jr. (ed.), *Japan Christian*, October 1949.

[14] Ibid., December 1949.

[15] A handwritten essay on Masaichi Kikuchi by Harry Robert Fox, October 2013. Special Collections, Beaman Library, Lipscomb University, Nashville, Tennessee.

[16] Harry Robert Fox, Jr. (ed.), *Japan Christian*, December 1949.

[17] Ibid.

[18] Harry Robert Fox, Jr. (ed.), *Ota Christian News*, January 1950. The name of Harry Robert Fox, Jr.'s paper changed in January 1950.

[19] Ibid., February 1950.

[20] Ibid.; E. W. McMillan, "Localities: Who and What in Japan," *Gospel Advocate*, April, 13, 1950, 226, 227.

[21] Harry Robert Fox, Jr. (ed.), *Ota Christian*, February 1950.

[22] Harry Robert Fox, Jr. (ed.), *Ota Christian*, March 1950.

[23] Harry Robert Fox, Jr., "My Life as a Missionary to Japan," unpublished essay. A copy is in Special Collection, Beaman Library, Lipscomb University, Nashville, Tennessee.

[24] Charles Doyle, "Ten Years in Japan—an Observation," *Firm Foundation*, January 21, 1958.

[25] Ibid.

[26] Ibid.

[27] Ibid.

[28] George C. Herring, *From Colony to Superpower: U.S. Foreign Relations since 1776* (New York: Oxford University Press, 2008), 637, 649, 657.

[29] E. W. McMillan, "The Restoration Movement in the Orient," *Harding College Lectures*, 1950, 98, 99.

[30] John W. Dower, *Embracing Defeat: Japan in the Wake of World War II* (New York: W. W. Norton, 1999), 541–46.

[31] Virgil Lawyer, "Japanese Worker Denies Rumors That War Crisis Is Jeopardizing Work," *Christian Chronicle*, October 11, 1950, 6.

[32] R. C. Cannon, "If War Comes. . . ?," *Firm Foundation*, February 6, 1951, 4.

[33] Because of military needs, private organizations could no longer use Army-Air postal service. "From General Headquarters Far East Command APO 500 to Church of Christ APO 500," *Firm Foundation*, September 26, 1950, 5. The *Firm Foundation* published the addresses of the missionaries in Japan, except Sarah Andrews and Hettie Lee Ewing.

[34] Charles W. Doyle, "You Are Mistaken about Japan," *Firm Foundation*, August 2, 1949, 2, 3.

[35] F. L. Rowe, "Are Japan Missions Worthwhile?," *Christian Leader*, February 27, 1945, 10.

[36] C. G. Vincent, "Are Japan Missions Worthwhile?," *Christian Leader*, March 27, 1945, 4, 5.

[37] E. J. Bonner, "Virgil Lawyer Preaches Full Sermon under an Umbrella," *Gospel Advocate*, August 9, 1951, 509.

[38] R. C. Cannon "1700 Different People Are Taught the Bible Each Month," *Firm Foundation*, January 30, 1951, 7.

[39] R. C. Cannon, "Special Bible Training Course for Native Japanese," *Firm Foundation*, September 11, 1951, 4.

[40] Logan J. Fox, "Tojo's Daughter Enrolls in Ibaraki Christian College," *Gospel Advocate*, May 31, 1951, 347.

[41] No author, "R. C. Cannons to Arrive in U. S. April 8 for Tour among Churches in Interest of Japan Evangelism," *Christian Chronicle*, April 4, 1951, 1; W. B. West, Jr., "R. C. Cannon Joins Harding Faculty," *Firm Foundation*, September 1, 1953, 6.

[42] Harry Robert Fox, Jr. (ed.), *Omika News-Letter*, September 1951.

[43] Ibid.

[44] Ibid., November 1951.

[45] Ibid., October 1951.

[46] Ibid., May 1952.

[47] Ibid., February 1952.

[48] No author, "Near 3,000 Baptisms and 30 New Congregations in Japan during Past Five Years," *Christian Chronicle*, May 7, 1952, 4; Reprint of article by Harry Robert Fox, Jr., in *Omika News-Letter*, "54 Baptisms in Summer Meetings in Japan; Needs More Personal Workers," *Christian Chronicle*, December 10, 1952, 5.

[49] Doyle Cannon, "Japan Worker Says He Went to Spend His Life in Evangelizing and He Has No Complaints," *Christian Chronicle*, January 31, 1951, 1.

[50] No author, "Doyles to Return for Furlough from Work in Japan," *Christian Chronicle*, March 5, 1952, 1.

[51] Harry Robert Fox, Jr. (ed.), *Omika News-Letter*, April 1952.

[52] Jesse W. Fox, "New Building Planned for Church in Japan," *Firm Foundation*, February 26, 1952, 10. Fox included a report from Virgil Lawyer.

[53] Ibid.

[54] Ibid., April 1952.

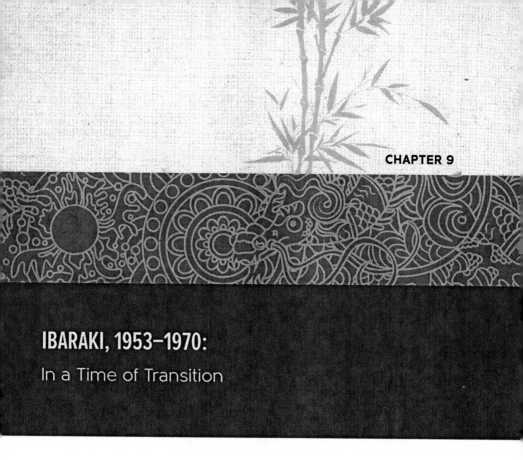

CHAPTER 9

IBARAKI, 1953–1970:

In a Time of Transition

January 1, 1953, marked five years and three months since Harry Robert and Gerri Fox arrived in Japan. Harry Robert was returning to the place of his birth, having left Japan with his family in 1935. Seven months later in April 1948, his brother Logan, accompanied by his wife Madeline, returned to Japan after a thirteen year absence. Earlier in 1948, Orville D. Bixler welcomed three young couples from Harding College. These young people—Virgil and Lou Lawyer, Joe and Rosa Belle Cannon, and Charles and Norma Doyle—were in a strange country without knowing the language and very little of Japanese culture and traditions. Stepping off the ship in Yokohama, they faced horrific destruction and despair. They had come to help the Japanese people conquer their despair through the message of the gospel of Jesus Christ. Not only would they be totally involved in evangelism; they were quickly commissioned to begin a high school in

253

Omika, Ibaraki Prefecture. In 1949, the Fox brothers and Carroll Cannon joined them in the inauguration of Ibaraki Christian College. What a daunting task!

From the time Harry Robert Fox arrived in Japan until 1953, twenty-one workers from Churches of Christ had come to Japan, with the majority of them settling in Ibaraki. The chief purpose in going to Japan was evangelism and establishing churches. They held an average of thirty "gospel meetings" per summer, with each man preaching multiple times on Sundays. During the week, these same men, plus an increasing number of Japanese preachers, held classes in homes, hospitals, sanatoriums, courts, schools, shops, and outdoor venues. From these evangelistic endeavors, over three thousand persons were baptized in Ibaraki. In all, the young missionaries and the native preachers established thirty-four churches in the state. To care for older people and orphaned children, Japanese Christians established an orphanage and an old folks' home.[1]

The years 1953 to 1970 were truly a time of transition for these six young families. Logan Fox told an eager audience at the Abilene Christian College Lectures in 1953 that "a nation which had been one of the most unfruitful mission fields in the world, in the space of four short, but awful years, became one of the most fruitful fields ever known." He told about the establishment of sixty churches in ten Japanese states, with twenty American missionaries, fifty Japanese preachers, and possibly as many as five thousand members. Fox indicated, "The people were hungry and cold and confused and afraid. Everything about them was changing and no one seemed quite sure about what to change and what ought not to change." Christianity offered people an answer to desperate needs: "Their nation had fallen, their gods had abdicated, their economy had collapsed, and their culture was outdated."[2]

The year 1953 was the beginning of a transition for Churches of Christ throughout Japan, but especially in Ibaraki. It was the time for one family, the Lawyers, to permanently return to the United States after five years in Japan without a furlough. Joe and Rosa Belle Cannon began a well-deserved furlough in 1953. The Cannons returned to Japan and Ibaraki Christian College in October 1954.[3] There had been several changes in administration at Ibaraki Christian College and High School. E. W. McMillan had served as the first president but spent most of his time in the United States raising funds for the schools. Shortly after McMillan was elected president of Ibaraki, he also accepted the presidency of Southwestern Christian College, a predominantly African American school in Terrell, Texas. The burden was so great that he asked to be relieved of his duties with Ibaraki Christian College.

On November 26, 1952, the board of directors, chaired by Harry Robert Fox, Jr., named E. W. McMillan president emeritus. At the same meeting, the board elected Logan Fox, who had served as dean since the college's inception, as president of the school. This was certainly a major transition for Ibaraki Christian College.[4] It was even more critical for Logan to be concerned about money matters. He had been elected president while he was in the United States engaged in raising funds for the college. He returned on April 3, 1953, to Japan.

Over the previous two or three years, the names of the missionaries had begun to change. The first to leave were Carroll Cannon and his family in 1951. In January 1953, Virgil Lawyer and his family returned to the United States without plans to return to Japan. The Lawyers settled in Justin, Texas, where in September 1953 Virgil Lawyer became the preacher for the Church of Christ in that community. Before moving to Justin, he traveled on behalf of the work in Japan and was the interim preacher, in the absence of Robert C. Jones, for the Southside Church of Christ in Fort Worth. This church had supported the Lawyers for the entire five years they were in Japan. With the return of the Lawyers, the church agreed to support Charles Doyle and family on their return to Japan.[5]

Max and Mildred Mowrer arrived in Yokohama on April 17, 1953, en route to Omika, Ibaraki, to join the faculty of the Ibaraki schools. Educated in the Bible and music, Mowrer and his wife came to Japan from Valdosta, Georgia, after graduating from Harding College in 1951. The Northside church in Wichita, Kansas, supported them in Japan.[6]

With the coming of the Mowrers, the five families living on campus decided to begin an American-style school for their children. Among the five families were eleven small children, and hopefully the families could provide their children "the same kind of education as they would [have] in the States." Mildred Mowrer was the preschool teacher of a class that included her own child and Kenny Fox.[7]

There was another very important consequence of the five families living on campus. The missionaries recognized the loneliness the women and children experienced, left by themselves in outlying areas while the men were out nights and weekends preaching or teaching classes. Now, Fox wrote, "the wives and children can have plenty of congenial associates and not get lonesome in a strange land." Harry Robert shared the feelings of the Ibaraki families with the churches in America supporting the work in Ibaraki: "[W]e are really thankful for the opportunity of living in the Omika community."[8]

The June issue of Harry Fox's report to his supporting churches and individuals carried a new name. Instead of the *Omika Newsletter*, he changed it to the *Kuji-Valley News*. The reasons for this change were multifaceted. The first title, *Japan Christian*, was given in 1947 when Harry Robert and Gerri arrived in Japan. This was too broad because the monthly publication was largely concerned with the state of Ibaraki. Then he changed it to *Ota Newsletter* because the Fox brothers were living and working out of Ota. When Harry Robert and Gerri returned to Japan in 1951, they chose to locate in Omika. Since they were no longer in Ota and Logan had already constructed a house on the campus, Harry and Gerri chose to build their home on campus as well. This meant that the newsletter needed a new name, thus *Omika Newsletter*. After two years, Harry Robert, very likely in consultation with Logan, chose to broaden the nature of the paper by calling it the *Kuji-Valley News*.

Adopting the title *Kuji-Valley News*, the publication more accurately described the "geographical bounds" of the Fox brothers' evangelistic work. Harry Robert recalls, "I have told you how the Kuji River has been called the 'Jordan River' of northwestern Ibaraki, [because] so many have been the baptisms that have taken place in it over the past thirty years." He remembered that almost all the evangelistic work of the pre–World War II missionaries had been along the Kuji River. The valley cuts across northern Ibaraki from the east to the northwest and extends to the neighboring state of Fukushima. Since returning to Japan in 1947 and 1948, the focus of the Fox men had been the interior regions of the Kuji River Valley and neighboring Tachigi Prefecture, the location of Shiauki and Karasuyama.[9]

The Fox brothers fully understood the limited nature of their time in Japan. Harry shared with American Christians the transitions taking place in Japan. "But more important, in the long run, than anything Logan and I can do for these churches is the work being done by the eighteen Japanese laboring among them." The future was before them. "From now on," stated Harry Fox, Jr., "I am more and more going to use the greater part of this news-letter to report the activities of these men in the Kuji Valley."

Harry Robert continued, "[T]he major turning point in [the Japanese preachers'] lives and in the history of the churches in the Kuji Valley occurred when they, Logan, and I met together on June 20 and 21, 1952 for a two-day retreat in the mountains near Daigo." It was at this retreat that Harry believed they were able to more fully "discern the will of the Lord for us." This was the first time the eighteen Japanese evangelists and the Fox brothers had met together. The two days together revitalized everyone: "The men returned to their respective home communities with a zeal and determination seldom seen among them."

One of the most important conclusions emerging from the retreat was a change in the future training of the evangelists. Instead of the School for the Evangelists at ICC, the preachers would begin meeting every Thursday at the Urizura church building for study and worship. The Fox brothers shared teaching responsibilities. They would engage in a systematic study of the Bible and related subjects. Other areas of Japan, especially in Tokyo, were also localizing learning opportunities for the evangelists.[10]

The Legacy of Japanese Evangelists

Native evangelists played an integral part in the development of the Churches of Christ ministry, establishing a long legacy of fellowship and collaboration between the two nations, even in the face of global conflict. Prior to World War II, there were only five or six native preachers who labored across the expanse of Japan, including Otoshige Fujimori, Yunosuka Hiratsuka, and Ryohachi Shigekuni. These men served throughout Japan beginning as early as 1897 when Fujimori and F. A. Wagner came to Japan as missionaries to Fujimori's native land. In August 1953, Logan Fox visited "Oto," then age eighty, at his home in Sawara in Chiba Prefecture. Basically inactive in evangelism following World War II, he continued with the small church in Sawara and traveled once a month to Tokyo. Fujimori was age twenty-five when he returned to Japan, where he began serving several churches in the state of Chiba. He was always ready when called by Sarah Andrews in Shizuoka, in Tokyo, and to the far north in Sapporo, Hokkaido. Logan Fox stated in 1953 that Fujimori "was known as our most capable evangelist in Japan before the war."

In his years before World War II, the Plum Street church in Detroit supported Oto. However, after the war, he insisted on being independent. He and his wife lived on rent money from accumulated property. According to Fox, Fujimori chose not to reconnect with the missionaries following the war. "I sensed in him some resentment against the domination of the work in Japan by American missionaries." Fujimori believed they had not sought advice from the older Japanese brothers. Living in the past, he affectionately remembered his teacher Frederick Wagner and his close working friendship with Sarah Andrews in Shizuoka.[11]

Later when Burton Coffman visited Japan, he mentioned that Oto Fujimori had been reading the *Christian Leader* for forty years—a paper Coffman had once edited. Throughout the years, Fujimori and Wagner reported their work through the pages of the *Leader* with an article every two weeks or so. Coffman stated that Fujimori continued to preach three Sundays a month for the church in Sawara and one Sunday for the Central church in Tokyo. As discovered by Logan Fox, Fujimori had little income— only money from rental properties, about 28 cents from the Sawara church each week, and 2,000 yen (about $5.50) each month from the Tokyo church. Coffman reported, "His knowledge embraces nearly sixty years of the unfolding drama of Church of Christ missionary activity in Japan."[12]

The last known contact American missionaries had with Fujimori was a letter declining an invitation to attend the 1955 annual summer retreat for Japanese Christians and American missionaries. Invited by Harry Robert Fox, Jr., he responded with a typed note:

Sawara, Sawara-Shi

June 22nd, 1955

Dear Brother Fox:

I thank you very much for the good and kind letter of the June 17th, 1955. Thank you for the invitation. I should accept it right at once, but I am getting too old one prepeal [the word is neither legible nor understandable].

You know I am 83 and 6 months old. I beg your pardon for not attending such a grand meeting. May God blessing upon the meeting and have a great success. Please, tell these brethren my christian [sic] love to them.

Your brother in Christ,
Otoshige Fujimori

In his own hand he added,

please pardon my poor English. OF.[13]

Otoshige Fujimori lived to be ninety years of age, dying on May 19, 1962.[14] The second of the prewar evangelists, Yunosuke Hiratsuka, preceded Fujimori in death, passing away on December 15, 1953, at the age of eighty years.[15] The deaths of Fujimori and Hiratsuka were certainly a huge loss and marked a time of transition among native preachers in Japan.

The youngest of the trio of long-term preachers of the gospel in Japan was Ryohachi Shigekuni. As a result of his younger age, his ministry continued even more intensely after World War II. Despite their declining membership and the fact that they met in a dormitory room of the old Bible school during the war years, the Ota church was kept alive by the Shigekuni family. Following the war, the Fox brothers and their families lived in Ota and attended the Ota church when they were not engaged in evangelism in surrounding communities.

For a while after the war, Shigekuni continued ministering to the Ota church. Harry Robert remembered listening to sermons given by Brother Shigekuni. Most of his sermons were on "Love." Fox said of the Japanese brother's preaching, "At first I began to feel tired of hearing a preacher preach on one subject for so many Sundays. But my feelings changed when I realized that Love is an inexhaustible subject which can't be preached too often."

As everyone came to appreciate, the defining characteristic of Ryohachi Shigekuni was his loving disposition. According to Fox, "He was one of the most loving, caring men I ever knew—and one who was among the most *genuinely* humble." And it was Shigekuni who advocated establishing the Christian high school and college in Omika. In fact, he gave the school its name—Shion Gakuen. When the super-rich Mitsui family offered O. D. Bixler the opportunity to operate their privately owned high school as a Christian school, Bixler persuaded Ryohachi to move to Tokyo to help operate the school. For a while, Shigekuni continued his relationship with the school and Bixler. Finding it difficult to work with Bixler, the Shigekuni family relocated to Yokohama, where he accepted an invitation to work with the Kanazawa and Nogeyama churches, planted by Erroll Rhodes. Ryohachi Shigekuni remained with the Nogeyama church for the remainder of his life.

In a 1964 letter to Harry Robert Fox, Jr., Shigekuni spoke of his work with the Yokohama church. His wife had died earlier in the year, and he was deeply impressed when more than two hundred people came "even [when] it was the coldest snowey [sic] day." Later he and his family traveled north to Ota where the Shigekunis had ministered so long. The church held a memorial for Fu-San, the name given to Hurako by the missionary children prior to World War II.[16]

In addition to Fujimori, Hiratsuka, and Shigekuni, a number of other Japanese preachers kept churches alive in the Kuji Valley and elsewhere during World War II. In Tokyo, S. M. Saito, along with Yunosuke Hiratsuka, preached for J. M. McCaleb's Zoshigaya church. In the state of Ibaraki, besides Ryohachi Shigekuni at Ota, a Brother Goto worked with the Omiya church. The Urizura church thrived because of Masaichi Kikuchi's ministering. At

Nagasawa, the Hiratsuka family kept the church alive, as did Brother Akutsu at the Ose church.[17] The efforts of these Christian men made it much easier for missionaries to reenter the state of Ibaraki following the war and inspired a new generation of Japanese evangelists post–World War II.

Passing the Torch: Young Evangelists Accept the Challenge

Beyond the devastation of World War II, young Japanese evangelists continued to heed the call to lead their people in the spirit of Jesus Christ, carrying on the long legacy of the native evangelists that came before them. By 1953, according to Logan Fox, there were as many as fifty Japanese preachers serving churches in various ways. With the exception of the men who had served the churches during the war, it was a new generation of men converted to Christ since World War II. Some were young men educated at Ibaraki Christian College. While students, many were converted to Christianity and then chose to preach the good news of Jesus Christ. Other men, somewhat older, chose to study in the special programs offered by the missionaries.

Yet few of these brave evangelists had as unique a backstory as Kiyoharu Tabata, a young man who began his young adult life in prison. Harry Robert Fox met Kiyoharu Tabata when Tabata was only eighteen years of age. Without a good nurturing home, his life had no direction. He and two friends tangled themselves in a prank when they interfered with the departure of a train in Tokyo, leading Tabata to be sentenced to two years in prison. Preparing for incarceration, Tabata listened to his cousin, who was a member of the Ota church, concerning the importance of Christ for his life. A few days before Tabata's imprisonment, Fox baptized him in the Kuji River.

While in the States on furlough, Fox had shared with a small group of members of the Ninth and Lime church in Long Beach his desire to enlist Tabata as his fellow worker in Japan. This special group of Christians quickly agreed to support this young man. Determined to raise $15 a month to support Tabata, these Christians collected and sold used newspapers.[18] Immediately on the Fox's return to Japan in the fall of 1951, Tabata became Harry Robert's "Timothy."

The relationship was a perfect fit for twenty-one-year-old Tabata. He accompanied Harry Robert on all his preaching engagements. He would canvass neighborhoods in preparation for preaching services. In January

1952, the young man had a special idea. He asked Fox to travel with him to his home village of Sakiku, where they would engage in a full day of meetings. The first assembly was a gathering of the village women, who met from 2:00 p.m. to 5:00 p.m. in the afternoon. At 6:00 p.m., Tabata spoke to a congregation of teachers. At 7:00 p.m., Fox met a gathering of young people, a meeting lasting until 10:00 p.m. In between the last two gatherings, Tabata took Fox to his home for a supper of raw fish. Through sheer willpower, Fox ate the fish and, surprised, enjoyed his meal. The three preaching sessions planted seeds but produced no visible results.[19]

By October 1953, Harry Robert believed Tabata was able, with assistance from his "Paul," to oversee and carry on the work of the small church in Ishizuka. Some three years earlier, Brother Kikuchi of Urizura had established the church. Because of a lack of leadership, the little church faltered. However, the confidence in Tabata was well founded; considering that Tabata had only been a Christian five years and in training for preaching for three years, his results were much more than anticipated.[20] Undaunted, in December 1953, Tabata, on his own initiative, held a several-day-long meeting at Ishizuka. Amazingly, he baptized fourteen people, doubling the size of the church.[21] The little church took on new life. In January 1954, Tabata baptized five more, and in February, Harry Fox announced that his "Timothy" had baptized twenty-five persons since going to Ishizuka in November. Fox pronounced this as the best work done by a native preacher in Ibaraki.[22] Another milestone was reached in 1953, when Tabata became the first Japanese preacher supported fully by Japanese churches. Four congregations pooled their resources to provide Tabata a full-time salary of $15 a month.[23]

A highlight of 1954 was the wedding of Tabata and Mitsuko Kikuchi. Held in the Ota church building, it was the first wedding since construction of the building two years before. Mitsuko was a longtime member of the Ota church. She had been partially responsible for her new husband becoming a Christian prior to his prison term. Members of both families attended the first Christian wedding any of them had ever witnessed. Following their wedding, Tabata and his bride moved to Ishizuka where they had rented a house. All the missionaries who knew Mitsuko believed she would be a great addition to the church in Ishizuka and a tremendous help for her husband.[24]

In the meantime, other young Christians, educated at ICC, were increasingly engaged in sharing the message of Jesus Christ with their own people. In 1956, a very special young man eagerly agreed to go to Okinawa as a missionary for a year. A graduate of both the Ibaraki high school and college, Yoshiaki Shigekuni was a second-generation Christian. His father was on the board of directors of Ibaraki Christian College and had been involved in Christian activities in Japan since 1927. The Yoyogi-Hachiman church in Tokyo, the largest Church of Christ in Japan, sponsored Yoshiaki, while other Japanese churches provided his travel expenses. Young Shigekuni, age twenty-four, had spent three weeks in the spring of 1956 on Okinawa with other Christians from Tokyo. This visit inspired him to return to Okinawa. Even at an early age, Shigekuni had impressed his teachers as qualified for his mission activities on the island. He had been an excellent student at Ibaraki Christian College and had been elected president of the student body. Charles Doyle added, "We feel that the mission of Ibaraki Christian College is being accomplished when we see young men like this going out to preach the gospel."[25]

The Rise of Omika and Increased Emphasis on Japanese Leadership

Omika became the center of missionary activity in Ibaraki with the establishment of the Christian schools. Most missionaries chose to live on campus. However, two missionaries, desiring to establish a church, constructed houses in Ishioka, some thirty-five miles southwest of Omika. Joe Bryant, who had moved to Ibaraki from Shizuoka in April 1952, and Richard Baggett began evangelizing the town. But they needed help. Several men, including George Gurganus and Ed Brown from Tokyo and Logan Fox, cooperated in May 1953 in a meeting in the village. Tabata, assisted preparation for the meeting by doing personal work among the town's residents. When the meeting concluded, it pleased everyone to report ten responses for baptism. The following Sunday, the church met to share communion in Ishioka.[26] In addition to their ministry in Ishioka, Bryant and Baggett made daily trips to Omika to teach Bible classes at Ibaraki Christian College.

With Omika becoming the center of the missionaries' work, it became even more important to remain in close contact with Japanese preachers located throughout the Kuji River Valley. Besides weekly meetings in Mito with native preachers, in late 1954 Ibaraki Christian College held a second annual lecture series for preachers. Joseph Cannon, the head of the Bible department, reported on the meetings. Twenty-five preachers gathered to hear discussions of such topics as

1. Keeping the unity of the Spirit
2. How to put our workers on a self-supporting basis
3. Progress report from the churches
4. The relationship between law and the gospel in Romans 2 through 9
5. Difficulties involved in our working together[27]

Leadership was the greatest need among the Japanese people. The American missionaries would not remain in Japan for an unlimited period of time.

Transition Time among College Students

The year 1953 was a transitional time among college-age students at Ibaraki Christian College and throughout Japan. It was the year of a truce between North and South Korea, continuing the division along the 38th parallel. With the conclusion of the Korean War and growing issues in Europe, the United States faced major concerns in both Europe and Asia.[28] The Korean War, so close to Japan, impacted students at Ibaraki Christian College. Harry Robert Fox reported in October 1952 on an oratorical contest on campus in which every student spoke on the subject of peace. "The younger generation is more pre-occupied with this problem than any other. And the stand they usually take is that Japan must at all costs honor the clause in their constitution which outlaws war." The students, probably mirroring the larger Japanese population, began questioning why the United States began military rearmament after World War II. Concluding, Fox noted in October 1952, "Increasing numbers of Japanese are beginning to look with as much alarm at what they think is a developing militarism in America as we in America looked at Japan with alarm in the 1930s."[29]

Secondly, communism was gaining support in Japan among young people who began referring to the American practices of "war-mongering capitalism." Japanese young adults denounced the rearmament of Japan and the stationing of American security forces in Japan. The year 1953 may have been the end of conflict in Korea, but criticism of the United Nations' handling of the Korean situation was alive among the young.

Considering the average American's perception of the difficulties in the Korean region of Asia, the missionaries felt it important to tell their people in the United States not to look through rose-colored glasses as they viewed world events. They urged Americans not to blindly defend the American capitalist system without recognizing that everyone is a sinner and we all make mistakes. The only answer, believed the missionaries living among the Japanese people, was to introduce young, idealistic students to the word of God without attaching it to any economic or political system. (This was difficult during the 1950s in the United States because of the Cold War that combined Christianity with democracy to counter communism and atheism.) With this approach in mind, Harry Fox stated firmly, "I think this is enough to give you [American Christians] some idea of the tremendous opportunities open to us in this part of the world at this particular time." He urged Christians in America not to become discouraged and think missionaries should be called home. He concluded, "Quite the contrary, that is all the more reason why more gospel preachers should come to these areas [of the world] and preach all the harder."[30]

Political and economic concerns were not the only issues facing Japan's younger generation. The young people, especially those who accepted the Christian religion, increasingly faced challenging conflicts within their families, especially from the older generations who clung to the past. Since the overwhelming numbers of converts to Christianity were young people between the ages of eighteen and twenty-five, the issue was especially important. Japanese adults, eight years after the conclusion of World War II and forgetting the emperor's statement that he was not a god, began returning to the religions practiced prior to the war. With this renewed interest in historic religions, the young people who had accepted Christianity had questions for the American missionaries, such as, "Can Christians participate in the Buddhist festival of Obon?" Their major concerns revolved around ancestor worship.

In midsummer, the Buddhist festival of Obon was a time when the spirits of ancestors returned to their homes, and all members of the families were to make offerings to them. At this time, young Christians came under the greatest pressure to compromise their Christian beliefs; it was almost impossible for Japanese young people to resist such pressures. Harry Fox indicated, "The average household cannot understand why Christians refuse to participate in the festivals of other religions."

There was another concern. Japanese Christians, at death, often found it impossible to find a cemetery that would accept their family members for burial. Most cemeteries were connected with Buddhist temples. The Buddhist priests used death as pressure to bring Christians back to Buddhism. The Fox brothers, recognizing the urgency of the issue, brought this problem to the weekly meeting of native preachers at Mito. Their suggestion was for at least one church to establish a cemetery so Christians would have a place of burial without confrontation with the Buddhists.[31]

Even with the changing attitudes in Japan, the numbers of students wishing to enroll in Ibaraki Christian College and High School continued to increase. Early in 1956, nearly a thousand young people took exams for the hundred places in the high school. In 1953, there were three hundred students in both college and high school. In 1956, there were six hundred students. The one thing that kept the enrollment from increasing was the lack of Bible teachers. As a result, there were constant calls for more college-trained Bible teachers, American or Japanese, for Ibaraki Christian College.[32] It was becoming more difficult to attract American Christians to mission work in Japan.

Not only were parents interested in their children attending a Christian high school; the parents and citizens of Hitachi and Mito began to financially support the school. An addition made to the home economics building was possible because of a contribution of $8,000 by the Ibaraki Christian College Helpers Association. This support came from business, professional, and civic leaders. Logan Fox, president of ICC, mentioned three members of the Helpers Association: Kameyama, president and founder of Japan's largest chain of rural banks; Matsuno, manager of the Hitachi Electrical Manufacturing Company; and Egami, manager of the copper mine that supplied the Hitachi company with raw materials—an impressive support group.[33]

The Parent Teacher Association of Ibaraki Christian High School in December 1955 agreed to raise 4,500,000 yen ($12,500) over the next five years to pay for an addition to the high school building. The investment allowed the board of directors to add seven large classrooms. The financial help given by the PTA and the Helpers Association was very encouraging to the faculty and administration of the college.[34]

The growth of Ibaraki Christian College and High School, since its founding in 1948, was made possible because the people of Ibaraki Prefecture were appreciative of an education for their children in a Christian environment. Soon the college was drawing students from as far away as the southern island of Kyushu. Many of the prospective students were unable to pay even the meager tuition of $7 per month. There was a constant call from the missionaries to Christians in America to sponsor a student with a contribution of $5; the student would be responsible for the remaining $2.[35] A small church in Pikeville, Tennessee, supported Yaki Iwauchi, one of the first persons Harry Robert Fox baptized when he arrived in Japan. Hideo Goto was a second-generation Japanese Christian. He graduated from Ibaraki Christian College in 1954. From a very poor family, he could not have attended Ibaraki without help from America.[36]

Without the coming of six young missionaries in 1947 and 1948, Ibaraki Christian College and High School would never have existed. As a result of these six young visionaries, the schools flourished during the formative years as other missionaries joined to assist. As they moved on toward 1970, the schools had a solid foundation, committed always to teaching the Bible to all who came to Omika for their education.

Ibaraki Continues to Grow

From the very beginning, the founders and staff of Ibaraki Christian College and High School aimed to provide quality educational institutions for Japanese students. The schools moved quickly toward accreditation, and to keep accreditation, it was necessary to have a qualified faculty. To accomplish that goal, the administrators had to hire non-Christian Japanese teachers for many of the nonbiblical subjects. However, from time to time, these non-Christians accepted Jesus Christ, responding for baptism. For instance, Professor Takiguchi, a teacher of Japanese language and literature at ICC for seven years, asked Harry Fox to baptize him in January 1957. The professor was from Mito, the center of right-wing political radicals. Accepting Christ, he faced being ostracized by his neighbors, his friends, and especially his family. Although his family was very traditional, Takiguchi accepted Christ without fear; he knew the difficulties he faced but still pressed on in his faith. Within a month, this teacher of language influenced another middle-aged teacher, Professor Terakado, to become a Christian. This new brother had retired from the public schools of Mito before coming to ICC to teach geography. Mentioning the conversion of these men, Harry Fox noted that both schools, the high school and the college, were approaching becoming all-Christian faculties.[37]

As mentioned, every missionary in Ibaraki taught the Bible either in the high school or in the college, and some in both. Two missionary families in 1956 were new to Ibaraki. Forrest Pendergrass, a graduate of Lipscomb, and his family had come to Japan in October 1953 but had settled in Yokohama for 2.5 years before moving to Omika. Sponsored by the Fairview church in Detroit, Michigan, with supporting help from churches in Indiana, they were a welcome addition to the Ibaraki community. They arrived in Omika on April 16, 1956, in time for Forrest to begin his Bible classes. On March 20, 1956, Joe Betts and family arrived in Yokohama and immediately made their way to Omika.[38] The Bettses were supported by the Paragould, Arkansas, church. This same church had supported Joe Bryant and his family while they were in Japan. Joe and Wilma Ruth Betts were both graduates of Harding College.[39]

Also in 1956, the Baggetts returned to Japan, but instead of going back to Ishioka where they had worked with the Bryants, they settled in Omika.[40] The houses occupied by the Bryants and the Baggetts in Ishioka were dismantled and moved to the campus of Ibaraki Christian College. With the Baggetts' return, there were now eight families with twenty children living on campus. There was an even greater need for a qualified American teacher.

The need for American-style education became a first priority. When the first missionaries arrived in Japan, there were few children. But as children reached school age, the families had to homeschool. With the crush of activities in all the homes, this became exceedingly difficult. Perhaps this was the reason the Bryants returned to the States after 4.5

years. There was a general agreement among the missionaries that they should not remain in Japan after a child turned age twelve. For Harry Fox's family, this meant 1960.[41]

Americans Visit Ibaraki

The missionaries in Japan, thousands of miles from home, were lonely. They had agreed to remain five years before returning home on furlough. Desiring to see someone from America, service men stationed in Japan were always welcomed for visits. The missionaries constantly called for members from their sponsoring churches to visit them. They were even more eager when they read of churches chartering airplanes to visit mission points in Europe. It was an exciting day in August 1953 when Mr. and Mrs. Herman Wilson, former minister for the Central church in Pasadena, California, visited the Ibaraki Christian campus. The Central church had sponsored the R. C. Cannons in Japan from 1948 to 1951. Harry Robert Fox stated forthrightly in his newsletter in July 1955, "Every time we receive a visit from one overseas we are reminded of how very desirable it would be if one of the elders or deacons from Uptown or one of the other contributing churches should come and see firsthand the work over here which you are making possible."

Mrs. O. P. Grant of Nashville, daughter of A. M. Burton, was on campus in February 1955. Burton, founder of Life and Casualty Insurance Company in Nashville, was a major benefactor of David Lipscomb College. Grant and her mother had befriended both Fox brothers while they were students at Lipscomb in the late 1930s and early 1940s. She and her mother had given generously toward the development of Ibaraki Christian College. Grant was so overcome by the worship by Japanese youngsters that she wept when she attended the high school chapel.[42]

Some well-known Americans also visited ICC. Burton Coffman, a well-known preacher among Churches of Christ on a tour of the Far East in 1953 in association with a trip organized by the US Air Force, visited the campus. On a second visit he presented a full scholarship for a student to attend Ibaraki Christian College. Named the Thelma Bradford Coffman scholarship, it was made possible by the military church on the island of Kyushu.[43] Coffman's visit to Japan was the beginning of a series of trips by well-known preachers, teachers, and editors sponsored by American military churches in Japan. Known as the Far East Fellowship, the programs focused on the Tokyo area. However, each person invited to Tokyo made the hundred-mile trip to Omika and the Ibaraki Christian College campus.

In 1955, the first of the visitors was Dr. James D. Bales of Harding College. Arriving in Tokyo a few days prior to his week-long Far East Fellowship at the Yoyogi-Hachiman church during the Thanksgiving week, he made a trip to Omika and Ibaraki Christian College. On November 16, 1955, Joe Cannon, one of Bales' former students, met his plane and accompanied him to Omika. He spent two days viewing the involvement of Churches of Christ throughout Ibaraki, visiting the Taga, Hitachi, and Motoyama churches. He spoke to both the high school and college chapels on both days. On the second day, he spoke to a combined student body on the lawn. It was a raw, blustery, cold day, but Bales, undaunted, spoke for an hour without a top coat. (The classrooms and auditorium of the school were also not heated.) Why hold such a meeting on the lawn? The administrators and teachers wanted Dr. Bales to see the entire student body at one time. Afterward, Joe Cannon chauffeured the visitor and several teachers on a visit of churches west of Omika. On the second-day tour, he had opportunity to see the orphans' home and the home for the aged. In the evening, Bales spoke to the Hitachi church, the largest in Ibaraki.

The next morning, Harry Fox accompanied Bales to Tokyo. Thanksgiving week, the remaining missionaries in Ibaraki traveled almost en mass to Tokyo. The missionaries were starved for American preaching. Fox mentioned this was the only gospel meeting he had heard in English since he had been in Japan. And it was the largest attendance of Americans he had experienced in all of his years in Japan. He added, "[I]n as much as we missionaries practically never get to hear anyone preach but ourselves it was a great treat to sit in the audience and be on the hearing end of a series of sermons."[44]

The following year, 1956, two Americans came to the campus on the same day. H. A. Dixon, president of Freed-Hardeman College, was the invited speaker for the Far East Fellowship that met from November 18 through 25. Before the Tokyo meeting, Dixon, along with Woodrow Whitten from Pepperdine College and two ladies from Southern California, Dot Nelson and Jackie Ludlum, visited Ibaraki and the Christian schools. Jackie was a classmate of Gerri and Harry Fox at Pepperdine in 1943. Because they were scheduled to be in Tokyo at 6:00 p.m. but wanted to see as much as they could, they made a speedy side trip to see the orphans' home. Arriving late at the school, they were greeted by the students in a hastily called twenty-minute session. After a short reception at the Richard Baggett home, the visitors moved quickly to catch the 1:00 p.m. train for Tokyo.

After returning home, Dixon wrote glowingly of his visit to Ibaraki. He mentioned every family connected with the Ibaraki schools. He was impressed that 34 churches with approximately 1,500 members were meeting in Ibaraki. As a president of a Christian college, he recognized the role of Ibaraki Christian College in the evangelization of Japan.[45]

The men of Ibaraki appreciated Dixon's short visit, but later in the same day, several of the Ibaraki men looked forward to meeting Reuel Lemmons of Austin, Texas, and editor of *Firm Foundation*, when he arrived in Tokyo at 7:10 p.m. Lemmons, at the invitation of E. W. McMillan, would lecture throughout Ibaraki and lead the celebration of the tenth anniversary of the initial announcement of the Ibaraki Christian schools. The party did not arrive in Omika until 1:00 a.m. Without much rest, the next morning being a Sunday, Lemmons preached for the Taga church, and later that evening he spoke to the missionaries and their families.

The following day, Lemmons traveled to Tokyo for a sight-seeing tour. He then traveled south to Shizuoka—where Sarah Andrews and Hettie Lee Ewing were long-term missionaries. Returning to Tokyo, he spoke on Thanksgiving for the Far East Fellowship. For the next week in Ibaraki, he was the featured speaker for the first Ibaraki Christian College Lectures. He concluded his visit on November 30.

It was a hectic week for Lemmons and the missionaries. Each school day, he spoke twice to the students about "The Restoration Movement in America." In the afternoons he spoke to area-wide meetings for Japanese Christians. He preached at the Ota church to an assembly of ninety-five Christians from nine congregations located up and down the Kuji River Valley. Fox wrote, "As usual he preached a powerful sermon and left a deep impression on all the Japanese brethren who heard him." On Thursday, November 29, he spoke to the preachers' study sessions at Mito, where twenty-six full-time Japanese and six part-time preachers gathered to hear him. There were also several other younger men who were in preparation to preach. While in Japan, Lemmons spoke to more than three hundred Japanese Christians from twenty-nine churches. Joe Cannon stated, "Through the informative and inspiring addresses given, the Japanese churches felt more than ever that they are a part of the rapidly growing brotherhood of New Testament Christians."[46]

In addition, Lemmons experienced one more, rather unusual, preaching opportunity while in Japan. He spoke to a group of people living in the caves of Izumigawa in Hitachi city. The Ibaraki missionaries had preached to the people on other occasions, converting a number of cave dwellers to Christianity: there were eleven Christians led by Brother Endo. Lemmons looked forward to the opportunity—it was the first time he had ever preached in a cave. The editor told the cave dwellers "the gospel is for all men regardless of their station in life." As a result of this visit, Joe Cannon called for American Christians to provide these homeless people with decent housing.[47] In March 1958, led by Brother Ota of Ibaraki Christian College, the Christians in Hitachi and Mito, along with Christians in America, constructed three duplexes for the people of Izumigawa. They no longer had to live in a cave. Once again, Christian fellowship had strengthened the resolve of former "enemies," both brothers and sisters in Christ, to rebuild the losses broken down by war and begin anew.[48]

By the time Harry Fox reported Lemmons's visit, the editor was back in America. He said of the editor's visit, on "Lemmons renewed our vision and revived our spirits and gave us a new sense of how important is this corner of the Lord's vineyard. He himself is so energetic and sees everything in such broad perspective and entertains such bright hopes that it is a tonic just to be around him."[49]

Reuel Lemmons wrote glowingly of his time in Japan. He penned his first editorial during his first week in the Far East country. After giving a short history of mission work in Japan, his writing style soared when he wrote about the opportunities for the gospel in Japan. Recalling the times before World War II, he wrote, "Opportunity doesn't last forever. It blazes like the sun and sinks behind the hills. It blossoms like a flower and fades. America sent only a trickling of missionaries. They did a wonderful amount of good. But what could a few expect to do with millions of bewildered people?" Lemmons answered his own question. He became optimistic about the work of the present missionaries and Ibaraki Christian College. Churches of Christ had made an impression on the Japanese people. He noted especially E. W. McMillan, Logan Fox, and his brother, Harry Robert Fox, for their work in establishing Ibaraki Christian College.[50]

Lemmons continued to report about Ibaraki Christian College and the young families who settled in Omika: "At Ibaraki Christian College seven young men and their wives are making great personal sacrifices to take advantage of our present opportunity." He noted that the schools already had six hundred students, and the only limit, he concluded, was the finances needed to construct buildings and provide tuition for students. He then added, "The seven young men who teach in Ibaraki Christian College, together with the forty plus Japanese preachers they have trained or are training, have planted 33 congregations in Ibaraki, and have baptized about 5,000 people. . . . Most of the young churches have buildings, and most of the young Japanese preachers are splendid faithful men."[51]

One year later, after flying 37 hours and 9,138 miles, Batsell Barrett Baxter, professor of speech and preaching at David Lipscomb College and minister of the Hillsboro Church of Christ, arrived on November 23, 1957, in Tokyo, Japan. As others before him, he came to Tokyo at the invitation of the Far East Fellowship. Among those who welcomed him to Japan were representatives from Ibaraki Christian College—Logan Fox, Charles Doyle, and Forrest Pendergrass. Following the lectures in Tokyo, Dr. Baxter traveled to Omika where from December 1 through December 5 he spoke to the faculty and students of Ibaraki Christian College and High School.

Each morning he spoke for an hour each to the high school and college students and faculty. Harry Fox said, "He made lasting impressions on all of us as he talked about such themes as 'Christ, the Lord of the Universe,' 'Christ, the Lord of History,' and 'Christ, the Lord of the Church.'" On Monday afternoon, the faculties of the two schools hosted a reception for the visitor from America. On Monday night he spoke at the Katsuta church to a large audience from several congregations in the area.

On Tuesday afternoon he spoke to the church at Ota. The Hillsboro church, where Baxter ministered, supported the young native preacher for the Ota church. On Tuesday evening the on-campus missionaries enjoyed visits with Baxter first in the Logan Fox home, and on Wednesday, they gathered in the home of Charles Doyle, where they "enjoyed a season of delightful fellowship."

On Thursday afternoon, Logan and Harry Robert Fox accompanied Baxter to Mito where he spoke to a gathering of Japanese preachers at their weekly study session. The discussion of the qualifications and work of preachers lasted thirty minutes. For the next hour, he answered questions from the Japanese preachers on a variety of subjects. Harry Fox recalled, "Out of his rich background of study and practice he was able to give them some good guidance."

Off campus, Baxter, along with his hosts, visited church-related facilities like the orphans' home in Nukada and the home for the aged in Urizura. And while they were on these visits, he was shown a number of church buildings constructed by funds made available by Christians in America. Logan Fox introduced him to a number of businessmen in the area. He was well received by the Rotary clubs of Hitachi and Mito. On the late afternoon of December 5, before he left for Tokyo, the Ibaraki Christian Helpers Association held a reception in his honor.[52]

After visiting in Ibaraki for five days, Baxter flew to Seoul, Korea, to help dedicate a new church building on December 8 before he traveled back to America. In March, Dr. Baxter published in the *Gospel Advocate* a lengthy article about his visit to Ibaraki Christian College. Impressed that after only ten years the school had enrolled 610 students—320 in high school and 290 in college—he mentioned that most students when they enrolled in the schools were Shinto, Buddhist, or atheist. However, when they graduated, 50–60 percent were Christian. Baxter, understanding the importance of a good faculty, called for more Christian teachers with a minimum of a master's degree to replace the 50 percent of the faculty who were non–Church of Christ. Secondly, the school needed more money to construct new residence halls to accommodate a larger number of students who could live on campus in a Christian environment. Besides places for the students to live, he called on Americans to contribute to the construction of a large auditorium for the church in Omika, which was meeting in inadequate facilities on campus. This building would serve the needs of both the church and the schools.

The seven Bible teachers impressed Baxter with their evangelization efforts at night, on weekends, and in the summer. They had established thirty-five churches within thirty-five miles of the campus. Twenty-three of the churches had buildings and were served by thirty native preachers. He mentioned kindergartens established in five communities and that two thousand students had been taught in the ten years since the initial six families moved to Ibaraki. He recalled visiting Urizura where the "Garden of Nazareth," founded by a Japanese Christian man, cared for sixty elderly people—fifty of whom were Christians. Baxter concluded his article: "Our prayer is that the day may come [when] there is a saturation of faithful Christian congregations in the city of Hitachi comparable to that of Nashville, Dallas, or Abilene. Toward that end we not only need to pray, but also to give our dollars and to send our young people as workers."[53]

Baxter had taught at Pepperdine College when Harry and Logan were students in the early 1940s. In a letter to Harry Robert, Baxter recalled his visit to ICC: "It was one of the greatest experiences of my life to get to make this trip and one of the highlights of the trip was being at Ibaraki." He added, "I wish that I could drop over often and work with you and drink in some of the stimulus and inspiration that your work affords."[54] Transitioning further and further away from a wartime philosophy bent on separation and nationalistic borders, more and more Americans traveled to engage in fellowship with their Japanese brothers and sisters in Christ. The result helped build up ICC and the Japanese people, rising from the ashes of a world broken by war.

Major Transitions for the Fox Brothers and Ibaraki Staff

In October before the Baxter visit, both Fox brothers and their families had returned from trips to the United States. Logan Fox, as president of Ibaraki Christian College, made two or three trips to the States to raise funds for the schools. When Logan became president of the college, E. W. McMillan and Fox in 1954 formed the Ibaraki Christian College Foundation. The desire was to form twenty chapters of the foundation across the expanse of the United States. On his 1957 trip, Logan's desire was to raise $200,000 to construct buildings and provide tuition for students to attend the schools.

It had been ten years since Harry Robert and Gerri arrived in Japan. In September 1957, to a gathering of 160 Christians at the Hitachi church building, Harry spoke optimistically: "Ten years ago there were no church houses; there were no Christians; there was no such meetings as this. By God's grace we have been led to this day, when such an audience of brethren in Christ can gather as a clear-cut demonstration of the progress of the gospel in Japan."[55]

When Harry and Gerri Fox and their children returned to Japan on September 2, 1957, Gerri was expecting. In America, Harry Robert had been asked to visit Formosa (Taiwan) to investigate what some referred to as a "restoration movement" in that island nation. He was already in Tokyo, waiting to board his plane, when he received a message that he should return to Omika immediately. Gerri had given birth to twins, born eight weeks prematurely.

When Harry Robert arrived the next day, four members of the staff of ICC met him at the train station. With this meeting, he concluded that bad news was awaiting him. The greeters revealed that one twin, Terry Paden, had died after living only ten hours. The other twin, Jerry Evan, faced difficulties, requiring 24-hour constant care. The doctors gave little hope of survival. But after four weeks, he had regained his birth weight and added 150 grams.

After the harrowing days and weeks spent with Gerri and the boys, Harry Robert resumed his Bible classes at ICC and his regular preaching responsibilities. In January 1958 he made his trip to Formosa. He could now report to Christians in Kansas City, Missouri, who had sponsored his trip to Formosa. He found scattered congregations in Formosa in need of an American presence who could provide leadership for the spiritual maturation of these groups.[56] Things, however, were not going well in Omika.

Those supporting Harry Fox's family in Japan must have been surprised when they received their monthly *Kuji-Valley News* from California. Gerri had showed signs of a nervous breakdown, and the doctors in Tokyo recommended her return to America as quickly as possible. They arrived in Los Angeles on March 4 and made medical appointments soon after arrival.

They brought only Jerry Evan with them. The other three children came with the Doyle family on March 6 when the Doyles returned to America on furlough. Harry Robert and his family would not return to Japan for full-time mission work, although Harry Robert returned to Japan for visits. In 1970, Gerri accompanied him to Japan. On this occasion, she shared with her Japanese friends her spiritual journey while in Japan as a young missionary's wife. In the midst of her lengthy recovery, in 1959 she composed a very moving and insightful poem. Even though she had suffered a nervous breakdown in early 1958, she recalled passionately the Japan she had left and the prayer she had for Japan and the Japanese people.

TO MY HOME ACROSS THE SEA
I want to thank you, Japan
For all you mean to me;
For what I received of your Soul,
Lovely island in the sea.

You have so much to contribute
To the aesthetic need of man:
In your great art, love of beauty,
And your patience with God's plan.

Someday your search for Life will find you
In the unwavering Hand of God.
Then you will understand the suffering
Of the road you have trod.

May I always be a part
Of God's great Gift to you:
In the gift of His salvation,
As He gives eternal life to you.[57]

Other missionaries left Ibaraki in 1958 for various reasons. As mentioned, the Doyles were on furlough. Leaving Ibaraki for a year, Joe Cannon accepted a visiting professor's position at Abilene Christian College. Three families faced health issues and had to return to America. Doctors diagnosed the young Mowrer child as having children's leukemia. She needed

American medical help. Forrest Pendergrass had been suffering from severe headaches. Doctors discovered he had a brain tumor. His family was able to return to the States in time for surgery to save his life. Mary Baggett was also thought to have a brain tumor. The family quickly returned to Memphis, Tennessee, for medical help.[58] It was a traumatic time for the Omika community.

With the exodus of the majority of the teachers at Ibaraki Christian College, only three American teachers remained. In 1958, President Fox quickly brought together a faculty. Added to those who remained were Richard Lyles, assistant to the president; Bill Decker, visiting exchange professor from Abilene Christian College; Bob Jolliff, with a master's from Harding College; and Joe Betts.[59] Jolliff would teach for two years. A California family, Elmer and Geneva Prout and their five children, left Torrence, California, in late 1958 to serve in Ibaraki. A graduate of George Pepperdine College, he had served as the minister for the Torrence church, which supported the family in Japan.[60] After arriving in Japan, he wrote his impressions of Omika, Ibaraki Christian College, and Japan. As a newcomer, the successes of the past ten years impressed him, but he noted rather quickly how few workers there were. Only four of the missionaries spoke the Japanese language.[61]

Late in 1958, E. W. McMillan, at the age of sixty-nine, returned to Japan for his first visit since 1949. Accompanying him were James T. and Oral Cone of Searcy, Arkansas. Cone served on the board of the Ibaraki Christian College Foundation. One Christian who had heard much about McMillan's work for Ibaraki Christian College remarked on meeting him, "Now I have met Moses." While in Ibaraki, he spoke of the $500,000 that had been raised in eleven years. He noted the school had grown from one hundred students and one temporary building to a campus with multiple buildings serving six hundred students. It pleased him that the faculty was 80 percent members of Churches of Christ. The next needed move was to become a senior college.[62]

The year 1959 saw the return of Joe Cannon to Ibaraki while Bill Decker resumed his teaching at Abilene. After an absence of over a year, Charles Doyle returned to Ibaraki Christian College as vice-president of the educational institutions. From Nashville, Tennessee, and David

Lipscomb College, Billy and Margaret Smith and their children, Donald and Marcia Lee, arrived in Japan on July 1, 1959. They were under the sponsorship of the Waverly-Belmont Church of Christ. A call that had been made for years was finally answered when Freda Gibson, sponsored by the Broadway and Walnut Street Church of Christ in Santa Ana, California, arrived in Japan on September 11 to instruct the children of missionaries. Robert and Dixie Yarbrough, graduates of Abilene Christian College and sponsored by the Northside church in Abilene, arrived on October 10. With the arrival of the newcomers, the Ibaraki staff increased to eighteen American adults.[63]

Logan Fox had come to Japan in 1948. He had been involved with Ibaraki Christian College since its inception. He spent his nights and weekends preaching up and down the Kuji River Valley. He had been responsible for establishing a number of churches. Because of his contributions to mission endeavors in Japan, Pepperdine College chose to confer on him an honorary Doctor of Law degree. Instead of Fox returning to Los Angeles for the conferring of the degree, Dr. M. Norvel Young, president of George Pepperdine College, on November 20, 1959, conferred the degree before an audience of seven hundred people in the Hitachi Civic Auditorium. Young was in Japan to speak on the Far East Fellowship in Tokyo. Said Young, "The Doctor of Law degree comes as a fitting tribute for the skill and dedication he has shown in subsequent years [after attaining an MA degree from the University of Chicago] both in scholarly activity and in work of a practical nature." All who attended the conferring of the degree agreed that he deserved the honor.[64]

Logan Fox's work was never finished. As president of Ibaraki Christian College, he had to spend time in the United States securing funds for the operation of the school. In May 1960 he was on a seven-week tour of the United States. After visiting Texas, Tennessee, Kentucky, Illinois, and Michigan, he would return to Japan on July 1. However, he would spend only two months in Japan. He, along with his family, moved to Los Angeles where they would live until their children finished school. Fox announced he would return to Japan during the summers, and then in 1972, he and Madeline would permanently move to Japan. While in the United States, he would remain president of Ibaraki Christian College. The day-to-day activities of the school would be under the oversight of Vice-President Charles Doyle.[65]

What Logan Fox had planned for his future never happened. In the midst of his trip to the United States, Fox resigned as president of the Japanese school. The reasons were not forthcoming in the religious papers. On January 11, 1961, Vice-President Charles W. Doyle, an original founder of the Ibaraki Christian High School in 1948, became the third president of Ibaraki Christian College.[66]

The men who dreamed about and built Ibaraki Christian College could not foresee what would happen in America during the 1960s. The Ibaraki Christian Foundation was unable to raise sufficient funds to guarantee the future of the schools. In 1971, the foundation announced it would no longer be able to contribute to the ongoing of Ibaraki Christian College. Although members of Churches of Christ continued on the faculty, the leadership of the college passed into Japanese hands.[67] It was the end of an era. Truly it was a time of transition.

Today, Ibaraki Christian University remains a viable college in Omika, Japan. It is a living legacy to E. W. McMillan and six idealistic young couples who would not accept an "it-can't-be-done" attitude when they were faced with the monumental task of building from the ground up a Christian high school and a Christian college in non-Christian Japan.

Endnotes

[1] Harry Robert Fox, Jr., "Work in Japan 1948–1953," *Firm Foundation*, November 10, 1953, 10.

[2] Logan Fox, "Made in Occupied Japan," *Abilene Christian College Lectures* (Austin, TX: Firm Foundation Publishing Company, 1953), 131–36.

[3] Harry Robert Fox, Jr. (ed.), *Kuji-Valley News*, October 1954.

[4] Harry Robert Fox, Jr., "An Announcement," *Gospel Advocate*, January 22, 1953, 44.

[5] Virgil H. Lawyer, No Subject, *Firm Foundation*, December 8, 1953, 15.

[6] Malcolm P. Hinckley, "Ready to Go to Japan," *Firm Foundation*, December 19, 1950, 8, 9.

[7] Harry Robert Fox, Jr. (ed.), *Kuji-Valley News*, October 1953.

[8] Harry Robert Fox, Jr. (ed.), *Omika Newsletter*, April 1953.

[9] Harry Robert Fox, Jr. (ed.), *Kuji-Valley News*, June 1953.

[10] Ibid.

[11] Logan Fox, "A Visit with Brother Fujimori," *Gospel Advocate*, October 22, 1953, 726.

[12] Burton Coffman, "Japanese Minister LEADER Reader 40 Years," *Christian Leader*, June 19, 1954, 12.

[13] A letter from Fujimori in response to an invitation tendered by Harry Robert Fox, Jr., June 22, 1955, original letter in Special Collections, Beaman Library, Lipscomb University, Nashville, Tennessee.

[14] An email from Yukikazu Obata. He quoted Rtuji Ebine, "Ko Fujimori Bokushi no Omokage [Reminiscences of the late Bro. Fujimori]," *Hikari to Inochi*, no. 155 (July 1962), 17–18.

[15] Clara Bishop, "Brother Hiratsuka," *Firm Foundation*, January 19, 1954, 7.

[16] Information gleaned from a letter sent to Robert Hooper by Harry Robert Fox, Jr., on May 23, 2013; Letter from Ryohachi Shigekuni to Harry Robert Fox, Jr., on March 24, 1964. Copy in possession Robert Hooper (Will go to Special Collections, Lipscomb University, Nashville, Tennessee).

[17] Letter from Harry Robert Fox, Jr., to Robert Hooper, March 8, 2013.

[18] Harry Robert Fox, Jr. (ed.), *Omika Newsletter*, November 1951.

[19] Ibid., January 1952.

[20] Harry Robert Fox, Jr. (ed.), *Kuji-Valley News*, November 1953.

[21] Ibid., December 1953.

[22] Ibid., February 1954.

[23] Ibid., December 1953.

[24] Ibid., June 1954.

[25] Charles W. Doyle, No Subject, *Gospel Advocate*, September 20, 1956, 787.

[26] Harry Robert Fox, Jr. (ed.), *Kuji-Valley News*, May 1953.

[27] No author, "Second Ibaraki Lectures Draw 25 Evangelists," *Christian Chronicle*, January 26, 1955, 1.

[28] George C. Herring, *From Colony to Superpower: U.S. Foreign Relations since 1776* (New York: Oxford University Press, 2008), 645.

[29] Harry Robert Fox, Jr. (ed.), *Omika Newsletter*, October 1952.

[30] Ibid., May 1953.

[31] Harry Robert Fox, Jr. (ed.), *Kuji-Valley News*, September 1953. When Bonnie Miller visited Sarah Andrews's tomb in Numazu, she noted that the cemetery was owned by the Numazu Church of Christ. Therefore there was at least one church-sponsored cemetery in Japan before 1961.

[32] Logan Fox, "New Building at Ibaraki Christian College," *Gospel Advocate*, August 23, 1956, 717.

[33] Ibid.; "Elders Report, Union Avenue Church of Christ, Memphis, Tennessee," *Christian Leader*, October 27, 1953, 9.

[34] Harry Robert Fox, Jr. (ed.), *Kuji-Valley News*, February 1956.

[35] Ibid., "Memphis Elders Report," *Christian Leader*, October 27, 1953, 1–9.

[36] Harry Robert Fox, Jr. (ed.), *Kuji-Valley News*, March 1954.

[37] Ibid., January and February 1957.

[38] Ibid., February 1956.

[39] Missionary Opportunities, "Joe Betts Family to Japan," *Firm Foundation*, December 6, 1955, 795.

[40] Richard Baggett, "Baggetts Return to Japan," *Gospel Advocate*, April 26, 1956, 404.

[41] Harry Robert Fox, Jr. (ed.), *Kuji-Valley News*, February 1955.

[42] Ibid.

[43] Ibid., November 1953.

[44] Ibid., November 1955; George Gurganus, "Far East Fellowship Meeting," *Gospel Advocate*, December 22, 1955, 1169.

[45] H. A. Dixon, "Far East Fellowship," *Gospel Advocate*, December 13, 1956, 972, 973; Harry Robert Fox, Jr. (ed.), *Kuji-Valley News*, December 1955.

[46] Charles W. Doyle, "Reuel Lemmons to Visit Japan," *Christian Leader*, November 20, 1956, 5; Joe Cannon, "Reuel Lemmons Addresses Japanese Brethren," *Gospel Advocate*, January 10, 1957, 28; Harry Robert Fox, Jr. (ed.), *Kuji-Valley News*, December 1956.

[47] Joe Cannon, No title, *Christian Leader*, December 18, 1956, 11; Cannon, "Reuel Lemmons," *Gospel Advocate*, January 10, 1957, 28.

[48] Charles W. Doyle, "Work Radiates from Omika," *Christian Chronicle*, March 25, 1958, 7.

[49] Ibid.

[50] Reuel Lemmons, "The Church in Japan," *Firm Foundation*, November 27, 1956, 762.

[51] Reuel Lemmons, "Ibaraki Christian College," *Firm Foundation*, December 11, 1956, 794.

[52] Harry Robert Fox, Jr. (ed.), *Kuji-Valley News*, November 1957.

[53] Batsell Barrett Baxter, "Ibaraki Christian College," *Gospel Advocate*, March 27, 1958, 200, 2011.

[54] Letter from Batsell Barrett Baxter to Mr. and Mrs. Harry Robert Fox, January 3, 1958.

[55] Joseph Cannon, No Subject, *Gospel Advocate*, October 17, 1957, 669.

[56] Harry Robert Fox, Jr. (ed.), *Kuji-Valley News*, January 1958.

[57] A copy of the poem is deposited in Special Collections, Beaman Library, Lipscomb University, Nashville, Tennessee.

[58] Conversation with Harry Robert Fox, Jr., February 2013.

[59] Logan J. Fox, "Missionaries at Ibaraki (Japan) Christian College," *Gospel Advocate*, December 11, 1958, 796.

[60] E. W. McMillan, "Elmer Prout Going to Japan," *Gospel Advocate*, July 3, 1958, 427.

[61] No author, "Elmer Prouts Reveal Plans to Work in Japan," *Christian Chronicle*, June 10, 1958, 1; Elmer Prout, "Prout Reports Impressions after Two Months in Japan," *Christian Chronicle*, January 20, 1959, 3.

[62] No author, "McMillan Sees Growth Tripled in Ibaraki CC," *Christian Chronicle*, January 6, 1959, 5; E. W. McMillan, "ICC, in 11th Year, Worth $250, 000," *Christian Chronicle*, March 31, 1959, 6.

[63] No author, "Cannons Returning to Japan College," *Christian Chronicle*, June 2, 1959, 5; No author, "Doyle Returns to Japan Post," *Christian College*, September 1, 1959, 1; No author, "New Workers Boost Total at Ibaraki to 18 Adults," *Christian Chronicle*, November 24, 1959, 5; Carroll Ellis, "The Smiths to Japan," *Gospel Advocate*, January 22, 1959, 56.

[64] No author, "Logan Fox Granted Pepperdine Degree," *Christian Chronicle*, December 22, 1959, 1.

[65] Chronicle Staff, "Logan Fox in U.S. for 7-Week Tour," *Christian Chronicle*, May 24, 1960, 6.

[66] Photograph of Charles W. Doyle, "Named to Post," *Christian Chronicle*, February 17, 1961, 4.

[67] Conversation with Harry Robert Fox, Jr., March 16, 2014.

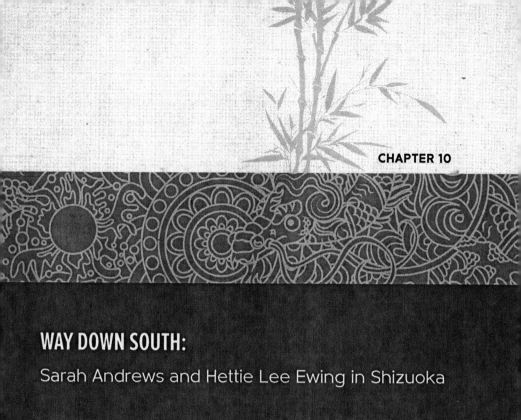

WAY DOWN SOUTH:

Sarah Andrews and Hettie Lee Ewing in Shizuoka

T here is no better way to close a study of missionary efforts in Japan by Churches of Christ than to return to the early years when the first missionaries arrived. Chapter 1 of this book focused on three women: Sarah Andrews, Lillie Cypert, and Hettie Lee Ewing. Of the missionaries who returned to Japan after World War II, two of the most prominent were Hettie Lee Ewing and Sarah Andrews. Both women returned to Japan in their fifties, looking to renew their relationships with Christians in Shizuoka. Members of Churches of Christ supported these women in missions doing things women in American churches would never be allowed to do. The establishment of churches in Shizuoka was the result of these two women aided by their Japanese Christian allies.

In the States, it was extremely difficult for single women to get the same kind of church support extended to married men and women. Yet when these women arrived in Japan, they quickly became members of the communities where they settled to do mission work, particularly because they offered kindergarten classes for small children. Getting to know Japanese families in this way broke down all barriers, including religious prejudices. This was true prior to World War II and was even truer after the women returned after the war. When Sarah Andrews left Shizuoka in 1946, the non-Christian women of the city urged her to return quickly. They were impressed by Andrews's unselfishness and her commitment to her God. Even though Hettie Lee Ewing did not remain in Japan as did Andrews, Japanese Christians urged her to come quickly to Japan. Her churches needed her leadership.

After World War II, both ladies returned to the churches they had established before the war. Andrews, as discussed in Chapter 1, spent the war years under house arrest in Japan. She left Japan in June 1946 for America, where she would regain her health, and then returned on May 20, 1949, after three years away from Shizuoka. Hettie Lee Ewing spent the World War II years in America, leaving Japan on October 4, 1940. She returned in July 1947 to Shizuoka, Japan.

Ewing in America

During the war years, Ewing worked in Washington, DC, and in the relocation camp for Japanese Americans near McGehee, Arkansas. Knowing their language and customs, she was perfectly suited to serve the Japanese Americans in their relocation to various places across the United States at the end of the war. Her language skills allowed her to converse with the older Japanese, who often had not learned the English language.[1]

While in the United States, Ewing remained concerned about the Christians in Shizuoka. Sometime in early 1946, she heard that her close associate, Kioshi Maeda, and his family had escaped the city before the destructive bombing on July 25, 1945. However, the army officer who relayed this information could not locate him. In 1941, Maeda had gone to Shimizu, a port city, to work in a fish factory. Hettie prayed that his family left the city before its destruction in 1945 by bombing. She also learned that Mr. Yoda, a mechanic she had befriended, had succumbed to pressures from governmental forces and denied the faith. She urgently needed to get back to Japan to care for these scattered Christians.[2]

After World War II, Ewing returned to Washington to seek government work in Japan. She discovered, however, that the government had a cutoff age of forty—in 1946 Hettie Lee Ewing was fifty years of age and too old to be considered for foreign employment. She hoped that J. M. McCaleb might use his influence with his contacts in Japan to ensure her return. Next she would attempt to return as a missionary. She had been led to believe the Cleburne, Texas, church would support her. They wanted a "*Non-Premillinial* [sic] worker on the ground floor."[3] The Cleburne church, however, had other interests. They decided to concentrate their missionary support in Europe and Africa.

Showing disappointment, Ewing voiced concern with American churches: "I do get impatient toward the churches for not looking ten and twenty years ahead and preparing for what we 'can do' if we prepare." She reminded the churches as to how much head start American evangelists had in Japan over Germany.[4] Sometime later, a small church in Bishop, Texas, agreed to support her. But before she could go, she needed an endorsement by Japanese Christians and a place to live in Japan before the occupational forces would consider her application.

Ewing Returns to Japan

The Church of Christ representative on the board to recommend missionaries for Japan, Orville D. Bixler, unsure of a single woman entering a war-torn country, turned her down.[5] But she would not be deterred. She turned elsewhere for assistance. Finally, after Jimmie Lovell, publisher of *West Coast Christian*, wrote Bixler "that if he wanted his support in the future, he should not block Ewing's application to return to Japan," Bixler relented and agreed to her going. However, getting to Japan was not easy; she had difficulty getting a passport. It was time for her ship to sail, and still she had no passport. The person who had helped her get her ticket told Ewing she would be on the ship. He called an airline to get a reservation to Hawaii on the day before the ship arrived.[6] From there, she finished her trip to Japan in late July 1947,[7] where she was met by her close friend Kioshi Maeda.

Ewing's food supply, coming by freighter, did not arrive for three or four weeks. Besides food, she had to await precious boxes of clothing and medicine supplied by churches in the States. When the shipment finally arrived, she did not delay the distribution of the much-needed items. A devastated Shizuoka had suffered heavy bombing in 1945, and she quickly began sharing the clothing with the needy, as winter was approaching. She distributed the clothing from Sarah Andrews's house, which remained unharmed by the bombing—first to Christians and then to townspeople.

Hearing that Ewing was back in Shizuoka, members of the churches she and Andrews had established began returning to the city from the hills where they had gone to escape the ravages of war.[8] They were a people without a shepherd.

It was time to bring the churches back to life. Dr. Shiba, who had performed surgery on Hettie Lee in 1932, offered land without rent on which she built a residence and a church meeting place to replace the one destroyed by the war. Additionally, her Christian helper, Maeda, one of the leaders of the church, constructed a house on the property for his family. They were able to use the land for ten years before they had to relocate because of the expansion of Shiba's hospital. Besides the Nakahara church, another congregation was begun in Nagoya. Later Ewing began a church in Osuka.[9] It was certainly a successful time for Churches of Christ and Hettie Lee Ewing in Shizuoka, with many barriers and trials overcome along the way.

Sarah Andrews in the States before She Returned to Japan

Sarah Andrews left her Christian friends at Shizuoka in June 1946, arriving in Tyler, Texas, on July 16.[10] It had been seven years since she had been in the United States. Over the next months, Sarah and her mother visited family and friends and then settled in Bartow, Florida. All the while, Sarah remained in contact with her Christian friends in Japan.

Andrews, responding to the interest of Christians in America, shared with the readers of the *Gospel Advocate* the situation in Japan and her desire to return. She remarked, "As soon as the dark curtain of war lifted and religious freedom was granted, there followed a revival of interest in the Christian religion among the Japanese such as had never been witnessed before." For instance, she had rented her home in Shizuoka to a

Christian couple who was teaching a sewing school with 250 students who also studied the Bible. A letter from a Japanese brother reported more and more people were attending Bible classes, and several had been baptized. Churches that had not met with regularity during the war were now meeting in Shizuoka and Okitsu.

Letters to Sarah from Japan included statements such as, "Democratic Japan is open to Christianity.... The newly appointed Premier is a believer in Christ." Andrews added, "People in Japan, even among the educated elite, are hungry for spiritual food." Reports from Shizuoka led her to believe the future was very promising. On her return to Japan, she planned to open a rest home in the hills near the three churches she had established. It would be a convalescent facility where the guests would be taught the Bible. In fact, the "minister of the Welfare Department at Shizuoka pleads that I return and carry out the plan."[11]

The year 1948 was quite meaningful to Sarah. Her mother died in May of that year. In a letter to J. M. McCaleb, Andrews mentioned that her weight was down to ninety-six pounds. She added: "I am feeling better now. I can't seem to throw off our sorrow. We miss Mother sorely and shall continue to miss her but I know we must remember our loss is her gain."[12] She told McCaleb that she wished to leave for Japan by the end of 1948.[13]

Andrews Returns to Japan

While awaiting her return to Japan, Andrews continued to prepare Bible study topics for the Japanese people.[14] On January 2, 1949, Sarah told Elizabeth McCaleb that she had her ticket for travel to Japan in March 1949.[15] However, she did not leave San Francisco until April 30, 1949, aboard the SS *Flying Scud*, a freighter with eight cabins for passengers. Noting Andrews's sailing date, Melvin Wise said knowingly, "Her more than thirty years of labor in this field gives her an insight into the needs that but few enjoy."[16]

After stops in Seattle, where the ship remained moored for several days, the *Flying Scud* stopped at Adak in the Aleutian Islands, then on to Yokohama, arriving there on May 20 in a heavy rain storm. She was met by her closest friend, O'iki San, her husband Brother Okada, Brother Sugiyama, and eleven others who had come from Shizuoka to welcome her. As the train passed through Okitsu, her Christian friends waved as she passed. She arrived in Shizuoka later in the day of May 24. Some fifty people met her, including members of the press. There were articles in several local newspapers noting her return to Japan. The next day, the church in Shizuoka held a reception for her, where sixty-five persons assembled to welcome her "home."[17]

Andrews's health was a constant concern. Her system was so upset when she arrived in Yokohama that she needed to travel to Tokyo for treatment. Returning to Shizuoka, she began unpacking the crates containing her supplies. She closed a letter to the McCalebs by saying, "It is surely nice to be home again and back at my post of duty." Sarah added, "I was so happy to be safely back again that I could hardly keep still."[18] The Japanese people were her people, not a former enemy. And her impact on Japan was widespread. Her Christian friends felt her love for them. All involved were neither American nor Japanese; they were Christian brothers and sisters.

While Sarah was away from her home in Shizuoka, the Sugiyamas, "a lovely Christian family," lived in her house. The house, however, was in need of repair, and she needed to wash down her smoke-stained walls with lye before repainting them. She gave the reason for the damage: "I had to use wood in an open fire box with no outlet for smoke during the war."

Among her first concerns were the churches she had left behind: "We hope to rebuild the house that was destroyed at Shimizu during the war, as soon as possible." The Lipscomb church and the Tyler, Texas, church had given her money "for whatever use I thought best to make of it." This money would go to Shimizu, although it was not sufficient to construct the meetinghouse. She believed the prospects for the church were great, but without a building, they could not have children's classes. She told the McCalebs that "Bro. Okada continues to preach here [Shizuoka] on Lord's day. The work seems to be on the up and up."[19]

The work in Shizuoka was much more than the two women could oversee. They needed help. Sarah called for two young families to locate in Shizuoka. She wrote Mack Craig, her nephew who was the principal of David Lipscomb High School. Evidently he was not interested. She added, "I'm hoping and praying that re-enforcements may come to this field ere long. The task is far too great for me, besides my years of service are dwindling."[20] Andrews had served longer than any current missionary in Japan, and only Bixler had served longer than Ewing.

Andrews told McCaleb with pleasure in August 1950 that "Bro. Toyoshima has completed his year at school in Ibaraki and is ready to give full time to the Lord's work in this section." A nice location for a church building in Shimizu had been located, but they could not get possession until November. Always on her mind was the rest home, but Sarah would not search for a location "until someone comes to relieve me" in Shizuoka.[21]

In July 1950, Sarah and her friend, a Sister Sugiyama, traveled to a hot spring for a three-days rest at a hotel. While in the mountains, "we visited a member of the church who lives there." The Christian sister took them to another hotel on the beach. While on her short vacation, the sister requested that Sarah and O'iki San come over to conduct Bible classes. The two preachers in Shizuoka would also go over for some evangelistic work. "The inhabitants of that village know nothing about Christianity." The Lord's work was always on Miss Andrews's mind.[22]

Less than a year later, the Lord answered Andrews's prayers. Joe Bryant and his family located in Shizuoka during the first months of 1951. Sponsored by the church in Paragould, Arkansas, and a graduate of Harding College, Joe was a young man who would give leadership to the native preachers and be available to aid Sarah Andrews and Hettie Lee Ewing in their teaching efforts. He reported that he was studying language in the morning, and in the evenings he taught Bible classes through an interpreter. He gave himself two years to learn the language. Kioshi Maeda, encouraged by Hettie Lee Ewing, studied language with Bryant.[23]

In December 1951, the Bryants, lonely for companionship, traveled 210 miles to be with the monthly meeting of missionaries in Omika.[24] But to the disappointment of Andrews and Ewing, the Bryants moved to Ibaraki in April 1952 to become a part of the largest contingent of missionaries in Japan.[25]

In July 1953, Harry Robert Fox, Jr., and Brother Tabata traveled to Shizuoka to hold a meeting for the Oiwa church. They arrived on a Saturday night, and they enjoyed dinner with the Japanese preachers in the city, hosted by Sarah Andrews. The preachers doubted if the meeting would be well attended because Shizuoka was an urban area, not rural like Ibaraki.

They were wrong. From the first night, the attendance grew each night until the largest gathering of eighty-six on Friday. Seven responded for baptism.

Fox related the fascinating story of Sarah Andrews and Hettie Lee Ewing to the readers of his newsletter. They were responsible for establishing five churches in the region—before and after World War II. Fox told of Andrews's heroic actions by remaining in Japan throughout the war. "She took on herself all of this suffering in order to hold the Japanese churches from apostasy during those days of strong pressure." He added: "Today the story of her heroic sacrifices on behalf of the cause of Christ brings tears to the eyes of any Japanese to whom it is told."[26]

During 1953, Sarah's dream, even before she returned to Japan, was coming to fruition. The home for older people was now a reality. In December the only thing lacking was to finish digging the well fed with water from the heights of Mount Fuji. In June 1954, she moved from her home of thirty years in Shizuoka to her new apartment in the home in Numazu,[27] which included a large room for a church to gather. Many of the residents in the home would not be Christians. By teaching the Christian religion in the home, Andrews believed these residents, seeing Christianity in practice, would accept Christ.

Harry Robert Fox, Jr., and his son Johnny, on their way to Kyushu, stopped in Numazu for a visit with Sarah Andrews. Knowing they were coming, "she had a good supper awaiting us."[28] From a letter she later wrote to Harry Robert and Gerri, the ever-humble Sarah seemed embarrassed when she was showing the home to Harry Robert. She thought the facility too elaborate. However, her longtime friend did not think it was pretentious at all.[29] After spending the night with Andrews, Harry Robert and Johnny left for Osaka for a preaching engagement.

The church at Numazu continued to prosper with a number of baptisms in 1955. But Sarah reported in December 1955 that she had been in bed for three weeks with a high fever. "When the fever subsided I was quite weak and had lost so much weight that I've had to be careful not to overtax myself." As a result, she had not heard from any of the other four churches. She had not been able to assist them for several weeks. She did announce that a Christian wedding was in process for December 20. Excitement pervaded the entire community awaiting the event.[30]

Andrews's health worsened over the next year. The doctors discovered she suffered from "chronic colitis and marked enteroptosis" (a disorder in which the intestines drop into the abdominal cavity). The doctors, unable to help her, suggested she return to the United States. In 1956 she returned home for the last time. Finding the help she needed, in 1958, at the age of sixty-five, she returned to Japan. Many of her friends, including O'iki San, met her in Yokohama and rode with her by train to Numazu. Others welcomed her by meeting the train: "How happy I was to see them all!" Everyone gathered at the church for a "welcome-home meal."[31]

There remained things Sarah Andrews wished to accomplish with the churches she had planted. The church in Shimizu continued to need a new meeting place to replace the building lost during the bombing in 1945. There were members of the churches who had become indifferent who needed to be reclaimed. She spent more and more time resting. In 1961, she suffered a number of strokes. The Japanese friends she had ministered to for over forty years now cared for her every need.

In those final days, Sarah never forgot why she came to Japan in 1916. Now at the point of death, the words from the Bible were even more meaningful to her than they had been to a twenty-one-year-old who was moved by the need for the gospel message by the people of Japan. Over the years, she had committed much of the Bible to memory. Especially important to her was Psalm 103. Often too weak to speak the words of the Psalm, she whispered them:

> Bless the Lord, O my soul: and all that is within me,
>   bless his holy name.
> Bless the Lord, O my soul. And forget not all his benefits:
> Who forgiveth all thine iniquities; who healeth all
>   thy diseases;
> Who redeemeth thy life from destruction; who crowneth
>   thee with loving kindness and tender mercies;
> Who satisfieth thy mouth with good things; so that thy
>   youth is Renewed like the eagle's.

The Psalm closes:

> Bless the Lord, all his works (KJV)

At the age of sixty-nine, on September 16, 1961, surrounded by the people she loved and who loved her, Sarah's earthly tent gave out. She breathed her last among people she loved and for whom she had given her life to share with them Jesus Christ. They grieved their loss. She would not be forgotten. Twenty years later, in 1981, one hundred Japanese people gathered at the memorial to Sarah Andrews to honor the woman who had shared Jesus with them. Her good works followed after her.

Two men, both writing in the *Gospel Advocate*, extolled Sarah Sheppard Andrews as a noble but humble Christian woman. E. W. McMillan, who had focused Churches of Christ on Japan after World War II, wrote, "Her body has been placed in the soil of the people she loved and served, and her life is enshrined in their affections. How better could any life be?"[32]

Now an old man, I. B. Bradley, who was told by a young Sarah when he baptized her that she was going to Japan when old enough, said, "She has done a great work. This is a work of our master, and this is a sacrificing and consecrated servant of the Lord."[33]

Only Hettie Lee Ewing Remains

Andrews's longtime companion in Shizuoka, Hettie Lee Ewing, remained in Japan until she became concerned about her retirement years. For three years, 1949 to 1952, she worked in Washington, DC. Returning to Japan at age sixty, she continued her work at her second home in Shizuoka. However, her unstructured work as a missionary did not qualify her for Social Security benefits. Therefore, at the age of sixty-eight, she returned to the United States to teach, first in 1965 at Fort Worth Christian School and then a semester at Alabama Christian in Montgomery. These employment opportunities qualified her for minimum Social Security benefits.[34]

In 1976, approaching her eightieth birthday, Hettie Lee Ewing journeyed to Japan to visit her Christian friends. She was living in the Christian Care Center in Mesquite, Texas, when she began dreaming about a return trip to Japan. Knowing her great desire to go, friends raised the funds for the trip. It was such a different trip than any she had ever made before. She flew to Japan on a Boeing 747, much different from the freighter ships she had traveled on in the 1920s and the 1930s. In Tokyo, she and her companions were met by the Maeda family. The next day at the Nakada Church of Christ, she met Sister Takaoka, who had worked with Miss Ewing from 1927 to 1972.

On Sunday, October 24, 1976, a group of forty Christian friends took Hettie Lee to the beach, where in a Japanese-style inn everyone celebrated the eightieth birthday of their mentor and dear Christian friend. On October 29, Ewing and her friends flew back to Texas where she was welcomed "home" by all her American friends.[35] What a highlight to a life given in Christian service to the Japanese people!

Hettie Lee Ewing passed away on September 15, 1986, age ninety, in Mesquite, Texas. She was remembered—and missed—most of all by her people in Japan who had learned Christian love by her instruction from the Bible and by the life she lived among them.

Never had two women accomplished so much in mission outreach as Sarah Andrews and Hettie Lee Ewing to a people across the Pacific Ocean, in Japan, "The Land of the Rising Sun." These two women committed their lives totally to Jesus Christ and the Japanese people, and like Mary, the friend of Jesus from Bethany, they will be remembered as long as the gospel is proclaimed.

Endnotes

[1] Oran and Nina Sawey (eds.), *She Hath Done What She Could: The Reminiscences of Hettie Lee Ewing* (Dallas: Gospel Teachers Publications, 1974), 100, 101.

[2] Letter, Hettie Lee Ewing to J. M. McCaleb, August 23, 1946.

[3] Letter, Hettie Lee Ewing to J. M. McCaleb, October 18, 1946.

[4] Letter, Ewing to McCaleb, August 23, 1946.

[5] Oran and Nina Sawey (eds.), *She Hath Done What She Could*, 101.

[6] Ibid., 116.

[7] Ibid., 116, 117.

[8] Ibid., 123, 126.

[9] Ibid., 131–36.

[10] Fiona Soltes, *Virtuous Servant: Sarah Sheppard Andrews, Christian Missionary to Japan* (Franklin, TN: Providence House Publishers, 2009), 64, 65.

[11] Sarah Andrews, "Report and Plans of Work in Japan," *Gospel Advocate*, November 20, 1947, 950.

[12] Letter from Sarah Andrews to J. M. McCaleb, May 26, 1948.

[13] Letter from Sarah Andrews to J. M. McCaleb, July 15, 1948.

[14] J. T. Marlin, "Sarah Andrews Prepares for Return," *Gospel Advocate*, April 29, 1948, 419.

[15] Letter from Sarah Andrews to Elizabeth McCaleb, January 2, 1949.

[16] No author, "Sarah Andrews Returns to Japan," *Firm Foundation*, June 14, 1949, 5.

[17] Ibid.

[18] Letter from Sarah Andrews to J. M. McCaleb, May 18, 1949.

[19] Ibid.

[20] Letter from Sarah Andrews to J. M. and Elizabeth McCaleb, August 5, 1950.

[21] Ibid.

[22] Ibid.

[23] Oran and Nina Sawey (eds.), *She Hath Done What She Could*, 144.

[24] Harry Robert Fox, Jr. (ed.), *Omika News Letter*, December 1951.

[25] Ibid., April 1952.

[26] Harry Robert Fox, Jr. (ed.), *Kuji-Valley Newsletter*, July 1953.

[27] Fiona Soltes, *Virtuous Servant*, 90, 91.

[28] Harry Robert Fox, Jr. (ed.), *Kuji-Valley Newsletter*, October 1954.

[29] Fiona Soltes, *Virtuous Servant*, 90.

[30] Letter from Sarah Andrews to friends, December 15, 1955.

[31] Fiona Soltes, *Virtuous Servant*, 92, 93.

[32] Fiona Soles, *Virtuous*, 93.

[33] Ibid.

[34] Oran and Nina Sawey (eds.), *She Hath Done What She Could*, 149–51.

[35] Hettie Lee Ewing, *Another Look at Japan: Reminiscences of Hettie Lee Ewing* (Dallas: Temple Publishing Company, 1777), 7–16.

A WORD FROM THE AUTHOR

n 1946, Sarah Andrews closed her final report from Japan with the words "A call comes ringing." All who read the article knew what she was quoting—a reference to the song "Send the Light," often sung in worship on Sunday mornings. To be honest, I have not heard the song in many years. And there are other songs we sang in the 1940s and the 1950s emphasizing mission work, including "Seeking the Lost," "Harvest Time," "Rescue the Perishing," and a song by the first missionary to Japan, J. M. McCaleb, "The Gospel Is for All." What has happened to these songs calling all Christians to share the good news of Jesus Christ with the world?

It was during this post–World War II era that I listened to Otis Gatewood in January 1951 tell a packed auditorium at Lipscomb about the impact of Christianity on the German people. That night introduced me to a new world I had never experienced. Even though I have never gone as a full-time missionary to a foreign country, I became determined to be involved vicariously, if in no other way than to know the history of missions among Churches of Christ. This interest led me to write the book you are holding in your hands.

The decade I grew to adulthood and began ministry and teaching was the era of religious optimism in the United States. This was equally true of Churches of Christ. Church growth was everywhere. Ira North, pulpit minister for the Madison, Tennessee, Church of Christ, wrote exultantly in 1955, "The church today is strong in its unity and fervent in its fellowship. The future is bright. Let us rejoice!"[1] Churches of Christ joined the mainstream of American Christianity. This optimism carried over into foreign missions in Europe; the Far East, including Japan; and Africa. Churches of Christ counted themselves as one of the fastest growing Christian churches in the United States. B. C. Goodpasture believed the membership reached 2,000,000 by the end of the 1950s, although his numbers may have been optimistic. The optimism of the late 1950s continued into the early years of the 1960s. Not as large as Billy Graham's crusades, well-known evangelists, including Willard Collins, Batsell Barrett Baxter, and Jimmy Allen, held large citywide arena-filled week-long meetings. For instance, the new Nashville Municipal Auditorium opened in 1963 with the Collins-Craig meeting. Almost ten thousand attended the first session, with several thousand turned away. The meetings continued for a week, with the arena near capacity each night.

The positive emphasis on missions in Japan and in Europe depended to a great extent on reports of the missionaries from foreign countries. These enthusiastic reports fit quite well into the optimism among churches during the 1950s and the early years of the 1960s. Who would not be excited by Sarah Andrews's story about remaining in Japan during the war, then being found alive by soldiers of the US Army? And once the young missionaries arrived in Japan, they began reporting hundreds of baptisms. What was happening in revivals in the States was happening in Europe and Japan. It was an exciting time to be members of Churches of Christ. Adding to these successes, the same missionaries established a Christian college in Japan. These reports filled the journals of Churches of Christ.

Whether in Germany or Japan, the conditions of the people appalled the young missionaries. Therefore, they called for clothing and food to care for the defeated people. Literally tons of clothing from churches crossed the oceans to clothe the near-naked people following the war. As was true in Germany, the Japanese people had lost everything during the war, including housing. The reports by the missionaries of people living in shacks and even in caves caused churches to respond to those needs with Christian compassion.

Beginning in 1947, E. W. McMillan had firsthand experience advocating for foreign missions. In 1956, he listed three things he believed impacted missions after World War II. The first was the Christian college, where young people caught the vision to carry the gospel to foreign people. Second, he believed the churches had elders, deacons, and preachers who believed the great commission. Third, he noticed the influence of the religious journals among Churches of Christ that reported in detail the efforts of missionaries in foreign countries.[2] He had no doubt such emphasis would continue for years to come.

An important happening in the United States must not be lost when hearing missionaries report on the rise of communism in Japan. The United States was caught up in the Cold War during the 1950s. President Harry Truman believed World War III was possible when North Korea invaded South Korea in 1950. During the presidency of Dwight David Eisenhower, Christianity became increasingly important. Christianity and democracy became the response to Soviet Union communism and atheism. Thus when the missionaries, and General MacArthur, warned against communism in Japan, this resonated with American churches, including Churches of Christ. G. C. Brewer, writing in the *Gospel Advocate,* emphasized the menace of communism: "Communism now reigns over about ten million square miles of territory, dominates three hundred million people, and is estimated to have ten million men under arms. If this does not constitute a threat to civilization, then it would be hard to imagine such a threat."[3]

In 1953, Brewer founded the *Voice of Freedom,* a journal focused on communism and Catholicism. However, Brewer urged Churches of Christ to join with Catholics until communism was defeated. This remained true until the election of 1960 when John F. Kennedy was the nominee of the

Democratic Party. In the October 1959 issue, editor L. R. Wilson warned: "We are concerned with our American system. . . . To make sure that we keep our present system, let us keep it out of Roman Catholic hands."[4] From the author's perspective, this anti-Catholic position was only a small part of the greater issues that would face Churches of Christ in the late 1960s and the 1970s.

From Optimism to Doubt and Pessimism

With so much optimism present in the 1950s, I likely know the question in your mind at this moment. You are asking why I so abruptly concluded my study with 1970. I joined the Lipscomb faculty in the fall of 1960. I had no idea at the time what the decade of the 1960s would be like. In 1970, looking back ten years, the United States had gone through one of the most disruptive decades since the Civil War. The decade began with the assassination in 1963 of President John Kennedy. The civil rights movement, gaining strength with the 1954 decision of the Supreme Court in *Brown v. School Board of Topeka, Kansas*, carried over during the last years of the 1950s into the 1960s, with the assassination in 1968 of Martin Luther King, Jr. The civil rights movement was disruptive to the American South, the area of greatest strength of Churches of Christ.

Without question, the most challenging happening in the 1960s was the divisive Vietnam War. The conflict divided families—children verses parents. It caused students to burn their draft cards. With the introduction of the lottery system, students with low numbers opted to leave the United States for Canada. The war became such a factious issue that President Lyndon Johnson chose not to seek the Democratic nomination in 1968. No matter, the party had to surround the Chicago convention center with barbed wire to keep the anti-Vietnam crowd from storming the convention. To make matters worse, Robert Kennedy, a candidate for the nomination of the Democrats in 1968, fell to an assassin's bullet. Add this assassination to the Memphis killing of Martin Luther King, and the decade ended with a divided and fractious nation.

The disruptive 1960s led to the decade of the 1970s when Churches of Christ faced numerous challenges. From 1906, when the US Census Bureau recognized Churches of Christ as a separate church group from

Disciples of Christ, the fellowship faced two major divisive movements. The first was premillennialism, and the second was the noninstitutional upsurge in the late 1940s and the 1950s. Not until the 1960s and the 1970s, however, was the mainstream challenged from within. Without question, the secularization of society impacted the fellowship.

On the other hand, within Churches of Christ arose men, using McCarthy-style methods, who attacked what they thought to be corruptness within the fellowship, leaving the "old paths." In 1962, Thomas Warren, writing in the *Gospel Advocate*, identified the issues: "Christianity Verses Relativism, Middle-of-the-Roadism, Neutralism, and Compromise." He asked, "Is our nation harmed by Middle of the Roaders?" He then quoted the reactionary Tom Anderson in his *Farm and Ranch* magazine: "America is losing its moral indignation." Warren applied Anderson's conclusions to Churches of Christ: "Is the church losing its sense of moral indignation? Is the church losing its intestinal fortitude? Is the silence that pervades us in the face of error taught on every hand (both without and within the church) golden or yellow?"[5]

Warren's position seemed mild to what Ira Rice, Jr., wrote in 1966 in his new book, *Axe at the Root*. He discovered while studying Mandarin Chinese at Yale University three young men—Derwood Smith, Robert Randolph, and Robert B. Howard—whom he felt were studying and teaching liberal theology. The first and second printings sold eight thousand volumes. There was concern among Churches of Christ for perceived liberalism. Rice's attack was much broader than three young men. He attacked all graduate education, with an emphasis on theology. He wrote, "We are about to see a brotherhood-wide division among us which will make the 1946 Anti-Cooperation Movement seem insignificant by contrast. I refer, of course, to this 'Educational Trojan Horse' which is being trundled into our midst from the denominational/secular, so-called 'Divinity' Schools intentionally via our Christian colleges."[6] Rice placed all Christian colleges, especially those offering graduate degrees, under a dark cloud.

In the same year Rice issued his *Axe at the Root*, Robert Meyer published *Voices of Concern*, a voice from the left in Churches of Christ. Included in the volume was an essay by Logan Fox, one of the first missionaries to enter Japan after World War II. Stating that he had been very conservative as a young man, as he matured, he played the politics of the brotherhood. He stated that by 1962 he would no longer play the games of the fellowship. At this point, he resigned from his position as president of Ibaraki Christian College and his teaching position at George Pepperdine College. He expressed a negative view toward Churches of Christ. They had accepted "a negative attitude toward education and scholarship, as typified by our opposition to a critical study of the scriptures."[7]

By 1974, leadership among Churches of Christ voiced concern. This led to J. D. Thomas publishing *What Lack We Yet?* He asked leaders across the wide span of the fellowship to share their views on the question posed in the title.[8] Reuel Lemmons, editor of *Firm Foundation*, emphasized a lack of leadership among Churches of Christ; plus he believed "the distance between the church and denominationalism is less than it used to be."[9] Batsell Barrett Baxter indicted the fellowship for the negativism. H. A. Dobbs and Glen Wallace feared the liberalism of the younger men who were becoming leaders in the church during the 1960s and the early 1970s.

It took an outsider looking at American Churches of Christ to focus on the problems across the brotherhood. Juan Monroy, of Madrid, Spain, wrote: "Vision and knowledge are gifts for which the Church should pray. Vision to see her own spiritual situation. Vision to see the needs of the world. Vision to understand the Church's possibilities at this critical hour. Vision to discover again God's power. And, knowledge to carry out her work with wisdom in a world overflowed with science and techniques."[10]

The concerns would not go away. Batsell Barrett Baxter, appearing in 1976 at Abilene Christian College, made a presentation titled "The Crisis." Emphasizing life cycles, Baxter suggested churches follow the same cycles: "vigorous youth, then mature, more sedate middle age, followed by a period of decline and ultimate death." Referring specifically to Churches of Christ, he spoke with urgency, "There is great vigor in the early years, followed by decline and ultimately disappearance. This must not happen to the Restoration Movement."[11] Monroe Hawley, of Milwaukee, Wisconsin, believed Churches of Christ should return to their roots in the Restoration Movement. He called the fellowship to become "JUST CHRISTIANS." He believed the heirs of the Restoration Movement must redig the wells of restoration just as Isaac "dug again the wells of water which had been dug in the days of Abraham his father" (Gen. 26:17).[12] In 1984, Rubel Shelly published *I Just Want to Be a Christian,* expanding on Hawley's theme. His book received scathing reviews from the more conservative within Churches of Christ.

The conflicts of the 1960s and 1970s impacted Churches of Christ in numerous ways. Juan Monroy, speaking at the West End church in Nashville, suggested fear as the cause of Churches of Christ—whether conservatives, moderates, or progressives—to turn inward. As a result, evangelism suffered. For instance, Willard Collins, then vice-president of David Lipscomb College, told me that interest in "gospel meetings" plunged in the early 1970s, both in attendees and in baptisms. In the 1950s, Collins held meetings when one hundred persons would respond for baptism. It was during the 1960s and 1970s when the idea of a one-week or two-week series of meetings began to disappear.

Having taken a look at the 1960s and the 1970s, it is time to return to the questions asked about ending this volume in 1970. Foreign missions have never been a first priority among Churches of Christ. As noted in this book, Japan was the first focus before World War II. After the war against the Axis Powers, Churches of Christ sent more missionaries to foreign countries than at any time before and then after 1975. One year following the end of World War II, there were 46 foreign missionaries. Seven years later, the number increased to 229. By the end of the 1950s, the numbers increased to 704 missionaries. The growth continued throughout the 1960s, reaching the highest number, 800, in 1975. For the most part, this number included the first and second generations of missionaries. After 1975, they were not replaced by a third generation. In 1982, the *Christian Chronicle* found only 374 foreign missionaries.[13]

Why such a precipitous decline in missionaries? The decline paralleled the difficulties experienced by all churches in the United States. The turning inward experienced by churches impacted missions. The Vietnam War and its attendant issues in the States impacted young people in churches and on college campuses, including Christian colleges among Churches of Christ. Young people were not as willing to commit to foreign missions as were their predecessors. And it must be noted that the war aroused anti-American feelings in international communities. The economic downturn of the 1960s also had immediate consequences. Churches began to spend more on their home needs. Evangelism abroad was no longer a first priority. And, as we have noted, the tension within the fellowship, causing tears in the fabric, impacted not only the larger brotherhood; it seeped down to the local congregation. And, of course, in Churches of Christ, the local church is the bedrock of the fellowship.[14]

Since the 1970s, several things have happened that continue to impact the fellowship of Churches of Christ. I can remember in 1953 when Columbia Broadcasting System asked Dr. J. P. Sanders, dean of David Lipscomb College, to present on their network a nationally broadcast sermon. I was so thrilled. Churches of Christ had never been featured on national radio or, the new medium, television. At first, a broadcast named *Herald of Truth*, born in the early 1950s, was only on radio, but in 1959 the Highland Church of Christ in Abilene, Texas, contracted with Batsell Barrett Baxter, a PhD in speech from Southern California and chair of the speech department at Lipscomb and pulpit minister of the Hillsboro Church of Christ, as a featured speaker of the TV version of *Herald of Truth*. Within the broad middle of Church of Christ, there was immediate support—Churches of Christ could be experienced by an entire nation. In the 1970s, *Herald of Truth* broadcast over 468 radio and 172 television stations.[15] In the twenty-first century, there is no longer a national TV *Herald of Truth*.

At one time, Churches of Christ supported multiple national and regional publications. The oldest, the *Gospel Advocate*, founded in 1855, continues to publish, but no longer as a weekly. For so much of my research, I depended on the *Gospel Advocate*. It was a treasure trove of information. But it no longer contains the information I need to do research on the history of Churches of Christ. The *Christian Leader*, the source of much information on missions in Japan, no longer exists. The same is true of the *Firm Foundation*. Barney Morehead's *World Vision*, a mission journal, is no longer published. The list could go on and on. The point to be made is this: The religious journals, oftentimes contentious, remained the vehicles that kept Churches of Christ informed and connected as a fellowship. Except for the *Christian Chronicle*, there is little that connects Churches of Christ today. Never in the history of the Restoration Movement, especially among Churches of Christ, have congregations been so independent, knowing little about a congregation down the street or across town. Congregations in the same cities rarely join in a citywide effort of any kind, especially in evangelism. The day of the cooperative citywide campaign is past.

Today, the only things that bring churches and individuals together are not congregationally focused. The colleges and universities associated with Churches of Christ offer their yearly lectureships and special programs emphasizing spiritual growth. There are numerous parachurch organizations that focus on a variety of good works, including mission work such as Continent of Great Cities and World Christian Broadcasting. These are good programs, but they are not congregationally centered. In Nashville, there are numerous organizations such as the Churches of Christ Disaster Relief that reach out to hurting people and communities who suffer floods, fires, and tornados. These are church-related but again not centered in local congregations. No longer are Churches of Christ as focused as E. W. McMillan believed they were in 1956.

Today Churches of Christ need to catch the vision of the early restorers of the nineteenth century, especially the Barton Stone Christians who went everywhere preaching the gospel. The Campbell movement caught the fire of evangelism from Walter Scott. Throughout the nineteenth century, the revivals of Stone and the gospel meetings of the Campbells reached across much of the eastern United States with a message of good news found in Jesus Christ. This emphasis continued into the twentieth century, with great revivals like N. B. Hardeman's tabernacle meetings in Nashville, Tennessee. The traveling gospel preacher, holding two-week meetings, was common to evangelism. It was not unusual for preachers like James A. Harding and T. B. Larimore to extend their meetings to four and six weeks. It was this enthusiasm for evangelism that caused the interest in foreign missions in the first half of the twentieth century. With the coming of the disruptive 1960s and the 1970s, evangelism suffered, including interest in foreign missions.

The need for today's world is no different from the world of the nineteenth and early twentieth centuries. How can the fellowship of Churches of Christ regain an interest in evangelism? There must be new means to reach out beyond local congregations to encourage the sharing of the gospel to neighborhoods, to our nation, and across the oceans. Evangelism must remain the driving force of our Christian commitment. The great commission Jesus gave his disciples, "Go into all the world," remains the clarion call for all Christians today. May we with fervor and conviction sing the old hymn often sung by American Christians in the years after World War II: "A call comes ringing over the restless waves, send the light, send the light"? The same gospel preached by the apostle Paul, by Walter Scott, by Barton Stone, by James A. Harding, by Harry Robert Fox, Jr., and by Batsell Barrett Baxter can bring the same results in the twenty-first century as it did in the near and far past. The world is in darkness. It needs the light only Jesus Christ can provide.

Endnotes

[1] Ira North, "Let Us Rejoice," *Gospel Advocate*, May 5, 1955, 348.

[2] E. W. McMillan, "Then and Now," *Firm Foundation*, November 27, 1956, 761.

[3] Quoted in Robert E. Hooper, *A Distinct People: A History of the Churches of Christ in the 20th Century* (West Monroe, LA: Howard Publishing Company, 1993), 246.

[4] L. R. Wilson, "Editorial Comment," *Voice of Freedom*, October 1959, 146.

[5] Thomas B. Warren, "Christianity Verses Relativism, Middle-of-the-Roadism, Neutralism and Compromise (No. 1)," *Gospel Advocate*, 1962, 342, 343.

[6] Ira Y. Rice, Jr., *Axe at the Root* (Dallas: Privately published, 1966), 2.

[7] Robert Meyers, *Voices of Concern* (St. Louis: Mission Messenger, 1966), 28, 29.

[8] J. D. Thomas (ed.), *What Lack We Yet?* (Abilene, TX: Biblical Research Press, 1974).

[9] Ibid., 12.

[10] Ibid., 32–37.

[11] Quoted in Clayton Pepper, "The Cycle of Growth and Decline of Religious Vitality as Related to Evangelism," *Personal Evangelism*, July, August, September 1979.

[12] Monroe Hawley, *Redigging the Wells* (Abilene, TX: Quality Printers, 1976), 15, 216.

[13] These figures are located in Hooper, *Distinct People*, 286; James O. Baird, "Missionary Decline Summarized," *Christian Chronicle*, August 1983, 14. Baird's article includes a chart showing missionary families from 1906 through 1982. The three decades when the number of missionary families of Churches of Christ reached the greatest number were 1959, 1967, and 1975. Thereafter, the next four decades showed decline.

[14] See the complete discussion of the topic in Hooper, *Distinct People*, chapter 13, titled "From 1950 toward the 21st Century," 281–306.

[15] *Herald of Truth*, accessed December 22, 2016, http://www.heraldoftruth.org.

INDEX

A

Abilene Christian College, 47, 113, 144, 145, 155, 207, 208, 222, 228, 254
Acadia, California, Church of Christ, 214
accreditation, 237, 267
Akamatsu, Sister, 220
Akutsu, Brother, 134, 261
Aladdin Company, in Portland, Oregon, 100
Alameda Salt Company, 132
Alien Enemy hearing boards, 148
Alien Land Law, in California, 131–132, 143
Allen, Jimmy, 296
Amache camp. *See* Camp Amache
American bombers, 53, 130
American military
  arrived in Japan in 1945, 204
  churches, 222–223, 270
  Churches of Christ and, 212–213
  looking for a church home, 168–169
  mission to find Sarah Andrews, 58
  recognized Bixler's weaknesses, 214
American occupation forces, 166, 172
Americans, in Japan, 53, 83, 129, 135
ancestor worship, 265–266
Anderson, Tom, 299
Andrews, Sarah Sheppard
  answering the call of Japan, 40–46, 95
  choosing to remain in Japan, 32, 35, 51–56, 57–59, 114
  established churches, 50, 51, 87
  health of, 44, 58, 287, 288, 290–292
  Oto Fujimori and, 82, 88, 137–138, 258

  travels to and from Japan, 40, 42, 43, 44, 45, 53, 82, 283, 284, 286–292
  work of, 36, 84, 124, 147, 292
anti-American sentiment, outpouring, 51
Armstrong, J. N., 96, 173
army, in internment camps, 151, 153
Asians, in California and other western states, 27, 131, 143
"assembly centers," 153
Auburn, Alabama, Church of Christ, 169, 177
Axe at the Root (Rice), 299
Azbill, Wilson K., 37, 95

B

Baggett, Mary, 268, 278
Baggett, Richard, 241, 263, 268
Bales, James D., 218, 270
Barton Stone Christians, 303
baseball games, 229
Baxter, Batsell Barrett, 219, 273–275, 296, 300, 302
"BE STILL AND KNOW GOD," 175
Beech, Emma, 108
Bell, James, 72, 73–74
Bell, R. C., 173
Bendetsen, Karl, 152
Benson, George, 172, 215
Betts, Joe and Wilma Ruth, 268, 278
Betts, W. H., 219
Bever, Arley, 157–158
Bible Center, conflicts at, 213

W

Y

Z

CPSIA information can be obtained
at www.ICGtesting.com
Printed in the USA
FFOW05n1618010517
35030FF